# RESOURCING INCLUSIVE EDUCATION

# INTERNATIONAL PERSPECTIVES ON INCLUSIVE EDUCATION

## Series Editor: Chris Forlin

### Recent volumes:

INTERNATIONAL PERSPECTIVES ON INCLUSIVE
EDUCATION VOLUME 15

# RESOURCING INCLUSIVE EDUCATION

### EDITED BY

## JANKA GOLDAN

*Faculty of Educational Sciences, University of Bielefeld,
Germany*

## JENNIFER LAMBRECHT

*Berliner Kita-Institut für Qualitätsentwicklung
(Berlin Kindergarten Institute for Quality Development),
Germany*

## TIM LOREMAN

*Faculty of Education, Concordia University of Edmonton,
Canada*

United Kingdom – North America – Japan
India – Malaysia – China

Emerald Publishing Limited
Howard House, Wagon Lane, Bingley BD16 1WA, UK

First edition 2021

**British Library Cataloguing in Publication Data**
A catalogue record for this book is available from the British Library

ISBN: 978-1-80043-457-8 (Print)
ISBN: 978-1-80043-456-1 (Online)
ISBN: 978-1-80043-458-5 (Epub)

ISSN: 1479-3636 (Series)

Printed and bound by CPI Group (UK) Ltd, Croydon, CR0 4YY

ISOQAR certified
Management System,
awarded to Emerald
for adherence to
Environmental
standard
ISO 14001:2004.

**ISOQAR**
REGISTERED

Certificate Number 1985
ISO 14001

INVESTOR IN PEOPLE

# CONTENTS

# ABOUT THE AUTHORS

**Dr Joseph Seyram Agbenyega** (EdD) is an Associate Professor of special education in the Division of Special Education, Guidance and Counselling and Education Neuroscience at Emirates College for Advanced Education (ECAE), Abu Dhabi, UAE. Before joining ECAE, Professor Agbenyega was the Director of Graduate Research Education at Monash University, Australia. His research focus is special education. He is interested in the psychological and sociological understandings of educational inclusion and inequality among children and youth. He explores how policy and government support for education orchestrate educational equity and quality.

**Dr Joanne Banks** is a lecturer and researcher in inclusive education at the School of Education in Trinity College Dublin. She has worked for over a decade in social research focussing on inclusive education, the school experiences of students with disabilities and educational inequality more generally. Her research focusses on inclusive education in policy and practice and examines system and school-level practices that promote quality and equity for all students. She has published widely on the school experiences of students with disabilities and those from socio-economically deprived backgrounds. Her work has been published in journals such as *Educational Assessment, Evaluation and Accountability, Child Indicators Research, British Journal of Sociology of Education, Journal of Youth Studies, International Journal of Inclusive Education, European Journal of Special Needs Education and Irish Educational Studies.*

**Dr Sheila Bennett**, D. Ed., is a Professor and Former Associate Dean of Professional and Undergraduate Programs Faculty of Educational Studies at Brock University, Canada. She has presented nationally and internationally and has authored and co-authored numerous books, chapters, monographs and articles including *Special Education in Ontario Schools*; including Students with Exceptionalities and A Canadian Perspective on the Inclusion of Students with Intellectual Disabilities in High Schools. Her research centres on inclusion for students with diverse needs. Upon completion of her graduate work at the University of Toronto, Dr Bennett held a number of school and school board–based positions prior to joining the Faculty of Educational Studies at Brock. She brings her practical experiences as an educator to the field of research, providing a blend of theory and practice essential to bridge the gap between what we do in classrooms and how we understand those actions in the larger context.

**Emily Butler** has a Master of Education (Counselling Psychology) from MUN, a Bachelor of Arts degree with a major in psychology and a Bachelor of Education.

She is a registered psychologist (provisional) and is interested in child psychology, play therapy and inclusive programmes for children with mental health concerns or special educational needs in early years' settings and K-12 school system.

**Nicholas Catania** is a doctoral candidate in special education at the University of South Florida (USF). His research interests include teacher preparation for social justice as well as pedagogical practices for meeting the needs of LBGTQ students. He has over 10 years of experience teaching in K-12 and higher education settings. Nicholas is also a visiting instructor for the Elementary Education programme at USF where he works with teacher candidates in their field placements providing them best practices while coaching them to improve their teaching skills. He has also presented his research at many national conferences.

**Dr Rupert Corazza**, Board of Education for Vienna, Austria, is an educational researcher and political advisor at the Board of Education for Vienna. As a member of the expert staff, he currently leads the implementation process of an extensive education reform in the field of special educational needs. He holds a doctorate in education and a master's degree in Philosophy. He is also lecturer at University College of Teacher Education in Vienna. Dr Corazza conducted numerous national and international research projects in the field of philosophy of education and student assessment. In a current project he develops an assessment tool for children with special educational needs according to ICF-CY. Drawing on Goffman's concept of framing, he regularly publishes scientific articles on the stigmatizing effects of educational categories like school dropout or learning disability.

**Professor Chris Forlin** is an international education consultant specializing in supporting governments and school systems to implement effective and quality inclusive education. She has worked in the field of education for more than 40 years as a teacher, university lecturer and government advisor. Her work with teachers is extensive and she is a frequently sought after as a keynote conference presenter. Her extant research and publications focus on policy development for education reform and systemic support for children and youth with disabilities and development of inclusive curriculum and pedagogy with a particular emphasis on inclusion in developing countries. Her most recent book, published by Emerald, *Promoting social inclusion: Co-creating environments that foster equity and belonging* was published in the *International Perspectives on Inclusive Education* series that she edits.

**Tiffany L. Gallagher**, PhD, is a Professor in the Department of Educational Studies at Brock University, Canada. Prior to this role, Tiffany taught in two school boards in Northern Ontario. Then, for 13 years, she was an administrator in private practice supplemental education providing remedial instruction for students with learning difficulties. She is recognized for her research that aims to enhance the learning of students with literacy difficulties and learning challenges. Supporting the professional learning of teachers through instructional and inclusion coaching are also a focus of her work. Longitudinal, multi-varied participant perspectives are the cornerstone of Tiffany's research projects. Her work seeks to inform targeted audiences such as students, teachers, administrators and policy makers. She has published more than 50 refereed articles/chapters, as well as eight books. Tiffany is also the director of the Brock Learning Lab that offers community-based tutoring for K-12 students and mentors undergraduate volunteer tutors.

**Dr Marie Gitschthaler**, Paderborn University, Germany, is an educational researcher at the Specialist Department for Inclusion, Diversity and Special Educational Needs at the Board of Education for Vienna since 2019 and is involved in the implementation process of an extensive education reform in the field of special education. Currently, she holds the position of an interim professor for Special Education with a focus on learning at University of Paderborn. For a decade, she worked as a researcher and lecturer at the Education Sciences Group at Vienna University of Economics and Business. Dr Gitschthaler conducted numerous national and international research projects on the causes of school dropout, the individual and social costs of inadequate education, social exclusion, education policies concerning inequality and good practices in school improvement. She is highly experienced in conducting longitudinal mixed-methods studies.

**Lisa Hoffmann** is a PhD student at the Institute for Educational Research at the University of Wuppertal, Germany, and special education teacher. Her research mainly focusses on the social participation of students with special educational needs in inclusive settings.

**Kiiko Ikegami** (PhD) is an Assistant Professor at the University of Saint Joseph, Macau, China. She is the Head of the School of Education and Programme Coordinator for the Master of Education at the University of St Joseph, Macau. Prior to moving to Macau, Kiiko was a teaching associate at the Faculty of Education, Monash University. Her specific research focusses on quality early childhood education theorized through the Soka education model and how educator's knowledge, beliefs and pedagogy practices contribute to quality education for young children.

**Dr Phyllis Jones** is a Professor in the Department of Teaching and Learning at the University of South Florida (USF). Phyllis taught and was a deputy head in schools in the UK for 15 years before she entered teacher education. She came to USF in 2003. She is author of *Curricula for Students with Severe Disabilities: Narratives of Standards-Referenced Good Practice, Inclusion in the Early Years: Stories of Good Practice*, co-author of *Collaborate Smart* and lead editor of *A Pig Don't Get Fatter the More You Weigh It*: Balancing assessment for the classroom, Leading for Inclusion, Creating Meaningful Inquiry in the Inclusive Classroom, Pushing the Boundaries: Developing Inclusive Practices through Integration of Insider Perspectives, co-editor of *The Routledge Companion to Severe, Profound and Multiple Learning Difficulties* and *The Foundations of Inclusive Education Research*. She is co-editor of *International Journal of Whole Schooling*, sits on the editorial board of *Disability & Society* and is a regular reviewer for *British Journal of Special Education, Journal of Child and Family Studies, International Journal of Inclusive Education, Journal of Teacher Education and International Review of Education*. Internationally, she has worked in England, Ireland, New Zealand, Thailand and Mexico. Phyllis has a current Fulbright application and has been successful at the US country level, with her application having been forwarded to Hong Kong for this review.

**Julia Kast**, MA, University of Vienna, Austria, has started her PhD at the Centre for Teacher Education at University of Vienna in 2018. Her research mainly focusses on inclusive education. In 2013, she graduated from Psychology with a focus on Educational Psychology at University of Vienna. Further topics include teachers' attitudes towards inclusive education and teachers' self-efficacy in inclusive educational settings. Her doctoral thesis focusses on the inclusion of students with different language abilities within the Austrian Education system.

**Dr Danielle Lane** is an Assistant Professor of special education at Elon University in North Carolina. Her research focusses on global understandings of disabilities in various cultural contexts. Specifically, she is interested in centralizing the importance of inclusive practices in educational provisions that are provided to students with disabilities. Danielle teaches courses in special education at the undergraduate level and serves as a university supervisor for pre-service teacher candidates. She also serves as the editorial assistant for *International Journal of Whole Schooling*.

**Kimberly Maich**, PhD, OCT, BCBA-D, is a Professor in the Faculty of Education at MUN, a certified teacher, a special education specialist, a board-certified behaviour analyst and a registered psychologist (provisional). Her research and writing is focused on special education in general and autism spectrum disorders, emotional/behaviour disorders, early learners and assistive technology more specifically. She engages in qualitative, mixed-methods and single case quantitative experimental research design and is committed to community-based knowledge mobilization of research findings and the use of case study in teaching and learning.

**Elisa Monteiro** is an Associate Professor in the Faculty of Social Sciences and Education in the University of Saint Joseph, Macao. She teaches various modules in the undergraduate and postgraduate education programmes and supervises in-service and pre-service teachers during their teaching practice at placement schools. Professor Monteiro has delivered several teacher professional development courses and workshops in the areas of instructional pedagogy and assessment. Most of her work has been developing and articulating teachers' professional knowledge and skills. Her research interests cover a range of topics in curriculum planning, pedagogy, instructional strategies, blended learning, assessment and inclusive education.

**Saskia Liebner** is a postdoc lecturer in the Faculty of Human Sciences, Unit Inclusion and Organization Development, at the University of Potsdam

(Germany). Her current research is concerned with teacher training and the professional development of pre- and in-service teachers in the field of inclusive education.

**Sharon C. Penney**, PhD, is an Associate Professor in the Faculty of Education at MUN, a certified teacher and registered psychologist with the Newfoundland and Labrador Psychology Board. Her research is focused on special education, autism spectrum disorders, home and school partnerships as well as positive mental health. She works primarily with qualitative methodologies and mixed-methods research.

**David Philpott**, EdD, is a Professor in the Faculty of Education at MUN and has enjoyed a career of more than 35 years in education and child development. He has worked in a range of teaching and management positions in special education, including a 25-year clinical practice in child mental health and assessment. He has an extensive national and international research/publication portfolio in areas such as inclusive education, assessment, Indigenous/Aboriginal education, family empowerment, international students, early child education and teacher training.

**Corine Rivalland** (PhD) is a lecturer in Early Childhood and Equity and Social Justice Education in the Faculty of Education, Monash University. Her research focus addresses alternative theories of child development and equity and social justice. Her work aims to contribute to the early childhood educational research with the view of implementing more equitable and socially just early childhood teaching and learning practices.

**Claudia Schmaltz** is a secondary school teacher in Baden-Württemberg, Germany. She completed her PhD at the University of Education, Freiburg, on the effect of in-service training on the teaching planning competence of teachers, with a particular focus on heterogeneity as a challenge for teaching.

**Susanne Schwab** is a Full Professor at the Centre for Teacher Education, University of Vienna, Austria, and extraordinary professor at the Research Focus Area Optentia, North-West University, Vanderbijlpark, South Africa. Her research specifically focusses on inclusive education, as well as teacher education and training. She has recently published a chapter about 'Inclusive and special education in Europe' in the *Oxford Research Encyclopedia of Education.*

**Sarah Semon** earned her PhD in Curriculum and Instruction in Special Education from the University of South Florida. She is a visiting instructor of special education in the Department of Teaching and Learning at USF and has over 20 years of experience teaching in K-12 and higher education settings. Sarah has dedicated her career to improving inclusive education services for diverse learners. She has extensive experience consulting, writing and managing federal and state grant projects. She has presented educational research findings at national conferences and has co-authored numerous journal articles and book chapters.

**Umesh Sharma** is Professor in the Faculty of Education at Monash University, Australia, where he is the academic head of the Educational Psychology and Inclusive Education Community. Umesh's research programmes in the area of disability and inclusive education span India, Pakistan, China, Bangladesh, Fiji, Solomon Islands, Vanuatu and Samoa as well as Australia, Canada, USA and New Zealand. He is the chief co-editor of the *Australasian Journal of Special Education* and the *Oxford Encyclopedia of Inclusive and Special Education*. His co-authored book *A Guide to Promoting a Positive Classroom Environment* was the recipient of the International Book Prize Award from the *Exceptionality Education International*. He was recently (2019) named the top special education researcher in Australia based on the impact of his work locally and internationally by the Australian Chief Scientist https://special-reports.theaustralian.com.au/1540291/.

**Sharlene Smith** earned her PhD in Curriculum and Instruction in Adult Education, and cognate in Autism Spectrum Disorder from the University of South Florida. She is a behaviour specialist at the Rutgers University Centre for Adult Autism Services. She is an advocate for inclusive and equitable communities to ensure every student receives the requisite resources to achieve success. For the past five years, she has been working with individuals with disabilities, specifically autism, and their families. Dr Smith is also a national and international scholar. She co-authored several peer-reviewed journals and book chapters. Her research centres on the adult education of general and special needs population. Some of her present research focus includes the professional development and continuing education of educators who work with individuals with special needs. She also serves as a reviewer for the *International Journal of Whole Schooling*.

**Monique Somma**, PhD, OCT, is an Assistant Professor and emerging scholar in the Department of Educational Studies at Brock University, Canada. Currently, she co-develops and teaches courses to teacher candidates on topics including child development, cognition and the inclusion of students with exceptionalities, in order to help prepare future teachers to effectively meet the needs of diverse learners in the classroom. Her research focusses on preschool to secondary educator preparedness for inclusive education, from attitudes and beliefs to learning and practice. She is the co-author of *Special Education in Ontario Schools, eighth edition, 2019*.

**Samantha Vlcek** is a research assistant at Monash University and is currently completing her PhD in the field of inclusive education at the University of Tasmania. She holds a BEd with first class Honours and a Graduate Certificate in Research. Samantha has taught in both primary schools and at a tertiary level. Her research and teaching are concerned with inclusive education and supporting the education of students with diverse needs. Samantha has comprehensive knowledge of disability legislation and policy, as well as a deep understanding of implementing evidence-based practices to support student experience and outcomes.

**Rebecca White**, BA, has completed a joint honours degree at the University of Ottawa, Canada, in history and political science. She is currently a project coordinator, research assistant and completing her Masters of Education at Brock University with a specialization in administration and leadership. Rebecca's research interests focus on improving inclusive education for students with exceptionalities in both policy and practice.

**Kathy Wlodarczyk**, PhD, has completed her studies at McMaster University, Canada. Her research, clinical and scholarly work focusses on understanding the mechanisms that contribute to effective outcomes and best practices in collaborative partnerships between the disciplines of rehabilitation and education. Kathy's work is edified with an inclusive, holistic and multidisciplinary lens.

**Gabrielle D. Young**, PhD, is an Associate Professor in a Canadian Faculty of Education, Memorial University of Newfoundland (MUN), where she teaches undergraduate and graduate courses surrounding understanding and supporting students with specific learning disorders, as well as the practicum in special education. Gabrielle's research interests surround the use of assistive and instructional technology in inclusive classrooms, applying the principles of universal design for learning to support students with exceptionalities in the general education classroom, and pre-service teachers' efficacy to support students in inclusive classrooms and facilitate positive mental health.

# ABOUT THE EDITORS

**Janka Goldan**, PhD, is a Researcher at the Faculty of Educational Science, University of Bielefeld. She studied in Frankfurt (GER) and London (UK) and holds degrees in education and business administration. Her research focusses on inclusive education, including funding and resourcing of special needs education. She received her PhD from the University of Wuppertal (GER) and is involved in several projects, among them also in education policy. Her key publications address issues of resourcing inclusive education and the assessment of resource perceptions.

**Jennifer Lambrecht**, PhD, is a Researcher at the Faculty of Educational Science, University of Potsdam, Germany. She studied in Hamburg and Berlin and holds degrees in education and philosophy. Her research focusses on inclusive education, educational inequalities and the role of institutional learning environments. In her dissertation, she developed a theory on inclusive education. Furthermore, she is involved in several projects, including science communication.

**Tim Loreman**, PhD, is President and Vice-Chancellor, and Professor of Education, at Concordia University of Edmonton. He studied at Monash and Deakin Universities in Melbourne, Australia. His active research interests include inclusive education, teacher education and pedagogy. In 2010, he was senior visiting research fellow at the University of Bologna and in 2013 was visiting research professor at Queens University Belfast. He has held a number of major Canadian research grants and participated in large cross-institutional and cross-national projects aimed at reform of education systems in Ukraine and various Pacific Island nations in order to better support inclusive education.

# SERIES INTRODUCTION

Edited by Janka Goldan, Jennifer Lambrecht and Tim Loreman

The adoption internationally of inclusive practice as the most equitable and all-encompassing approach to education and its relation to compliance with various international declarations and conventions underpins the importance of this series for people working at all levels of education and schooling in both developed and less developed countries. There is little doubt that inclusive education is complex and diverse and that there are enormous disparities in understanding and application at both inter- and intra-country levels. A broad perspective on inclusive education throughout this series is taken, encompassing a wide range of contemporary viewpoints, ideas and research for enabling the development of more inclusive schools, education systems and communities.

Volumes in this series on *International Perspectives on Inclusive Education* contribute to the academic and professional discourse by providing a collection of philosophies and practices that can be reviewed considering local contextual and cultural situations in order to assist governments, educators, peripatetic staff and other professionals to provide the best education for all children. Each volume in the series focusses on a key aspect of inclusive education and provides critical chapters by contributing leaders in the field who discuss theoretical positions, quality research and impacts on school and classroom practice. Different volumes address issues relating to the diversity of student need within heterogeneous classrooms and the preparation of teachers and other staff to work in inclusive schools. Systemic changes and practice in schools encompass a wide perspective of learners to provide ideas on reframing education to ensure that it is inclusive of all. Evidence-based research practices underpin a plethora of suggestions for decision-makers and practitioners, incorporating current ways of thinking about and implementing inclusive education.

While many barriers have been identified that may potentially constrain the implementation of effective inclusive practices, this series aims to identify such key concerns and offers practical and best practice approaches to overcoming them. Adopting a thematic approach for each volume, readers will be able to quickly locate a collection of research and practice related to a topic of interest. By transforming schools into inclusive communities of practice, all children can have the opportunity to access and participate in quality and equitable education to enable them to obtain the skills to become contributory global citizens. This series, therefore, is highly recommended to support education decision-makers, practitioners, researchers and academics, who have a professional interest in the inclusion of children and youth who are marginalizing in inclusive schools and classrooms.

Volume 15 in the *International Perspectives on Inclusive Education* series adds to the collection by addressing a very demanding aspect of how to resource inclusive education to ensure it is equitable, fair, manageable and effective. All governments and education departments are faced with issues surrounding resourcing inclusive education, usually within a defined budget and fiscal constraints. This is heightened further for financial administrators, during transition periods where governments are moving from a segregated to a more inclusive education system. By critiquing an extensive range of optional funding models, funding formulas and human resourcing approaches, this book offers a comprehensive review of how appropriate resourcing, within a country's given restraints and specific cultural and contextual issues, can support more effective inclusive education.

Presented in two sections, the authors firstly address the evolving challenges associated with funding inclusive education by considering evidence from a range of countries which have endeavoured to respond to these in diverse and positive ways. The issues of developing effective policy and of establishing accountability mechanisms that ensure equitable distribution of funding across all schools are treated empathetically, citing relevant and useful research and evidence. The latter half of the book provides a life-long learning perspective on how to improve inclusion by focussing on enhanced human resourcing through better teacher education and professional learning. The importance of appropriate and effective teacher education for inclusion has been identified in all systems. Key international documents continue to highlight that inclusive education requires teachers who are appropriately trained, motivated, enjoy teaching and who are backed by well-managed and resourced education systems. Any inclusive educational reform model must be focussed on these areas. Both sections of the book are, therefore, critical, as the dynamic interaction between the two is essential to ensuring effective and sustainable implementation of quality inclusive education.

A tangible strength of this volume is that it explicitly contemplates resourcing inclusive education through the application of realistic funding approaches and improved professional learning. Of importance, though, is that while focussing on dollar expenditure, it also considers how better resourcing will help students to develop twenty-first century skills of academic self-concept, social inclusion and general well-being. It also highlights the strong link between effective funding management and teachers' self-efficacy and attitudes towards becoming effective and positive inclusive practitioners.

Volume 15 is a critical book for all stakeholders concerned with how to resource inclusive education, to provide quality education for all learners. This is addressed effectually through reviewing how resourcing can be managed to ensure equitable access regardless of geographical region or students' needs. This book provides excellent, current and practical approaches while reviewing global trends that will appeal to support school staff, administrators, economists, district coordinators, other stakeholders and school board personnel to make best possible decisions regarding funding regimes. This volume will also appeal to university academics, students and researchers who are tasked with investigating best practice ways of resourcing inclusive schools. Within the book, selected chapters enable the reader to choose a specific area of resource interest and to explore options derived from research and best practice evidence-based ideas presented by leading international experts in the field. Volume 15 will be an important international resource providing immediate access to a wide range of germane approaches across many disciplines to enable good decisions to be made to better resource inclusive education. I highly recommend and endorse it as an excellent addition to the *International Perspectives on Inclusive Education* series.

Chris Forlin
Series Editor

# INTRODUCTION

## Janka Goldan, Jennifer Lambrecht and Tim Loreman

With the ratification of the Convention on the Rights of Persons with Disabilities (UN-CRPD; United Nations, 2006), the signatory states have committed themselves to guarantee equal access to the general education system for students with and without special educational needs. In order to achieve this goal, states have to ensure that '[r]easonable accommodation of the individual's requirements is provided' (UN-CRPD Art. 24, 2c). This raises the critical question of the provision of appropriate resources for inclusive education.

This volume addresses the issue of funding and resourcing from two perspectives: The first section of the volume considers financial resourcing of education systems in terms of funding formulas. The second part focuses on human resourcing with regard to professional development and teacher training.

In the first section, leading international experts address the challenges of funding that have emerged with the implementation of a more inclusive school system. The different objectives to be achieved through specific modes of funding including demand-orientation, fairness and effectiveness are often accompanied by unintended side effects, such as the labelling of students with special educational needs that might lead to stigmatization (Banks, Frawley, & McCoy, 2015; Fletcher-Campbell, 2002; Goldan, 2019; Meijer, 1999). Further, it is not only important to consider different funding modes on the level of policy making but also how resources are distributed and perceived within schools (Goldan & Schwab, 2018; Lambrecht, Bosse, Henke, Jäntsch, & Spörer, 2016).

In this book, Joanne Banks addresses the question of unintended side effects by examining a funding model for inclusive education in Ireland that provides support without labelling children on the basis of disability for inclusive education. Young, Philpott, Maich, Penney and Butler focus on the latest research with regard to the role of early childhood education in ameliorating subsequent special educational needs through early interventions. The following chapters are concerned with questions regarding the use of resources. Catania, Lane, Semon, Smith and Jones take a closer look at the policies guiding the education and funding of students with special educational needs in the United States, while

Resourcing Inclusive Education
International Perspectives on Inclusive Education, Volume 15, 1–3
Copyright © 2021 by Emerald Publishing Limited.
All rights of reproduction in any form reserved
ISSN: 1479-3636/doi:10.1108/S1479-363620210000015002

Sharma and Vlcek report on how funding is used in schools around the world to facilitate inclusive education. The first section concludes with two chapters focussing on the perception of resources. Gitschthalter, Kast, Corazza and Schwab examine the reasonableness of resourcing from a subjective point of view, asking if teachers are satisfied with the resources provided. Goldan, Hoffmann and Schwab explore the relationship between students' perception of resources in inclusive education and its effect on school well-being, academic self-concept and social participation.

The second part of the book is focused on international perspectives of teacher training and professional development for inclusive education, ranging from early childhood education to post-secondary teacher training. As Sharma and Vlcek (Chapter 5) point out, resources for inclusive education are mainly spent on professional development. This raises questions about resource allocation to foster professional development. Accordingly, Bennett, Gallagher, Somma, White and Wlodarczyk introduce the second part of the book by presenting a resource model in which internal school district funding was reallocated to convert teaching positions into inclusion coach positions. They show how a specific school district was able to successfully transit beliefs and practices from segregated special education to full inclusion for students with special education needs. In the following chapter, Agbenyega and Ikegami offer a different approach to the dominant Western philosophies of education and grounding early childhood education and teacher education in Nichiren Buddhist (Soka) philosophy, arguing that this can help improve the effectiveness of the inclusive educational experience for all children. The final two chapters analyze the implementation of changes in teacher education. Opalinski and Schmaltz provide an overview of the current status of the curricular implementation of inclusion-oriented teacher training in Germany. Monteiro and Forlin investigate the effect of a revised Post-Graduate Diploma in Education (PGDE) programme on teachers' pedagogical practice and knowledge transfer for inclusive education.

This volume provides a broad selection of topics and perspectives on resourcing for inclusive education, considering not only financial models but also approaches that make best use of the personnel resources which are essential for the successful implementation of inclusive education.

# REFERENCES

Banks, J., Frawley, D., & McCoy, S. (2015). Achieving inclusion? Effective resourcing of students with special educational needs. *International Journal of Inclusive Education, 19*(9), 926–943. doi: 10.1080/13603116.2015.1018344

Fletcher-Campbell, F. (2002). The financing of special education: Lessons from Europe. *Support for Learning, 17*(1), 19–22. doi:10.1111/1467-9604.00227

Goldan, J. (2019). Demand-oriented and fair allocation of special needs teacher resources for inclusive education – Assessment of a newly implemented funding model in North Rhine-Westphalia, Germany. *International Journal of Inclusive Education.* doi:10.1080/13603116.2019.1568598

Goldan, J., & Schwab, S. (2018). Measuring students' and teachers' perceptions of resources in inclusive education – Validation of a newly developed instrument. *International Journal of Inclusive Education, 14*(2), 1326–1339. doi:10.1080/13603116.2018.1515270

Lambrecht, J., Bosse, S., Henke, T., Jäntsch, C., & Spörer, N. (2016). Eine inklusive Grundschule ist eine inklusive Grundschule? Wie sich inklusive Grundschulen an Hand ihres Umgangs mit Ressourcen unterscheiden lassen [*Is an inclusive primary school an inclusive primary school? How to cluster inclusive schoolsby their use of resources.*] *Zeitschrift für Bildungsforschung, 6*(2), 135–150.

Meijer, J. W. (1999). *Financing of special needs education. A seventeen-country study of the relationship between financing of special needs education and inclusion.* Middelfart: European Agency for Development in Special Needs Education.

United Nations (UN). (2006). *Convention on the rights of persons with disabilities an optional protocol.* New York, NY: United Nations.

# SECTION 1

# FUNDING AND RESOURCING INCLUSIVE EDUCATION

# A WINNING FORMULA? FUNDING INCLUSIVE EDUCATION IN IRELAND

Joanne Banks

## ABSTRACT

*Increasingly, countries around the world are reforming their traditional 'special educational needs' funding models, many of which contradict the overarching principles of inclusive education as set out in the United Nations Convention on the Rights of Persons with a Disability (UNCRPD). There is growing awareness across countries that the way education systems are financed directly shapes the extent to which schools can be inclusive. Spiralling costs have also influenced governments who have begun calling for 'cost control' and greater transparency and accountability in how resources are distributed and monies are spent. In Ireland, calls for a more equitable resource model for students with disabilities in mainstream education resulted in the introduction of a new system of funding which removed the need for diagnosis to receive supports. However, since ratification of the UNCRPD in 2018, Ireland's system of special education is being considered for full reform with the possibility of moving to a system of inclusive education and the removal of special schools and classes. This raises the question: can two separate funding streams, one for general education and one for special education ever exist in an inclusive system? Having one funding model for all students, although the logical choice, is the source of much concern among parents and disability advocates, many of whom fear it will lead to children with disabilities 'falling through the cracks' and used by government as a mechanism to reduce spending overall.*

**Keywords**: Inclusive education; funding systems; school autonomy; Universal Design for Learning

Resourcing Inclusive Education
International Perspectives on Inclusive Education, Volume 15, 7–19
ISSN: 1479-3636/doi:10.1108/S1479-363620210000015003

# INTRODUCTION

Internationally, inclusive education policy stresses that all learners of any age should have the right to a meaningful, high-quality education in their local school alongside their peers (European Agency, 2015, 2019). A key principle of inclusive education is that school is an environment where students with disabilities engage on an equal basis to their peers, where they can reach their potential and be accepted (Sharma, Furlonger, & Forlin, 2019). Article 24 of the UN Convention on the Rights of Persons with Disabilities (CRPD; UN, 2006) has meant that for the 181 countries, inclusive education is now a legally binding obligation. The 'reform journey' (de Bruin, 2019) or the transition from special education to inclusive education is complex, varies from country to country and, for many, the right to an inclusive, quality education remains 'unfinished business' (Slee, 2019, p. 7). In Ireland, the special education 'sector' is currently in a state of flux. Students with disabilities can attend either mainstream schools, special classes in mainstream schools or special schools. Two separate funding streams exist, one for general education and another for special education. Recently, however, demands for a more equitable funding model for students with disabilities in mainstream education led to the introduction of a new system of resource allocation. Significantly, the new model removed the need for diagnosis or 'labelling' of students to receive supports and devolved much of the decision-making power around resources to schools. Just a couple of months after its introduction however, Ireland ratified the UNCRPD which refocused attention on the continued use of special classes and special schools as a form of provision. Public consultation is now underway about whether Ireland can move to a fully inclusive system thus removing the need for specialized provision. This chapter examines this time of transition and change in Ireland as it begins its 'reform journey' towards inclusive education. Using Article 24 of the UNCRPD as a framework, it examines current funding structures and raises the question: can two separate funding streams, one for general education and one for special education ever exist in an inclusive system? Using Ireland's new funding model as an example, the chapter explores the key characteristics of inclusive funding models and highlights the need for systemic reform where schools can provide resourced mainstream provision with meaningful inclusion of all students regardless of their levels of need.

# EDUCATION FUNDING MODELS: POLICY AND PRACTICE

How education systems are financed is just one part of these structural reforms but thought to directly influence the extent to which inclusive education can be realized (European Agency, 2016a, 2016b; OECD, 2012; UNESCO, 2009). Funding mechanisms influence school-level decision-making about how students with disabilities are identified and often labelled (Ebersold, Watkins, Óskarsdóttir, & Meijer, 2019). The UNCRPD makes explicit that governments should create:

> ...a funding model that allocates resources and incentives for inclusive educational environments to provide the necessary support to persons with disabilities (GC No. 4 to Article 24, p. 22)

Despite these policy developments, it is generally accepted that the way funding is provided can incentivize the placement of some students in separate educational settings such as special classes or special schools (Slee, 2019). Furthermore, many countries continue to operate a dual funding system of general and special education with many reporting dramatic increases in the amount spent on these supports each year (Graham & Sweller, 2011; Jahnukainen, 2011; Parrish et al., 2003). To date, much of the research in this area has assumed the continuation of dual funding and focussed on the most equitable way to resource students with disabilities in mainstream education (Banks, Frawley, & McCoy, 2015; Engstrøm Graversen, 2015; Goldan, 2019; Gubbels, Coppens, & De Wolf, 2017; Jahnukainen, 2011; Parish & Bryant, 2015; Pijl, 2016; Pulkkinen & Jahnukainen, 2016; Sharma, Forlin, & Furlonger, 2015). Debates have tended to examine the pros and cons of input, throughput or output funding, the value of categorical versus general funding or whether to have a centralized or national funding model as compared to a district, local authority or school-level system of support. There is some agreement that input funding, where individual students or their parents receive funding or resources based on a specific weighted category of disability, is based on the medical model of disability and therefore problematic. This type of support is, however, often favoured by students and their parents as it guarantees the resources that they were assigned (Goldan, 2019; Lamb, 2009). With increases in the numbers of students with disabilities in mainstream schools over the last two decades, various stakeholders expressed concerns over this funding model mainly due to spiralling costs, the need to label and diagnose students to access support, the waiting time to access supports, as well as the associated inequities with the categorical nature of this type of funding (Engstrøm Graversen, 2015; Topping & Maloney, 2005).

Other funding models have since been introduced such as school- or area-level funding (known as throughput funding) where central governments allocate base funding to schools or local authorities who are responsible for how funding is spent and resources allocated (Pulkkinen & Jahnukainen, 2016; Sharma et al., 2015). More recently, some governments have modified their input or throughput models to include outcome-based funding which is based on student performance in school (EASNIE, 2016a, 2016b). Increasingly, countries are adopting a combination of methods in an attempt to counter the negative aspects of each approach (Jahnukainen, 2011; Sharma et al., 2015). Some are moving to a combination of bounty (where resources are linked to a diagnosis) and base funding with others shifting to base funding only. There remains little consensus however with little evidence pointing to the value of one system over another.

# FUNDING INCLUSIVE EDUCATION IN IRELAND

Special education in Ireland is in a state of flux. In line with most other European countries, the Irish education system aims to be inclusive (NCSE, 2014, 2019), and over the past 15 years there has been significant policy development (national and international) in the area of disability and special education (Government of Ireland, 2004, 2005; NCSE, 2006, 2011, 2014, 2019; UN, 2006; UNESCO, 1994). Introduced in 2004, the Education for Persons with Special Educational Needs (EPSEN) Act is now considered a landmark document as it broadened the definition of special educational needs beyond medical disability categories (NCSE, 2006) and subsequently changed the profile and in particular the level of diversity in mainstream classrooms (Banks & McCoy, 2011). Over the past 15 years, the prevalence of students with disabilities increased and is currently estimated to be between 25 and 27% or 1 in 4 of the school population (Banks & McCoy, 2011; Cosgrove et al., 2014). Although not all students with disabilities require supports, there has been a consistent increase in the amount spent on special education which has brought with it increasing levels of scrutiny from government (DPER, 2017, 2019). In line with spending patterns internationally, during Ireland's economic recession, spending on special education increased. The EASNIE (2016a, 2016b) suggests that these patterns may reflect the tendency by education systems to label learners for the purpose of accessing supports rather than an increasing investment in inclusive education systems (EASNIE, 2016a, 2016b, 2018b; Soriano, Watkins, & Ebersold, 2017). In an attempt to understand these increases, Ireland's Department of Public Expenditure and Reform (DPER) has carried out two reviews of spending on special education in recent years. They (DPER, 2017, 2019) highlighted a dramatic rise in the cost of special education over time with a 52% increase between 2011 and 2019, from €465 million to €1.9 billion representing 19% of the Department of Education's budget (DPER, 2019). Perhaps the most controversial aspect of the report was the finding that spending on special education was higher than that spent on higher education (€1.58 billion) (DPER, 2017). The pressure to curb spending has been the source of much debate on whether the system is simply playing catch-up of years of under-resourcing or if it is over-spending in the area of resource allocation for students with disabilities in mainstream schools (Banks & McCoy, 2017).

*Special Schools and Classes*

In line with patterns of provision internationally (Graham & Sweller, 2011; Le Laider & Prouchandy, 2012), and despite the significant investment in special education in mainstream education, the number of students attending special schools in Ireland had not decreased but remained static (DPER, 2017). Furthermore, there has been significant investment in a model of special class provision over the last decade with a particular focus on the provision of classes or 'units' for students with a diagnosis of autism. Despite the lack of evidence that special classes are the optimum setting for all students who are placed in these settings (Banks et al., 2016; McCoy et al., 2014), there are now over 1,600 special classes in early childhood education, primary schools and secondary schools.

Between 2011 and 2019, there was a 91% increase in special education teachers at primary level and a 190% increase at secondary level (DPER, 2017). It is worth noting, however, that these (SET) teachers are not required to have any specialist training, and research suggests newly qualified teachers are often placed in these positions where other staff are reluctant (Banks et al., 2016; Hick et al., 2018; NCSE, 2019). Since Ireland's ratification of the UNCRPD in 2018, the role of special schools and special classes has come under increased scrutiny, given national and international policy commitments to inclusive education. General Comment 4 to the CRPD leaves little room for uncertainty as to how we define segregation:

> ...when the education of students with disabilities is provided in separate environments designed or used to respond to a particular or various impairments, in isolation from students without disabilities. (para 11)

## A New Funding Model to Improve Equity?

In an attempt to address inequities in the system, the Irish National Council for Special Education (NCSE) introduced the Special Education Teaching (SET) model in 2017 replacing the traditional, predominantly input model. This new model was broadly welcomed as a more equitable system of resource allocation combining elements of different funding formula (input, throughput and output) and removing the need for assessment for students with disabilities. The key features of the model are that it combines baseline funding (which goes to all schools regardless of the need for resources) with a weighted component based on the school's educational profile (Table 1).

In order to fully support students with higher levels of need, the SET Allocation model takes account of the number of students with complex needs enrolled in the school. The students include those who have enduring conditions that 'significantly affect their capacity to learn' (NCSE, 2014, p. 32). In identifying students with complex needs, the model does not use categories of disabilities in an attempt to reduce the 'incidence of inappropriate diagnosis and unnecessary labelling of children' (NCSE, 2013, 2014). These students are expected to be identified either at birth or by the time they enter primary school by the health service rather than the education system (NCSE, 2014). Although the new model is just over two years in operation, figures from the Department of Education already show some adjustment to the allocation at primary level. In particular, there is a decline in the

**Table 1.** Primary Level Allocation under the SET Model.

| | |
|---|---|
| Baseline | 20% |
| Complex Needs | 42.5% |
| Standard tests | 27.85% |
| Disadvantage | 5.5% |
| Gender | 4.35% |

*Source:* DES (2017).

amount allocated to students with complex needs since its introduction from 50% of funding allocated in 2017 to 42.5% in 2019 (DES, 2017, 2019).

An interesting new aspect of the SET Allocation model is that it seeks to measure student progress or outcomes through standardized test results in an effort to build the school's educational profile (NCSE, 2014). This measure sees a shift in focus towards school accountability for funding received, but it may be problematic. An increased emphasis on testing may be to the detriment of the educational experiences of these students, since such tests can create anxiety for students generally (Banks & Smyth, 2015). Funding based on student achieve-ments in standardized tests may also act as a disincentive for schools to perform well, as doing so will risk a reduction in funding. Furthermore, test results may not have any real meaning for some students with disabilities, who may not be given the opportunity given the test. For some students, progress in school is perhaps more appropriately measured in other ways. Measuring outcomes such as enjoyment in school, academic engagement or peer relations might, for some students, be a more accurate reflection of their progress and performance. This is particularly important in the context of research findings which show that some children with disabilities are more likely to report not liking school (McCoy & Banks, 2012) and have more negative peer relations (Banks, McCoy, & Frawley, 2018). A final component of the school's 'educational profile' is based on the social context of the school, including the social mix of students, the level of disadvantage and the gender-mix of the school. Much of this information will be obtained from a 'social context' survey completed by school principals. This includes information about students' family background including whether they have a medical card, those living in social housing and those with an unemployed head of household. Although the social profile elements of the SET Allocation model are innovative in how it is trying to target supports more effectively, its success depends on the use of accurate data and the willingness or capability of principals to provide detailed social background information about students. Other aspects of the school profile are available centrally in the Department of Education and Skills, such as its disadvantaged status and gender-mix.

### Ireland's Reform Journey: Moving to Inclusive Education?

Irish special education is now at a crossroads. Prompted by new obligations under the UNCRPD Article 24 and questions around the future of special schools and classes, the National Council for Special Education is currently engaging in a consultative and research process. In their draft policy paper (NCSE, 2019), they pose the question as to whether Ireland should move to inclusive education thus removing special schools and classes as a form of provision. Part of this process has involved visits and consultations with stakeholders in other national contexts such as New Brunswick in Canada and Portugal where inclusive education systems are in operation (NCSE, 2019). This consultation has been the source of much debate and concern among parents, education stakeholders, teacher unions and advocates of students with disabilities who argue that inclusive education is not viable and will lead to children with disabilities 'falling through the cracks' and out of the education system altogether. Others fear the transition to inclusive education suits the government who will use this as an opportunity to spending overall (*Irish Examiner*, 2019; *Irish Times*, 2019).

# CHARACTERISTICS OF INCLUSIVE FUNDING MODELS

Research has consistently shown the extent to which education funding models are linked to the level of inclusion (Ebersold et al., 2019). International debates have evolved and begun to emphasize on how best to implement inclusive funding mechanisms thus removing the need for a dual funding structure of special and general education (Ebersold et al., 2019; Soriano et al., 2017). The question has naturally shifted from how we resource special education to how we resource inclusive education. Based on this growing body of literature (Ebersold et al., 2019; Sharma et al., 2019; Soriano et al., 2017), it is possible to compare funding models, such as the Irish SET model, to inclusive finance mechanisms with a view to identifying gaps and highlighting future goals. There are a number of characteristics to these kinds of systems, some of which Ireland has introduced in the SET model:

- They have **devolved funding structure** which increases the level of school autonomy and level of responsibility for school leaders.
- Inclusive funding models tend to incorporate investment in **school development or capacity building** involving school leaders and management and teachers working with increased diversity. Investment is also made in the promotion of innovative teaching and learning strategies such as Universal Design for Learning or Multi-Tiered Systems of Support.
- **Systems of accountability and transparency** in how and why funding is allocated are important elements of inclusive funding mechanisms.

*Devolved Funding Structure*

Inclusive finance mechanisms have a devolved funding structure which ensures flexibility in decision-making at school level thus reducing the need for labelling students in order to access supports. Increased autonomy brings new responsibilities for schools around governance, policies, budgeting, accounting and teacher autonomy (Ebersold et al., 2019). Without the need for diagnosis to receive resources, schools however now have control over decision-making around funding, and attention can be given to the individual needs of students within local contexts (Sharma et al., 2019). This flexibility is thought to create greater opportunities for developing more innovative forms of inclusive education by providing flexible learning and support opportunities in addition to strengthening school governance (NESSE, 2012; Stubbs, 2008).

Research has highlighted however that delegating funds to schools does not always guarantee that the funds will be used to support inclusive educational practices (Riddell, Tisdall, & Kane, 2006). Using a mix of base funding and a weighted funding 'school profile' formula, Ireland's SET model has meant greater responsibility on school principals to implement effective resource mechanisms within the context of inclusive education policy. Previous Irish research has shown that without sufficient supports, school-level funding may lead to inefficiencies and failings if principals lack clarity around how to approach inclusive education (Banks, 2020; Banks et al., 2016). International research also highlights the importance of school leadership and culture in the success of any funding model (Zollers, Ramanathan, & Yu, 2010) regardless of the underlying demographic and contextual factors (Parish & Bryant, 2015). In response to these issues, frameworks for inclusive funding mechanism stress the need to incorporate school capacity building in any system of inclusive education (Ebersold et al., 2019). Based on an analysis of six European countries, the FPIES (Financing Policies for Inclusive Education Systems) project suggests this is done by enabling 'all school stakeholders to become competent inclusive practitioners' including the provision of leadership advice and consultancy 'both at the system level, school level, practitioner level' (Ebersold et al., 2019, p. 11).

### School Development or Capacity Building

Teacher capacity is viewed as one of the key factors in the implementation of inclusive education (European Agency, 2015; UNESCO, 2017). International research has consistently pointed to the need for support for classroom teachers to enable students with disabilities to have the same opportunities to develop as their peers (Banks et al., 2016; Hick et al., 2018; Sharma et al., 2019; Slee, 2010). The World Forum on Education Incheon's (2015) declaration emphasizes the need for inclusive education teachers to be 'empowered, adequately recruited, well-trained, professionally qualified, motivated and supported within well-resourced, efficient and effectively governed systems' (UN, 2015, p. 8). Irish research has shown, however, that teachers report not feeling equipped to teach students with disabilities and practice inclusion in their schools (Banks et al., 2016). There remains little understanding of teacher capacity and qualifications and the role played by initial teacher education and continuous professional development in developing teacher capacity and confidence to practice inclusion (with the exception of Hick et al., 2018). As part of the SET model, there is no additional provision for capacity building for teachers working in inclusive education beyond professional development programmes offered by the National Council for Special Education and further and higher education providers. Furthermore, in many systems, funding to schools is often utilized to employ education assistants or special needs assistants to meet the needs of individual students (Sharma et al., 2019; NCSE, 2018), but there is limited evidence about the effectiveness of their role improving student outcomes within the context of inclusive education (Blatchford, 2009 cited in Sharma et al., 2019). Some inclusion advocates claim that these kinds of roles in schools are still part of a compensatory approach to 'help the teacher' and make the student with the disability 'fit in' with the existing system (EASNIE, 2016a, 2016b). In addition to capacity building and development at school level, frameworks for inclusive education funding systems highlight the importance of investment in capacity building for teachers as part of their funding structure. This can be done through the delivery of in-service training, technical support and other supports (Ebersold et al., 2019).

An integral part of any inclusive funding model is the promotion of innovative teaching and learning strategies (Sharma et al., 2019). The FPIES project highlights the importance of capacity building in teaching through the creation of 'inclusive and flexible learning environments' where all school stakeholders engage in Universal Design for Learning (UDL) (Rose, Meyer, & Hitchcock, 2005) thus making the curriculum accessible to a wider more diverse student body (Ebersold et al., 2019; Florian, 2019). UDL is most associated with higher education in Ireland through the work of AHEAD (Association for Higher Education Access and Disability) but is now also embedded in the Irish pre-school curriculum (Access and Inclusion Model) and is part of the reforms of the curriculum at lower secondary level in Junior Cycle (DES, 2015). By investing in the identification of school-based methods and approaches for flexible and adaptive teaching such as UDL, inclusive funding models thus remove the need for external support linked to the labelling of learners.

*Systems of Transparency and Accountability*

The idea of quality assurance and the monitoring of school policies through an inclusive lens is relatively new (EASNIE, 2018a). Systems of accountability are an important part of any funding model (Busemeyer & Vossiek, 2015) but remain absent from the SET model in Ireland. Although baseline information is collected from schools on student numbers and levels of support in primary and second level, no metrics or indicators are being used to evaluate whether the model is effective in reaching its objectives (DPER, 2019). Perhaps part of this problem is the lack of any real debate about what the objectives of additional supports are within the context of inclusive education policies in school. Without these data, no monitoring of expenditure can take place, and funding cannot be linked to inclusion goals. Ireland is not alone however. Few countries collect budgetary data in their national data collection systems or can connect sums spent on inclusive education with placements, achievements or learning outcomes (EASNIE, 2011 cited in Ebersold et al., 2019). As a result, some argue there is a need to 'regulate processes for allocating funds to ensure that resources effectively reach the learner for whom they are intended and that they are well spent' (Ebersold et al., 2019, p. 244). This would then incentivize the development of a whole-school approach to inclusion where schools are compliant with regulations and standards (Ebersold et al., 2019).

# CONCLUSION

Debates about funding inclusive education are dynamic and continually evolving. In the past, much of the discussion focussed on a lack of funding for students with disabilities in mainstream education (Boyle & Anderson, 2014). There is now an increasing awareness of the need for inclusive funding mechanisms to be in place for this funding to be effective (EASNIE, 2016a, 2016b; Fletcher-Campbell, Pijl, Meijer, Dyson, & Parrish, 2003; Parish & Bryant, 2015). The reasons are many and include the high cost of special education and the tendency for educations systems to segregate or exclude students with disabilities from mainstream education. Furthermore, by providing special education as a separate form of provision, it removes the need for mainstream education to adopt flexible teaching approaches in response to diverse needs. What is clear from existing research is that inclusive funding models are complex when compared to special education mechanisms as they involve multiple stakeholders and an inert-agency, inter-departmental, cross-sectoral approach (Ebersold et al., 2019). They go beyond the provision of supports for individual students to include other components that can relate to physical infrastructure, involve specialist support, capacity building through staff development and training, monitoring and accountability and supports to enhance teaching and learning (Ebersold et al., 2019).

Ireland's special education funding system has undergone much scrutiny in recent years as a result of spiralling costs and new obligations around inclusion since ratifying the UNCRPD. By moving to the proposed new model of inclusive education, teacher unions, parents and disability advocates have expressed concerns about moving from the current systems of special education to inclusive education (NCSE, 2019). Particular areas of concern are the potential closure of special schools and classes and the policy of government to provide a 'continuum of service provision' where parents have the choice where to send their children to school. By moving to inclusive education, the fear remains that the education system would be unable to provide adequate supports in a meaningful way.

The SET Allocation model fulfils some of the 'cross-sectoral issues' as identified by Ebersold et al. (2019) in that the new funding model is non-categorical and has a devolved structure with greater autonomy and flexibility at the school level. Regardless of whether Ireland adopts an inclusive funding model in the future, there are gaps in the extent to which schools have the leadership or teaching capacity to respond to an increasingly diverse student population. Furthermore, there is little investment in supporting schools to adopt more flexible teaching and learning strategies such as Universal Design for Learning or Multi-Tiered Systems of Support which 'work' not just for students with disabilities but for all students. Finally, the newly introduced SET model has no system of monitoring or accountability. Without transparency in how funds and resources allocated, it will be difficult for schools and the National Council for Special Education to refine supports and ensure those that require them, receive them.

As part of the ongoing consultation around building an inclusive education system in Ireland, greater attention needs to be given to the role of how education supports are funding and the in-built incentives in some funding approaches. Evidence shows that the way in which we fund supports in education directly impacts on whether we can achieve inclusion in our schools (Ebersold et al., 2019; Sharma et al., 2019; Slee, 2019). By having two funding streams (general and special), both funding models enact a medical model of disability whereby students with disabilities receive supports to integrate into an unreconstructed mainstream education system. Instead of financing 'special' and 'mainstream' education, perhaps the Irish education systems should remove incentives for segregation and ensure that inclusive education funding models apply to any student at risk of exclusion from education.

## REFERENCES

Banks, J. (2020). Examining the cost of special education. In *Oxford Research Encyclopedia of Education*. Oxford University Press. doi:10.1093/acrefore/9780190264093.013.1025.

Banks, J., Frawley, D., & McCoy, S. (2015). Achieving inclusion? Effective resourcing of students with special educational needs. *International Journal of Inclusive Education, 19*, 926–943.

Banks, J., & McCoy, S. (2011). *A study on the prevalence of special educational needs.* Trim: NCSE.

Banks, J., & McCoy, S. (2017). Playing catch-up or overspending? Managing the cost of special education. *Education Matters, Ireland's Yearbook of Education, 2017–2018, 30*, 236–242.

Banks, J., McCoy, S., & Frawley, D. (2018). One of the gang? Peer relations among students with special educational needs in Irish mainstream primary schools. *European Journal of Special Needs Education, 33*(3), 396–411.

Banks, J., McCoy, S., Frawley, D., Kingston, G., Shevlin, M., & Smyth, F. (2016). *Special classes in Irish schools, phase 2: A qualitative study.* Trim: ESRI/NCSE.

Banks, J., & Smyth, E. (2015). 'Your whole life depends on it?': Academic stress and high-stakes testing in Ireland. *Journal of Youth Studies, 18*, 598–616.

Boyle, C., & Anderson, J. (2014). Disability funding in schools shouldn't be based on state. Commentary in The Conversation, The Conversation Media Group, Melbourne, Australia. Retrieved from https://theconversation.com/disability-funding-in-schools-shouldnt-bebased-on-state-30018

Busemeyer, M., & Vossiek, J. (2015). *Reforming education governance through local capacity-building: A case study of the "learning locally" programme in Germany.* OECD Education Working Papers, No. 113. OECD Publishing, Paris.

Cosgrove, J., McKeown, C., Travers, J., Lysaght, Z., Ní Bhroin, O., & Archer, P. (2014). *Educational experiences and outcomes for children with special educational needs: A secondary analysis of data from the growing up in Ireland study.* Trim: NCSE.

de Bruin, K. (2019). The impact of inclusive education reforms on students with disability: An international comparison. *International Journal of Inclusive Education, 23*(7–8), 811–826.

DES. (2015). *Framework for junior cycle 2015.* Dublin: Department of Education and Skills.

DES. (2017). *Circular to the management authorities of all mainstream primary schools special education teaching allocation.* Dublin: Department of Education and Skills.

DES. (2019). *Circular No. 007/2019 to the management authorities of all mainstream primary schools special education teaching allocation.* Dublin: Department of Education and Skills.

DPER. (2017). *Spending review 2017 special educational needs provision.* Dublin: Department of Public Expenditure and Reform.

DPER. (2019). *Spending review 2019 monitoring inputs, outputs and outcomes in special education needs provision.* Dublin: Department of Public Expenditure and Reform and Department of Education.

Ebersold, S., Watkins, A., Óskarsdóttir, E., & Meijer, C. J. W. (2019). Financing inclusive education to reduce disparity in education: Trends, issues and drivers. In M. J. Schuelka, C. J. Johnstone, G. Thomas, & J. A. Artiles (Eds.), *The Sage handbook of inclusion and diversity in education.* Thousand Oaks, CA: SAGE Publications.

Engstrøm Graversen, M. (2015). *Accounting for the Danish public school system: Incentives and practice.* Aalborg: Institut for Økonomi og Ledelse.

European Agency for Special Needs and Inclusive Education. (2015). *Empowering teachers to promote inclusive education.* Odense: European Agency for Special Needs and Inclusive Education.

European Agency for Special Needs and Inclusive Education. (2016a). *Financing of inclusive education: Mapping country systems for inclusive education* (S. Ebersold, Ed.). Odense: European Agency for Development in Special Needs Education.

European Agency for Special Needs and Inclusive Education. (2016b). *Financing of inclusive education background information report*. Brussels: European Agency for Special Needs and Inclusive Education.

European Agency for Special Needs and Inclusive Education. (2018a). *Financing policies for inclusive education systems: Resourcing levers to reduce disparity in education* (S. Ebersold, E. Óskarsdóttir, & Watkins, Eds.). Odense: European Agency for Development in Special Needs Education.

European Agency for Special Needs and Inclusive Education. (2018b). *Evidence of the link between inclusive education and social inclusion: A review of the literature*. Odense: European Agency for Development in Special Needs Education.

European Agency for Special Needs and Inclusive Education. (2019). *Financing policies for iInclusive education systems: Final summary report* (E. Óskarsdóttir, A. Watkins & S. Ebersold, Eds.). Odense: European Agency for Development in Special Needs Education.

Fletcher-Campbell, F., Pijl, S. J., Meijer, C., Dyson, A., & Parrish, T. (2003). Distribution of funds for special needs education. *International Journal of Educational Management, 17*, 220–233.

Florian, L. (2019). On the necessary co-existence of special and inclusive education. *International Journal of Inclusive Education, 23*(7–8), 691–704.

Goldan, J. (2019). Demand-oriented and fair allocation of special needs teacher resources for inclusive education – Assessment of a newly implemented funding model in North Rhine-Westphalia, Germany. *International Journal of Inclusive Education*. doi:10.1080/13603116.2019.1568598. Retrieved from https://www.tandfonline.com/doi/abs/10.1080/13603116.2019.1568598?journalCode=tied20

Government of Ireland. (2004). *'Education for Persons with Special Educational Needs Act', (EPSEN)*. Dublin: DES.

Government of Ireland. (2005). *'Disability Act', (EPSEN)*. Dublin: DES.

Graham, L. J., & Sweller, N. (2011). The inclusion lottery: who's in and who's out? Tracking inclusion and exclusion in New South Wales government schools. *International Journal of Inclusive Education, 15*, 941–953.

Gubbels, J., Coppens, K. M., & De Wolf, I. (2017). Inclusive education in the Netherlands: How funding arrangements and demographic trends relate to dropout and participation rates. *International Journal of Inclusive Education, 22*, 1137–1153.

Hick, P., Solomon, Y., Mintz, J., Matziari, J., Ó Murchú, F., Hall, K., ... Margariti, D. (2018). *Initial teacher education for inclusion phase 1 and 2 report*. Trim: NCSE.

*Irish Examiner*. (2019). Let's get real about the kids who can't do mainstream schools. Victoria White, November 20. Retrieved from https://www.irishexaminer.com/opinion/arid-30965526.html

*Irish Times*. (2019). Is Ireland ready for a 'total inclusion' approach for special education? Carl O'Brien, December 17. Retrieved from https://www.irishtimes.com/news/education/is-ireland-ready-for-a-total-inclusion-approach-for-special-education-1.4109360

Jahnukainen, M. (2011). Different strategies, different outcomes? The history and trends of the inclusive and special education in Alberta (Canada) and in Finland. *Scandinavian Journal of Educational Research, 55*, 489–502.

Lamb, B. (2009). *Lamb inquiry: Special educational needs and parental confidence*. Nottingham: DCSF.

Le Laider, S., & Prouchandy, P. (2012). La scolarisation des élèves handicapés et l'éducation inclusive. *Revue Internationale D'éDucation De Sèvres, 59*, 10–14.

McCoy, S. & Banks, J. (2012). Simply academic? Why children with special educational needs don't like school. *European Journal of Special Needs Education, 27*, 81–97.

McCoy, S., Banks, J., Frawley, D., Watson, D., Shevlin, M., & Smyth, F. (2014). *Understanding special class provision in Ireland*. Trim: NCSE/ESRI.

NCSE. (2006). *Implementation report: Plan for the phased implementation of the EPSEN Act 2004*. Trim: NCSE.

NCSE. (2011). *Inclusive education framework a guide for schools on the inclusion of pupils with special educational needs*. Trim: NCSE.

NCSE. (2013). *Supporting students with special educational needs in schools*, NCSE Policy Advice Paper No. 4. Trim: NCSE.

NCSE. (2014). *Delivery for students with special educational needs: A better and more equitable way*. Trim: NCSE.

NCSE. (2018). *Comprehensive review of the special needs assistant scheme a new school inclusion model to deliver the right supports at the right time to students with additional care needs*, NCSE Policy Advice paper No. 6. Trim: NCSE.

NCSE. (2019). *Progress report – Policy advice on special schools and classes, an inclusive education for an inclusive society*. Trim: NCSE.

NESSE. (2012). *Education and Disability/Special Needs: Policies and practices in education, training and employment for students with disabilities and special educational needs in the EU*. Brussels: European Commission.

OECD. (2012). *Equity and quality in education: Supporting disadvantaged students and schools*. Paris: OECD Publishing.

Parish, N., & Bryant, B. (2015). *Research on funding for young people with special educational needs*. London: Department for Education.

Parrish, T., Harr, J., Wolman, J., Anthony, J., Merickel, A., & Esra, P. (2003). *State special education finance systems, 1999–2000. Part II: Special education revenues and expenditures*. Palo Alto, CA: The Center for Special Education Finance (CSEF).

Pijl, S. J. (2016). Fighting segregation in special needs education in the Netherlands: The effects of different funding models. *Discourse: Studies in the Cultural Politics of Education, 37*, 553–562.

Pulkkinen, J., & Jahnukainen, M. (2016). Finnish reform of the funding and provision of special education: The views of principals and municipal education administrators. *Educational Review, 68*(2), 171–188.

Riddell, S., Tisdall, K., & Kane, J. (2006). *Literature review of educational provision for pupils with additional support needs*. Edinburgh: Scottish Executive Social Research.

Rose, D. H., Meyer, A., & Hitchcock, C. (2005). *The universally designed classroom: Accessible curriculum and digital technologies*. Cambridge, MA: Harvard Education Press.

Sharma, U., Forlin, C., & Furlonger, B. (2015). *Contemporary models of funding inclusive education for students with autism spectrum disorder: A report commissioned by the Program for Students with Disabilities Review Unit of the Department of Education and Training for the State of Victoria*. Victoria: Review Unit of the Department of Education and Training for the State of Victoria.

Sharma, U., Furlonger, B., & Forlin, C. (2019). The impact of funding models on the education of students with autism spectrum disorder. *Australasian Journal of Special and Inclusive Education, 43*, 1–11.

Slee, R. (2010). Political economy, inclusive education and teacher education. In C. Forlin (Ed.), *Teacher education for inclusion: Changing paradigms and innovative approaches*. London: Routledge.

Slee, R. (2019). *Defining the scope of inclusive education think piece prepared for the 2020 Global Education Monitoring report, inclusion and education*. Paris: UNESCO.

Soriano, V., Watkins, A., & Ebersold, S. (2017). *Inclusive education for learners with disabilities*. Brussels: European Parliament, Directorate General for the Internal Policies Department C: Citizens Rights and Constitutional Affairs.

Stubbs, S. (2008). *Inclusive education: Where there are few resources*. Oslo: The Atlas Alliance.

Topping, K. J., & Maloney, S. (2005). *The Routledge Falmer reader in inclusive education*. Abingdon: Routledge Falmer.

UN. (2006). *Convention on the rights of persons with disabilities*. New York, NY: United Nations.

UN. (2015). *Incheon declaration, World Education Forum (WEF)*. Paris: UNESCO.

UNESCO. (1994). *The Salamanca statement and framework for action on special needs education*. Paris: UNESCO.

UNESCO. (2009). *Policy guidelines on inclusion in education*. Paris: UNESCO.

UNESCO. (2017). *A guide for ensuring inclusion and equity in education*. Paris: UNESCO.

Zollers, N. J., Ramanathan, A. K., & Yu, M. (2010). The relationship between school culture and inclusion: How an inclusive culture supports inclusive education. *International Journal of Qualitative Studies in Education, 12*, 157–174.

# QUALITY EARLY CHILD EDUCATION MITIGATES AGAINST SPECIAL EDUCATIONAL NEEDS IN CHILDREN

Gabrielle D. Young, David Philpott, Sharon C. Penney, Kimberly Maich and Emily Butler

## ABSTRACT

*This paper examines whether participation in quality early child education (ECE) lessens special education needs and insulates children against requiring costly, intensive supports. Sixty years of longitudinal data coupled with new research in the United Kingdom and Canada were examined to demonstrate how quality ECE reduces special education needs and mitigates the intensity of later supports for children with special education needs. Research demonstrates that quality ECE strengthens children's language, literacy/numeracy, behavioural regulation, and enhances high-school completion. International longitudinal studies confirm that two years of quality ECE lowers special education placement by 40–60% for children with cognitive risk factors and 10–30% for social/behavioural risk factors. Explicit social-emotional learning outcomes also need to be embedded into ECE curricular frameworks, as maladaptive behaviours, once entrenched, are more difficult (and costly) to remediate. Children who do not have the benefit of attending quality ECE in the earliest years are more likely to encounter learning difficulties in school, in turn impacting the well-being and prosperity of their families and societies.*

Resourcing Inclusive Education
International Perspectives on Inclusive Education, Volume 15, 21–34
Copyright © 2021 by Emerald Publishing Limited.
ISSN: 1479-3636/doi:10.1108/S1479-363620210000015004

**Keywords**: Early childhood education; special education needs; inclusive education; early intervention and prevention; long-term benefits; early years policy development

The World Health Organization (2018) estimates that 15% of the global population live with disabilities. Within the school population, this equates to approximately 13% of students with special education needs, 60% of who manifest delays in highly preventive areas such as speech/language skills, emotional/behavioural regulation, or academic achievement skills (National Center for Education Statistics, 2018). Children with low socio-economic status are at a significantly higher risk of developing special education needs (New Jersey Council on Developmental Disabilities, 2016). International researchers have reached consensus that participation in quality early child education with intentional play-based pedagogy improves human development, especially for children from disadvantaged backgrounds (McCain, Mustard, & McCuaig, 2011; Melhuish, 2016; Melhuish et al., 2013; Pascal, 2009; Pelletier & Corter, 2018). A significant body of research literature supports investing in the early years, as investing in the early years has proven to have lasting societal and economic impact for families, communities, and economies (Alexander & Ignjatovic, 2012; Aos, Lieb, Mayfield, Miller, & Pennucci, 2004). The benefits of early intervention have informed economic policy (Barnett, Jung, Youn, & Frede, 2013; Peters, Bradshaw, et al., 2010; Peters, De, et al., 2010; Reynolds, Temple, Robertson, & Mann, 2001; Reynolds, Temple, White, Ou, & Robertson, 2011; Sylva, Melhuish, Sammons, Siraj-Blatchford, Taggart, et al., 2004). Inclusive early child education settings are essential in reducing special education needs and improving the quality of children's lives (Campbell et al., 2012; Sammons et al., 2003; Taggart, Sylva, Melhuish, Sammons, & Siraj, 2015). This paper examines the research literature on how participation in quality early child education mitigates against the development of special education needs in children.

This paper is based on an extensive review of established national and international literature, with particular attention to longitudinal studies. The long-term benefits of investing in children's lives at a young age was examined to display the social, emotional, academic, and economic benefits that early child education has for the general population. New research in the United Kingdom and Canada was also examined to further inform an argument that quality early child education can reduce special education needs. The initial online literature search used Google Scholar, Education Resources Information Centre, Psych-Med, PubMed, and PsyINFO. Keywords and phrases such as *longitudinal studies, early childhood education, benefits of early childhood education, special education enrolment, inclusive education, special education enrolment trends,* and *inclusive early child education* were used in these literature searches to ensure a comprehensive overview of relevant knowledge. Particular attention was paid to more recent data as presented by Melhuish et al. (2019) and Pelletier and Fesseha (2019). Influential longitudinal studies were also examined that investigated early child education programs and their impact on adversity, behaviour, and children's self-regulation skills, all of which are vital to positive child mental health (Hall et al., 2009; McCain et al., 2011; National Scientific Council on the Developing Child, 2008/2012; Ravers, 2003; Schonkoff & Garner, 2012). Search terms in this case included *pre-school children, young children, at-risk, mental health, behaviour/behaviour problems, social-emotional development/learning, childcare, early childhood education, pre-school programs, teacher stress,* and *kindergarten.*

Quality early child education was defined as as regulated early learning for children aged 0–6, delivered by qualified early child educators with an explicit curriculum framework. Inclusive early childhood education for children aged 0–6 requires small group instruction, low staff-to-child ratios, adherence to health and safety policies, highly trained staff, fair salaries, explicit curriculum frameworks, and well-planned physical environments.

## EXAMINING THE INTERSECTION OF EARLY CHILD EDUCATION AND SPECIAL EDUCATION NEEDS

A series of longitudinal studies allowed insight into 60 years of data on the benefits of early child education. Table 1 profiles a series of these studies and their findings. These studies were conducted in: Ontario, Canada (Better Beginnings, Better Futures, 1993); the United States – Michigan (Schweinhart & Weikart, 1997; Belfield, Nores, Barnett, & Schweinhart, 2006), North Carolina (Campbell & Ramey, 1995; Campbell, Ramey, Pungello, Sparling, & Miller-Johnson, 2002), Chicago (1986), New Jersey (Barnett et al., 2013); and the United Kingdom (The Effective Provision of Pre-School Education, 1997; Effective Pre-school, Primary, and Secondary Education, 1997; Early Years Transition and Special Educational Needs, 1997). What emerges is unanimity on the long-term impact on children's development in the very areas where children develop special education needs (language, literacy, mathematics, and social-emotional skills), especially for those with low socio-economic status (an over-represented group in special education). While each of these studies commented to various degrees on the ability for early child education to lower special education needs, the true impact emerges when they are examined collectively.

Attention to these studies from the special education perspective is not new. In 2017, a research team examined American longitudinal studies, with a specific look at the impact on special education needs, grade retention, and high-school graduation (McCoy et al., 2017). Through a meta-analysis of 22 early child education programs from the 1960s to 2016, they concluded that enrolment in quality early child education reduced participation in special education programs by more than 8%, decreased grade retention by 8%, and increased high-school graduation by more than 11%. These outcomes stem from the finding that skills typically targeted by early child education programming, including cognitive skills in language, literacy, mathematics, and social-emotional capacities

***Table 1.*** Longitudinal Studies on the Benefits of Early Child Education.

| Longitudinal Study | Enhanced Literacy/ Numeracy | Enhanced language Skills | Enhanced Social/ Emotional Skills | Greatest Gains for Low SES Children | Reduction in Special Education | Control Group Used | Cost Benefits |
|---|---|---|---|---|---|---|---|
| Abbott[a] | Yes | Yes | | Yes | Yes | Yes | Yes |
| BBBF Project[b] | Yes | Yes | Yes | Yes | Yes | Yes | Yes |
| Chicago study[c] | Yes | Yes | | Yes | Yes | Yes | Yes |
| High/scope[d] | Yes | Yes | Yes | Yes | Yes | Yes | Yes |
| EPPE Project[e] | Yes | Yes | Yes | Yes | Yes | Yes | |
| EPPSE 316+[f] | Yes | Yes | Yes | Yes | Yes | Yes | Yes |
| EYTSEN[g] | Yes | Yes | Yes | Yes | Yes | Yes | |
| Abecedarian[h] | Yes | Yes | Yes | Yes | Yes | Yes | Yes |

*Note:* EPPE, Effective Provision of Pre-school Education; EYTSEN,Early Years Transitions & Special Educational Needs; EPPSE, Effective Pre-school, Primary and Secondary Education; BBBF, Better Beginnings, Better Futures.
[a]Barnett et al., 2013.
[b]Peters, Bradshaw, et al., 2010; Peters, De, et al., 2010.
[c]Reynolds et al., 2001; Reynolds et al., 2011.
[d]Schweinhart & Weikart, 1997; Belfield et al., 2006.
[e]Sylva, Melhuish, Sammons, Siraj-Blatchford, & Taggart, 2004; Sylva, Melhuish, Sammons, Siraj-Blatchford, Taggart, & Elliot2004; Sylva et al., 2009
[f]Taggart et al., 2015.
[g]Sammons et al., 2003.
[h]Campbell & Ramey, 1995; Campbell et al., 2002.

(self-regulation, motivation, engagement, and persistence) are likely precursors of children's abilities to maintain positive academic trajectories (Heckman, Pinto, & Savelyev, 2013). As a result, educational outcomes are theoretically relevant as more distal targets of early child education programming (McCoy et al., 2017).

Another examination of these studies through the lens of economic impact of early child education concluded that quality early child education positively affects economies and families and advantages individual children by enhancing educational outcomes, high-school completion, post-secondary education, and the socio-economic status of individual students (Alexander, Beckman, Macdonald, Renner, & Stewart, 2017). Two years of quality early child education before age six is crucial, especially for children with low socio-economic status. Quality early child education positively impacts families by supporting human capital skills, education, employment, and earnings (Alexander et al., 2017). High quality birth-to-five programs for disadvantaged children can deliver a 13% return on investment through increased school and career achievements as well as reduced remedial education, and health and justice system costs (García, Heckman, Leaf, & Prados, 2019). These findings build on earlier research conclusions that children who did not attend early child education programs required costly supports later in school and that investment in the early years more than pays for itself in reduced social programs and loss of earning potential (Barnett et al., 2013; Mahnken, 2017; Reynolds et al., 2011; Taggart et al., 2015).

Longitudinal findings indicated that when low-income children participated in early childhood interventions starting at age three, rather than receiving the standard educational interventions, the total return to society was $10.83 per dollar invested (Reynolds et al., 2011). For children who started the intervention at school age instead of during the pre-school years, the return to society was $3.97 per dollar invested the earlier the intervention, the better the social and economic benefits (Reynolds et al., 2011).

More recently, a review of longitudinal studies in the European Union (EU) (Ulferts, Wolf, & Anders, 2019) noted similar findings and stressed the importance of quality of early child education and professional development. This review assessed 17 studies from 9 countries to examine the outcomes of 1600 children (excluding programs for highly targeted groups, such as new immigrants and students with special education needs). Although 60% of these studies did not track past elementary school, highest gains within their chosen time frame were made in language, literacy, and mathematics, and these gains persisted over time. While early child education is more inclusive and universal in EU, the authors concluded that 'Policy aiming at improving regular provision can have widespread implications for societies and economies given the enormous and increasing number of children in regular ECE' (p. 1485). These findings were consistent with earlier research (Bauchmüller, Gørtz, & Rasmussen, 2014) indicating high quality early child education offers the key to lasting impact on special education needs.

Perhaps the largest study on the importance of high quality early child education on influencing a lasting impact for child development emerged in *The Effective Provision of Pre-School Education (EPPE) Project* in the UK, which tracked more than 3,000 children beginning in 1997 to graduation. It led to a series of studies and investigations of children's development in relation to a comparison group (Sammons et al., 2003; Sylva, Melhuish, Sammons, Siraj-Blatchford, Taggart, & Elliot, 2004; Taggart et al., 2015). The study was the first to raise the importance of high quality as well as the importance of two years of exposure. Students with two years of high quality early child education demonstrated higher literacy, numeracy, language, self-regulation, social skills, graduation, post-secondary education attainment, citizen involvement, incomes, and lower crime and violence; the impact was greatest for children with low socio-economic status. At age four, 30% of children were identified with special education needs; at age six, it was 20% (Taggart et al., 2015).

The *Early Years Transition and Special Educational Needs* (EYTSEN), a sub-study of the EPPE Project, looked more deeply at the special education needs impact (Sammons et al., 2003). Children in the EPPE Project were tracked until Grade 1 for special education needs. Low socio-economic status participants had the highest risk and those with early child education before age four had the biggest gains. Children without early child education were more likely than children with two years of early child education to be at risk for cognitive (51% versus 21%), reading (44% versus 23%), mathematics (37% versus 16%), and social issues (51 versus 21%). The EPPE Project studies confirmed the lasting benefits of early child education on child development, particularly in academics, language, and social-emotional development. Again, children with low socio-economic status showed the biggest gains, and there was a significant reduction in special education needs (Sammons et al., 2003).

The EPPE Project database remains operational; therefore, the research team revisited it in 2018 with the intention of tracking special education needs across the children's full school experience. Students who scored more than one standard deviation from the mean on measures of cognition and internalized/externalized behaviours were tracked and compared to the control group. Melhuish et al. (2019) concluded that risk for special education needs based on cognitive development and social-behavioural needs can be dramatically reduced by enrolment in early child education, and even more so by high quality early child education, with demonstrated reductions in cognitive risk at age five (36% vs 45%), by age 16 (40% vs 55%), and in social/behavioural risk by age 11 (5% vs 39%). These findings were particularly strong for students with high quality early child education and those with low socio-economic status.

The impact of high quality early child education, in addition to quantity, is currently being explored in the Canadian context by a team of researchers tracking the phase-in of a two-year play-based kindergarten (Pelletier, 2012; Pelletier & Corter, 2018). This longitudinal study comments on the quality and quantity of early child education in relation to the phase-in of full-day kinder-garten and junior kindergarten in the province of Ontario (Pelletier & Corter, 2018). Using a natural control group for comparison, a diverse group of 600 students were examined, with quality early child education being defined as: early child education and Kindergarten teacher co-teaching, using play-based curriculum, and mixed groups for two years of extended day programming. These same students were examined in Grade 3 (Pelletier & Corter, 2018), and in comparison to students who received half-day kindergarten, students that received full-day kindergarten performed significantly higher in language, reading (provincial tests), self-regulation, and social skills, and performed significantly higher on measures of number knowledge, writing, and drawing.

As with the EPPE Project dataset, the research team requested a re-examination of the Ontario study with a particular look for students who scored more than one standard deviation from the mean on measures of cognition and behavioural regulation. Pelletier and Fesseha (2019) reported similar findings as Melhuish et al. (2019). Data indicated a significant reduction in special education needs; half-day kindergarten students were significantly more likely than full-day kindergarten students to be performing one standard deviation below the mean on measures of vocabulary (one and a half times), reading (two times), and self-regulation (three times more likely).

Multiple lines of evidence demonstrate the pre-emptive nature of early child education on special education needs; however, the quality of early child education determines the amount of the impact. The prevalence and cost of special education, grade retention, and high-school dropout is significant (Levin, Belfield, Muennig, & Rouse, 2007). Rich and diverse data confirm the utility of quality early child education in reducing education-related expenditures and promoting childhood well-being. Research continues to indicate that the early years are of utmost importance for improving academic and developmental trajectories, especially for at-risk children (Von Hippel, Workman, & Downey, 2018).

## A BROADER ECONOMIC IMPACT

The data are conclusive in defending an argument of the pre-emptive nature of early child education on special education needs, especially when the benefits of high quality early child education directly target the learning needs of children who now populate special education programs. However, the financial return for children with identified special education needs is equally significant. Central to special education programs is a philosophy of early identification and intervention. What would the impact be for *earlier* intervention, during the early years? The Organisation for Economic Co-operation and Development (OECD, 2018) identified that fewer than 25% of children with identified exceptionalities had access to early child education programs.

While Alexander et al. (2017), as outlined above, argued for the lasting economic impact on individuals, there is also an immediate economic impact on families, especially for both employment rates as well as expenses associated with having a child with special education needs (Halfon & Friendly, 2013; Hanvey, 2002; Mayer, 2009). This is especially true for mothers, who continue to be overwhelmingly responsible for the care of young children and are more likely than fathers to stay home or work part-time to care for children (Halfon & Friendly, 2013). In fact, families who have children with special education needs are more inclined to experience poverty, are subject to higher financial costs related to special education needs, and are more likely to experience barriers to employment (Hanvey, 2002). This pattern is particularly true for families with children who have more pervasive needs such as Autism Spectrum Disorder. In Canada, one in 66 Canadians aged 5 to 17 is diagnosed with Autism Spectrum Disorder; and more than half of Autism Spectrum Disorder diagnoses (56%) occurred by age six with 75% by age eight (Public Health Agency of Canada, 2018). More than half of children with Autism Spectrum Disorder are diagnosed during the early years, highlighting the need and possibilities for active levels of participation and access to early intervention within early child education programs. Practical applications of inclusion-related learning within early child education programs and K-12 settings are an ongoing issue, although inclusion is considered to be the best-practice approach in Canada (Halfon & Friendly, 2013; Killoran, Tymon, & Frempong, 2007). Social communication is essential within and beyond the early years and inclusive environments can provide social, cognitive, and other opportunities for skill development, as well as effective interventions that help some subgroups of children with Autism Spectrum

Disorder. Children with more severe impairments (e.g., social skills and adaptive behaviour) may benefit more from inclusive early child education programs and transition to school more seamlessly (Hanline & Correa-Torres, 2012; Isaacs, 2012; Rogers & Johnson, 2018; Wolfe & Hall, 2003). While 'early intervention has been recognized as the best indicator for optimal outcome' (Booth & Keenan, 2016, p. 16), major longitudinal studies that discuss the benefits of early child education have overlooked Autism Spectrum Disorder (Barnett et al., 2013; Peters, Bradshaw, et al., 2010; Peters, De, et al., 2010). Inclusive early child education programs with trained educators can and should play a pivotal role in supporting, reinforcing, and generalizing interventions to everyday settings and situations; in turn, decreasing later demands on school-based supports and interventions. Special education services in the K-12 system would be directly impacted if these high needs children received access to quality early child education programs with intensive programs earlier in their development.

A similar argument can be made for the benefits of early interventions on lessening the impact and cost of mental health challenges in students. The estimate of mental health issues globally range from 14% to 20% of the population, carrying an associated disease burden that ranges from 7% to as much as 14% in some countries, consuming a significant amount of health-care budgets (Center on the Developing Child at Harvard University, 2016; National Research Council and Institute of Medicine, 2009; Ritchie & Roser, 2018; World Health Organization, 2017). The onset for more than half of these disorders in adulthood began in early childhood or adolescence (Collishaw, 2015; Moffitt et al., 2011; Whitley, Smith, & Vaillancourt, 2012). In the early years, it is estimated that between 10% and 25% of young children have mental health issues that interfere with their daily social and environmental interactions (Jones, 2013; Malla et al., 2019). One research study noted that children entering kindergarten often do not have the necessary social and emotional skills to be successful at school (Whitted, 2011). For many of these children, mental health promotion, prevention, early identification, and intervention may be key to preventing social-emotional difficulties and behavioural challenges from persisting and worsening and from impacting the individuals, their families, and the broader society (Breitenstein, Hill, & Gross, 2009; Conners-Burrow et al., 2013; Reynolds et al., 2011; Schonkoff & Garner, 2012). Positive social-emotional development in the early years can lead to good educational attainment, financial stability, and health and wellness (Moffitt et al., 2011).

Quality early child education has been associated with the learning of positive behaviours, such as self-regulation and prosocial skills. For example, the ratio of adults to children within a given setting affects a child's experience in early education/daycare program or kindergarten class and likely impacts children's social and behavioural outcomes, including responsiveness to adults and peers, initiative, and cooperative behaviours (Friendly, Ferns, & Prabhu, 2009). Low ratios allow for more quality individual child-educator interactions and support a positive relationship between the two, factors that contribute to positive developmental outcomes in young children. Child-to-adult ratios influence developmental outcomes such as academic achievement, cognitive competence, and social-emotional skills. However, other considerations such as staff training and experience, staff compensation, and access to support staff have also been shown to affect children's achievement in the classroom setting (Browne, Magnuson, Schindler, Duncan, & Yoshikawa, 2017; Eleni & Giotsa, 2018; Friendly et al., 2009; O'Brennan, Bradshaw, & Furlong, 2014).

Research in behavioural and social sciences, epigenetics and neuroscience has established clear links between early mental health and later developmental outcomes (Schonkoff & Garner, 2012). The inability to regulate emotions, an essential part of healthy social-emotional development in early years, can be a predictor of poor educational attainment, reduced financial stability, and compromised health in adulthood (Moffitt et al., 2011). Low socioe-conomic status can create barriers to accessing safe affordable housing, health and social services, and quality child care: factors that influence a child's early social-emotional development and mental health (Meins, Centifanti, Fernyhough, & Fishburn, 2013).

Mental health concerns in young children often go unrecognized and are not remediated (National Scientific Council on the Developing Child, 2004; Poulou, 2015). Disruptive behavior in early childhood is a common precursor for up to 60% of mental health issues observed across the lifespan (Wakschlag et al., 2014). Treatment is more effective and less costly if problem behaviours are identified and treated early (Conroy & Brown, 2004; Eyberg, Nelson, & Boggs, 2008; Gleason, Goldson, & Yogman, & AAP Council on Early Childhood, 2016; Moffitt et al., 2011). The pre-school period is considered an optimal time to identify and reduce problem behaviours (Hall et al., 2009; Poulou, 2015; Sylva, Melhuish, Sammons, Siraj-Blatchford, & Taggart, 2009; Taggart et al., 2015). Researchers, experts, and direct service providers agree that promoting mental health across the lifespan and acting early to prevent mental illness leads to a stronger society and economy (Heckman et al., 2013; Reynolds et al., 2011).

## *Summary*

When intervention is considered for young children, research is explicit in showing that quality early child education correlates with overall better academic, behavioural, social, and developmental outcomes. Research is equally conclusive in recognizing the positive and long-term financial impact of this intervention on personal and family incomes, as well as economies. Universal early child education programs should be considered for public policy as they reduce stigma and mitigate long-term consequences for children most at risk. Related literature supports a collaborative approach to working with families and caregivers to provide seamless services, as well as expert assistance, in evidence-based practices for all children. This is especially true for children most at risk of developing special education needs. The burgeoning expenses of special education as well as the long-term educational and employment outcomes for children with special education needs underscore the importance of exploring the pre-emptive nature of early child education. While existing research is rich with evidence, further research is required on how best to utilize the early years in optimizing human development. Importantly, this approach includes best practices for adequately training educators on responding to diverse needs and in making education an inclusive and rewarding experience for all children. Collaboration, collegial practice, and a continuum of pedagogy and policy collectively can aid with this process. These benefits are especially true for children with more challenging special education needs, including Autism Spectrum Disorder and significant behavioral and/or mental health issues. Services during the early years hold the key to effective intervention. Front-loading investments are not only wise for financial planning, but in preventing maladaptive behaviours from becoming entrenched. There will always be a need for special education programs, but earlier intervention can significantly lessen the supports children require later in school and can produce optimal outcomes. The extent of this preemption rests with the quality of the early child education experience.

# REFERENCES

Alexander, C., Beckman, K., Macdonald, A., Renner, C., & Stewart, M. (2017). *Ready for life: A socio-economic analysis of early childhood education and care*. Ottawa, ON: The Conference Board of Canada.

Alexander, C., & Ignjatovic, D. (2012, November 27). Early childhood education has widespread and long-lasting benefits (TD Economics special report). Retrieved from https://www.td.com/document/PDF/economics/special/di1112_EarlyChildhoodEducation.pdf

Aos, S., Lieb, R., Mayfield, J., Miller, M., & Pennucci, A. (2004). *Benefits and costs of prevention and early intervention programs for youth*. Olympia, WA: Washington State Institute for Public Policy. Retrieved from http://www.wsipp.wa.gov/

Barnett, W. S., Jung, K., Youn, M. J., & Frede, E. C. (2013). Abbott preschool program longitudinal effects study: Fifth grade follow-up. Retrieved from http://nieer.org/wp-content/uploads/2013/11/APPLES205th20Grade.pdf

Bauchmüller, R., Gørtz, M., & Rasmussen, A. W. (2014). Long-run benefits from universal high-quality preschooling. *Early Childhood Research Quarterly, 29*(4), 457–470.

Belfield, C., Nores, M., Barnett, S., & Schweinhart, L. (2006). The high/scope Perry preschool program: Cost–benefit analysis using data from the age-40 followup. *The Journal of Human Resources, 41*(1), 162–190. Retrieved from http://www.jstor.org/stable/40057261

Booth, N., & Keenan, M. (2016). Autism spectrum disorder post-diagnosis experience in Northern Ireland: Views from caregivers. *Špeciálny Pedagóg, 1*(5), 15–33.

Breitenstein, S. M., Hill, C., & Gross, D. (2009). Understanding disruptive behavior problems in preschool children. *Journal of Pediatric Nursing, 24*(1), 3–12. doi:10.1016/j.pedn.2007.10.007

Browne, J. B., Magnuson, K. A., Schindler, H. S., Duncan, G. J., & Yoshikawa, H. (2017). A meta-analysis of class sizes and ratios in early childhood education programs: Are thresholds of quality associated with greater impacts on cognitive, achievement, and socioemotional outcomes? *Emotional Evaluation and Policy Analysis, 39*(3), 407–428.

Campbell, F. A., Pungello, E. P., Burchinal, M., Kainz, K., Pan, Y., Wasik, B. H., ... Ramey, C. T. (2012). Adult outcomes as a function of an early childhood educational program: An Abecedarian project follow-up. *Developmental Psychology, 48*(4), 1033–1043. doi:10.1037/a0026644

Campbell, F., & Ramey, C. (1995). Cognitive and school outcomes for high-risk African-American students at middle adolescence: Positive effects of early intervention. *American Educational Research Journal, 32*(4), 743–772. doi:10.3102/00028312032004743

Campbell, F., Ramey, C., Pungello, E., Sparling, J., & Miller-Johnson, S. (2002). Early childhood education: Young adult outcomes from the Abecedarian project. *Applied Developmental Science, 6*(1), 42–57. doi:10.1207/S1532480XADS0601_05

Center on the Developing Child at Harvard University. (2016). From best practices to breakthrough impacts: A science-based approach to building a more promising future for young children and families. Retrieved from www.developingchild.harvard.edu

Collishaw, S. (2015). Annual research review: Secular trends in child and adolescent mental health. *Journal of Child Psychology and Psychiatry, 56*(3), 370–393. doi:10.1111/jcpp.12372

Conners-Burrow, N., McKelvey, L., Sockwell, L., Ehrentraut, J. H., Adams, S., & Whiteside-Mansell, L. (2013). Beginning to "unpack" early childhood mental health consultation: Types of consultation services and their impact on teachers. *Infant Mental Health Journal, 34*, 280–289. doi:10.1002/imhj.21387

Conroy, M. A., & Brown, W. H. (2004). Early identification, prevention, and early identification with young children at risk for emotional and behavioural disorders: Issues, trends, and call for action. *Behavioral Disorders, 29*(3), 224–239.

Eleni, D., & Giotsa, A. (2018). Early detection of externalizing problems in preschool children according to their teachers. *Psychology, 8*(2), 60–73.

Eyberg, S. M., Nelson, M. M., & Boggs, S. R. (2008). Evidence-based psychosocial treatments for children and adolescents with disruptive behavior. *Journal of Clinical Child and Adolescent Psychology, 37*, 215–237.

Friendly, M., Ferns, C., & Prabhu, N. (2009). Ratios for four and five year olds: What does the research say? What else is important? University of Toronto Childcare Resource and Research Unit. Retrieved from http://childcarecanada.org/sites/default/files/BN_ratios.pdf

García, J. L., Heckman, J. J., Leaf, D. E., & Prados, M. J. (2019). Quantifying the life-cycle benefits of a prototypical early childhood program. NBER Working Paper No. 23479. JEL No. C93,I28,J13. Retrieved from https://heckmanequation.org/www/assets/2017/01/w23479.pdf

Gleason, M. M., Goldson, E., Yogman, M. W., & AAP Council on Early Childhood (2016). Addressing early childhood emotional and behavioral problems. *Pediatrics, 138*(6), e20163025. doi:10.1542/peds.2016-3025

Halfon, S., & Friendly, M. (2013). *Inclusion of young children with disabilities in regulated child care in Canada. A snapshot: Research, policy and practice.* Occasional paper no. 27. Childcare Resource and Research Unit, Toronto, ON. Retrieved from http://www.childcarecanada.org/sites/default/files/Occasional%20paper%2027%20FINAL.pdf

Hall, J., Sylva, K., Melhuish, E., Sammons, P., Siraj-Blatchford, I., & Taggart, B. (2009). The role of pre-school quality in promoting resilience in the cognitive development of young children. *Oxford Review of Education, 35*(3), 331–352.

Hanline, M. F., & Correa-Torres, S. M. (2012). Experiences of preschoolers with severe disabilities in an inclusive early education setting: A qualitative study. *Education and Training in Autism and Developmental Disabilities, 47*(1), 109–121.

Hanvey, L. (2002). Children with disabilities and their families in Canada: A discussion paper commissioned by the national children's alliance for the first national roundtable on children with disabilities. Retrieved from http://citeseerx.ist.psu.edu/viewdoc/download?doi=10.1.1.457.3999&rep=rep1&type=pdf

Heckman, J., Pinto, R., & Savelyev, P. (2013). Understanding the mechanisms through which an influential early childhood program boosted adult outcomes. *The American Economic Review, 103*(6), 2052–2208. doi:10.1257/aer.103.6.2052

Isaacs, J. B. (2012). *Starting school at a disadvantage: The school readiness of poor children.* Washington, DC: Center on Children and Families at Brookings. Retrieved from https://www.brookings.edu/research/starting-school-at-a-disadvantage-the-school-readiness-of-poor-children/

Jones, P. (2013). Adult mental health disorders and their age of onset. *British Journal of Psychiatry, 201*(S54), S5–S10. doi:10.1192/bjp.bp.112.119164.

Killoran, I., Tymon, D., & Frempong, G. (2007). Disabilities and inclusive practices within Toronto preschools. *International Journal of Inclusive Education, 11*(1), 81–95. doi:10.1080/13603110500375473

Levin, H., Belfield, C., Muennig, P., & Rouse, C. (2007). *The costs and benefits of an excellent education for all of America's children* (Vol. 9). New York, NY: Teachers College, Columbia University.

Mahnken, K. (2017, July 4). Intensive preschool programs can yield massive returns, especially for boys, Nobel Laureate's study shows. *The 74*. Retrieved from https://www.the74million.org/article/intensive-preschool-programs-can-yield-massive-returns-especially-for-boys-nobel-laureates-study-shows/

Malla, A., Shah, J., Iyer, S., Boksa, P., Jooper, R., Anderson, N., & Fuhrer, R. (2019). Youth mental health should be a top priority for health care in Canada. *The Canadian Journal of Psychiatry, 63*(4), 216–222. doi:10.1177/0706743718758968

Mayer, D. (2009). Disability and inclusion: Changing attitudes—Changing policy. *Our Schools/Our Selves, 18*(3), 159–168.

McCain, M. N., Mustard, J. F., & McCuaig, K. (2011). *Early years study 3: Making decisions, taking action*. Toronto, ON: Margaret & Wallace McCain Family Foundation.

McCoy, D., Yoshikawa, H., Ziol-Guest, K., Duncan, G., Schindler, H., Magnuson, K., & Shonkoff, J. (2017). Impacts of early childhood education on medium- and long-term educational outcomes. *Educational Researcher, 46*(8), 474–487. doi:10.3102/0013189X17737739

Meins, E., Centifanti, L. C. M., Fernyhough, C., & Fishburn, S. (2013). Maternal mind-mindedness and children's behavioral difficulties: Mitigating the impact of low socioeconomic status. *Journal of Abnormal Child Psychology, 41*(4), 543–553.

Melhuish, E. (2016). Longitudinal research and early years policy development in the UK. *International Journal of Child Care and Education Policy, 10*(3), 1–18. doi:10.1186/s40723-016-0019-1

Melhuish, E., Barnes, J., Gardiner, J., Siraj, I., Sammons, P., Sylva, K., & Taggart, B. (2019). A study of the long-term influence of early childhood education and care on the risk for developing special educational needs. *Exceptionality Education International, 29*, 22–41. Retrieved from https://ir.lib.uwo.ca/eei/vol29/iss3/3

Melhuish, E., Quinn, E., Sylva, K., Sammons, P., Siraj-Blatchford, I., & Taggart, B. (2013). Preschool affects longer term literacy and numeracy: Results from a general population longitudinal study in Northern Ireland. *School Effectiveness and School Improvement, 24*(2), 234–250. doi:10.1080/09243453.2012.749796

Moffitt, T. E., Arseneault, L., Belsky, D., Dickson, N., Hancox, R. J., Harrington, H., & Sears, M. R. (2011). A gradient of childhood self-control predicts health, wealth, and public safety. *Proceedings of the National Academy of Sciences, 108*(7), 2693–2698. doi:10.1073/pnas.1010076108

National Center for Education Statistics. (2018). Fast facts: Students with disabilities [Web page]. Retrieved from https://nces.ed.gov/fastfacts/display.asp?id=64

National Research Council and Institute of Medicine. (2009). *Preventing mental, emotional, and behavioral disorders among young people: Progress and possibilities*. Washington, DC: The National Academies Press. doi:10.17226/12480

National Scientific Council on the Developing Child. (2004). Children's emotional development is built into the architecture of their brains. Working paper no. 2. Retrieved from www.developingchild.harvard.edu

National Scientific Council on the Developing Child. (2008/2012). Establishing a level foundation for life: Mental health begins in early childhood. Working paper no. 6 (Updated ed.). Retrieved from www.developingchild.harvard.edu

New Jersey Council on Developmental Disabilities. (2016). Homelessness, poverty, and special education [Web page]. Retrieved from https://www.njcommonground.org/homelessness-poverty-and-special-education/

O'Brennan, L., Bradshaw, C., & Furlong, M. (2014). Influence of classroom and school climate on teacher perceptions of student problem behavior. *School Mental Health, 6*(2), 125–136. doi:10.1007/s12310-014-9118-8

Organisation for Economic Co-operation and Development (OECD) (2018). *Education at a glance 2018: OECD indicators*. Paris: OECD Publishing. doi:10.1787/eag-2018-en

Pascal, C. (2009). *With our best future in mind: Implementing early learning in Ontario*. Toronto, ON: Queen's Printer for Ontario.

Pelletier, J. (2012). New directions in integrated early childhood services in school-as-hub models: Lessons from Toronto first duty and peel best start. In N. Howe & L. Prochner (Eds.),

*New directions in early childhood care and education in Canada* (pp. 367–396). Toronto, ON: University of Toronto Press.

Pelletier, J., & Corter, J. (2018). A longitudinal comparison of learning outcomes in full-day and half-day kindergarten. *The Journal of Educational Research, 112*(2), 192–210. doi:10.1080/00220671.2018.1486280

Pelletier, J., & Fesseha, E. (2019). The impact of full-day kindergarten on learning outcomes and self-regulation among kindergarten children at risk for placement in special education. *Exceptionality Education International, 29*, 42–56. Retrieved from https://ir.lib.uwo.ca/eei/vol29/iss3/4

Peters, R., Bradshaw, A., Petrunka, K., Nelson, G., Herry, Y., Craig, W., & Collins, W. (2010). The better beginnings, better Futures project: Findings from grade 3 to grade 9. *Monographs of the Society for Research in Child Development, 75*(3), 1–176. Retrieved from http://www.jstor.org/stable/40984372

Peters, R., De, V., Nelson, G., Petrunka, K., Pancer, S.M., Loomis, C., & Van Andel, A. (2010). Highlights of better beginnings, better futures research findings at grade 12. Retrieved from http://bbbf.ca/Portals/15/pdfs/Grade%2012%20report% 20FINAL%20version.pdf

Poulou, M. S. (2015). Emotional and behavioural difficulties in preschool. *Journal of Child and Family Studies, 24*, 225–236. doi:10.1007/s10826-013-9828-9

Public Health Agency of Canada. (2018). Autism spectrum disorder among children and youth in Canada 2018: A report of the national autism spectrum disorder surveillance system. Retrieved from https://www.canada.ca/en/public-health/services/publications/diseases-conditions/autism-spectrum-disorder-children-youth-canada-2018.html

Ravers, C. C. (2003). Young children's emotional development and school readiness. *Society for Research in Child Development's Social Policy Report, 16*(3), 3–19.

Reynolds, A. J., Temple, J. A., Robertson, D. L., & Mann, E. A. (2001). Long-term effects of an early childhood intervention on educational achievement and juvenile arrest: A 15-year follow-up of low-income children in public schools. *Journal of the American Medical Association, 285*(18), 2339–2346, doi:10.1001/jama.285.18.2339

Reynolds, A. J., Temple, J. A., White, B. A. B., Ou, S., & Robertson, D. L. (2011). Age 26 cost–benefit analysis of the Child-parent center early education program. *Child Development, 82*(1), 379–404. doi:10.1111/j.1467-8624.2010.01563.x

Ritchie, H., & Roser, M. (2018). Mental health [Online resource]. Retrieved from https://ourworldindata.org/mental-health.

Rogers, W., & Johnson, N. (2018). Strategies to include students with severe/multiple disabilities within the general education classroom. *Physical Disabilities: Education and Related Services, 37*(2), 1–12.

Sammons, P., Taggart, B., Smees, R., Sylva, K., Melhuish, E., Siraj-Blatchford, I., & Elliot, K. (2003). *The early years transitions &special educational needs (EYTSEN) project*. London: Institute of Education, University of London. Retrieved from http://dera.ioe.ac.uk/18204/1/RR431.pdf

Schonkoff, J. P., & Garner, A. C. (2012). The lifelong effects of early childhood adversity and toxic stress. *Pediatrics, 129*(1), e232–e246. doi:10.1542/peds.2011-2663

Schweinhart, L. J., & Weikart, D. P. (1997). The High/Scope Preschool curriculum comparison study through age 23. *Early Childhood Research Quarterly, 12*(2), 117–143.

Sylva, K., Melhuish, E., Sammons, P., Siraj-Blatchford, I., & Taggart, B. (2004). *The effective provision of pre-school education (EPPE) project: The final report*. Technical paper 12. Institute of Education, University of London, London.

Sylva, K., Melhuish, E., Sammons, P., Siraj-Blatchford, I., & Taggart, B. (2009). *Effective Pre-School and Primary Education 3–11 (EPPE 3–11) project. Final report from the primary phase: Pre-school, school, and family influences on children's development during Key Stage 2 (age 7–11)*. Institute of Education, University of London, London.

Sylva, K., Melhuish, E., Sammons, P., Siraj-Blatchford, I., Taggart, B., & Elliot, K. (2004). The effective provision of pre-school education (EPPE) project: Findings from the pre-school period to end of Key Stage 1. Retrieved from https://ro.uow.edu.au/cgi/viewcontent.cgi?article=3155&context=sspapers

Taggart, B., Sylva, K., Melhuish, E., Sammons, P., & Siraj, I. (2015). Effective Pre-school, Primary and Secondary Education 3–16 (EPPSE 3-16+) project: How pre-school influences children and young people's attainment and developmental outcomes over time. Retrieved from http://dera.ioe.ac.uk/23344/1/RB455_Effective_preschool_primary_and_secondary_education_project.pdf

Ulferts, H., Wolf, K. M., & Anders, Y. (2019). Impact of process quality in early childhood education and care on academic outcomes: Longitudinal meta-analysis. *Child Development*, *90*(5), 1474–1489.

Von Hippel, P., Workman, J., & Downey, D. (2018). Inequality in reading and math skills forms mainly before kindergarten: A replication, and partial correction, of "are schools the great equalizer?" *Sociology of Education*, *91*(4), 323–357.

Wakschlag, L. S., Briggs-Gowan, M. J., Choi, S. W., Nichols, S. R., Kestler, J., Burns, J. L., & Henry, D. (2014). Advancing a multidimensional developmental spectrum approach to preschool disruptive behaviour. *Journal of the American Academy of Child & Adolescent Psychiatry*, *53*(1), 82–97.

Whitley, J., Smith, D., & Vaillancourt, T. (2012). Promoting mental health literacy among educators: Critical in school-based prevention and intervention. *Canadian Journal of School Psychology*, *28*, 56–70.

Whitted, K. S. (2011). Understanding how social and emotional skill deficits contribute to school failure. *Preventing School Failure*, *55*(1), 10–16. doi:10.1080/10459880903286755

Wolfe, P. S., & Hall, T. E. (2003). Making inclusion a reality for students with severe disabilities. *Teaching Exceptional Children*, *35*(4), 56–60.

World Health Organization. (2017). *Depression and other common mental disorders: Global health estimates*. World health Organisation, Geneva. Retrieved from https://apps.who.int/iris/bitstream/handle/10665/254610/WHO-MSD-MER-2017.2-eng.pdf.

World Health Organization. (2018). Disability and health [Web page]. Retrieved from http://www.who.int/en/news-room/fact-sheets/detail/disability-and-health

# WHAT'S IN THE BUDGET?: A LOOK AT FUNDING FOR INCLUSIVE INITIATIVES IN ESSA AND IDEA

Nicholas Catania, Danielle Lane, Sarah Semon, Sharlene Smith and Phyllis Jones

## ABSTRACT

*This chapter explores two policies guiding the education and funding related to students with and without disabilities in the United States. The Individuals with Disabilities Education Act (IDEA) of 2004 serves as the nation's primary legislation outlining policies, procedures and funding for the education of students with disabilities. Thus, IDEA 2004 is integral in understanding inclusion throughout the United States. The Every Student Succeeds Act (ESSA) of 2015 is regarded as the primary educational legislation concerned with funding to provide all students with access to a well-rounded education. The chapter begins with a brief overview of the laws in relation to inclusion and funding for teacher professional development (PD) and argues in support of funding specifically aimed at the PD of highly effective classroom teachers. Preparing, recruiting and retaining high quality teacher candidates must be a top priority in PK-12 education. In the current political climate, there is a need to examine how to use available resources in a time of shrinking budgets, teacher shortages and increasing equity gaps.*

*This chapter will examine budgets from the most recent five years available and make connections to issues related to funding for inclusive programming, including professional development of teachers. While ESSA does not guide PD of teachers, it guides the funding for said programmes. Through budget evaluations and analysis of the President's rationale for decreasing funding under Title II of ESSA, we demonstrate that the current President is decreasing funds for PD, recruitment, preparation and more on the basis that*

Resourcing Inclusive Education
International Perspectives on Inclusive Education, Volume 15, 35–49
Copyright © 2021 by Emerald Publishing Limited.
ISSN: 1479-3636/doi:10.1108/S1479-363620210000015005

*Title I funding of ESSA covers these activities. With a new election set to take place next year, this chapter explores how the budgets have impacted funding for inclusive programming while looking to the future and its impact on the preparation and development of teachers.*

**Keywords**: Professional development; inclusive education; policy; budgetary analysis

## INTRODUCTION

This chapter explores the policies guiding the education and funding of students with and without disabilities in the United States with a critical eye towards two major policies focused on funding for inclusive programmes. To begin, we discuss the role of professional development for promoting inclusion and highlight the relevant federal legislation. We then take an exploratory approach to understanding the budget proposals from the most recent five years available, with an attempt to identify spending focused on inclusion initiatives. Further, we explore how the budgets have impacted funding for inclusive programming while looking to the future and its impact on the preparation and development of teachers. We conclude with an argument in support of funding specifically aimed at providing inclusion-focused professional development (PD) to prepare, recruit and retain high quality teachers and teacher candidates in PK-12 education.

The role of professional development in inclusion is paramount for teachers to gain continuous training and knowledge in the field and promote collaborative teaching among general and special educators. Several studies assert a need for special educators to be more involved in designing collaborative instruction and supporting inclusion (Lowrey, Hollingshead, Howery, & Bishop, 2017; Quirk, Lea Ryndak, & Taub, 2017). Furthermore, Woodcock and Hardy (2017) explored how professional development of special educators positively influenced their perception of inclusion and inclusive pedagogy. Additionally, special educators in the US increasingly work alongside regular educators in general education classrooms to support students rather than in the self-contained or resource settings (Faraclas, 2018; Lowrey & Smith, 2018). They have become inclusion teachers, facilitators and consultants, among other titles and roles (Shepherd, Fowler, McCormick, Wilson, & Morgan, 2016; Woolf, 2019). Special educators need to develop and implement specially designed literacy interventions for a variety of students with extremely disparate needs within general education settings. For example, special educators may need to provide specially designed instruction and intervention to students in a fourth grade mathematics classroom, emergent readers in a kindergarten classroom, students identified with learning disabilities struggling with comprehension in third grade and students in need of remediation for phonemic awareness in first and second grade, perhaps also while supporting a student who has hearing or vision loss in an upper grade. This example illustrates how professional development for inclusion should be ongoing and responsive, allowing special and general educators to work collaboratively and effectively to meet the educational needs of students.

# RATIONALE FOR EXPLORING FUNDING FOR INCLUSION

Funding for public education in the United States is provided by the government. However, these funds are rarely sufficient and may be supplemented by state and local taxes or by private funders (parents, wealthy donors, foundations, etc.), which often leads to increased disparities between high- and low-income neighbourhoods (Kitzmiller, 2019). Amidst this backdrop, the recent federal administrations have been actively promoting the privatization of education, which is known as the 'school choice' movement (Darling-Hammond, 2017). Under the guise of reducing the burden of federal interference, we question whether cutting programmes and associated accountability and reporting requirements is effectively rolling back protections established to ensure compliance. Without funding what happens to compliance?

Due to the movement towards inclusive education in the United States, it is imperative for teachers to be prepared to work effectively with students with disabilities, particularly since student outcomes are linked to teachers' effective teaching in some states (Smith & Tyler, 2011). Therefore, teachers must continue to engage in professional development to remain current and knowledgeable in the field in order to address the educational needs of all students, including those with special needs (Smith & Tyler, 2011). Berry, Petrin, Gravelle, and Farmer (2012) conducted a study of 373 administrators in 43 states and 203 special educators from 33 states to determine issues in special education teacher recruitment, retention and professional development needs of rural special educators. The findings revealed challenges in hiring qualified teachers for rural districts, difficulties in retaining teachers and the need for appropriate professional development. The majority of the teachers interviewed expressed appreciation for the monthly trainings received which greatly assisted them in special education processing, such as writing IEPs, technology and general curriculum content. However, the areas of professional development teachers identified as needing the most were working with paraprofessionals, working with parents, training in a specific disability category and including students with disabilities in the general education curriculum. The teachers indicated the need for continuous professional development in those areas so they can confidently and effectively meet the educational needs of all of their students. This study showed that ongoing professional development for inclusive education is paramount for teachers to effectively teach a class of students in a general setting, which include students with special needs (Berry et al., 2012).

# THE POLICY CONTEXT

The Individuals with Disabilities Education Act (IDEA), originally authorized in 1976 and recently reauthorized in 2004, serves as the nation's primary legislation outlining policies, procedures and funding for the education of students with disabilities. Thus, IDEA 2004 is integral in understanding inclusion throughout the United States. The Elementary and Secondary Education Act (ESEA), originally authorized in 1965 and most recently reauthorized as the Every Student Succeeds Act (ESSA) of 2015, is a federal law regarded as the primary educational legislation concerned with funding to provide all students with access to a well-rounded education. These two major pieces of legislation intersect and structure education in the United States, and combined with additional civil rights protections, form a policy framework intended to support the inclusion of students with disabilities in general education settings (Schuh et al., 2018).

> Although ESEA is often thought of as the general education law, in fact, it sets clear national policy for the public education of every child in the United States. The IDEA layers on ESEA to provide additional supports and services to students with disabilities, while reinforcing the right to equal educational opportunity that students with disabilities are entitled to, procedural safeguards and the responsibilities of states and districts. Permeating all school settings are the nation's other civil rights laws that prohibit discrimination against specific groups of people. These different federal laws complement each other to create the federal policy framework to which all schools, districts and states must adhere. (Schuh et al., 2018, p. 1)

The federal government approves ESSA and IDEA funding annually, contingent on state compliance with the regulations. Significantly, we note that there is little coordination of activities between these policies given the separate nature of the educational systems in the US (US Government Accountability Office, 2009). In order to conduct a critical analysis of the budgets as they relate to funding inclusion initiatives, we first examine the socio-historical context of each policy.

## Historical Context for IDEA

Aforementioned, IDEA 2004 is the nation's primary legislature guiding inclusion in the United States. While the legislature does not use the term inclusion and does not specifically define inclusion, the current policy states,

> Each public agency must ensure that (i) to the maximum extent appropriate, children in public or private institutions or other care facilities, are educated with children who are nondisabled; and (ii) special classes, separate schooling or other removal of children with disabilities from the regular educational environment occurs only if the nature or severity of the disability is such that education in regular classes with the use of supplementary aids and services cannot be achieved satisfactorily. (IDEA)

IDEA was originally titled the Education for All Handicapped Children Act of 1975 (EAHCA), before being reauthorized in 2004. Understanding the significance of this legislation requires a brief explanation of the history of societal perceptions of disability, which continue to influence special education today. As explained by Spaulding and Pratt (2015), education for children with disabilities has not followed a steady path of improvement, as education often mirrors societal and cultural trends. Throughout history, people with disabilities experienced extreme hardship, exploitation, ridicule, exclusion or worse (Baynton, 2013). As recent as the 1940s, disability was still viewed as deviance to be removed or eliminated in a new era of institutions and horrific eugenic advancements (Baynton, 2013; Spaulding & Pratt, 2015). Spaulding and Pratt (2015) explain, however, that from 1950 to present, philosophical developments and political pressures for disability rights and awareness led to contemporary legislative and educational reforms. In many ways, EAHCA increased educational access for students with disabilities. Indeed, according to the preamble in the Reauthorization of IDEA (2004), the US Congress defined the following vision:

> Improving educational results for children with disabilities is an essential element of our national policy of ensuring equality of opportunity, full participation, independent living and economic self-sufficiency for individuals with disabilities. (IDEA, 20 U.S.C. 1400(c) (1))

Reflecting on the intent of IDEA, former director of the Office of Special Education Programs (OSEP), Melody Musgrove, indicated that additional policy changes continue to be necessary for ensuring positive life outcomes for children with disabilities. In her 'perfect world', 'Every child could go to school and get what they need-without an IEP (Individualized Education Plan)' (Musgrove, 2017, p. 136).

## Historical Context for ESSA

Spanning back to the 1960s, the Elementary and Secondary Education Act (ESEA) of 1965 has been reauthorized by a number of US Presidents (Sharp, 2016), each version breathing new life into teacher and school leader recruitment, preparation, training and development. In 2016, the US President added his version of the act to the growing list. According to the United States Department of Education, the President signed the renamed Every Student Succeeds Act (ESSA) on December 15, 2016. Unlike previous versions, ESSA featured a shift in educational decision-making from the federal government, back to state and local levels (Sharp, 2016). With fewer federal regulations, the path taken by each state to build an educational system that increases the equitable outcomes for its diverse student populations varied (Sharp, 2016; Weiss & McGuinn, 2016).

Following the 2016 reauthorization, ESSA's full implementation began with the 2017–2018 school year. Teacher education associations across the nation supported ESSA and began planning for a more differentiated and individualized approach to improve student learning. However, the nation was on the cusp of political turn-taking as a new President of the United States was chosen and took office in January of 2017, and the impact on ESSA was profound.

With the 2017 change in administration came a list of changes to the Department of Education. Since the start of his term, our current President's administration has worked to undo many of the progressive actions taken by the previous administration. One of the current administration's first significant policy moves was to effectively rolling back ESSA by, '...voting to repeal crucial regulations associated with the Every Student Succeeds Act' (Goldstein, 2017, p. 1). While our current President has not yet terminated ESSA completely, as he enters his final year in his first term in office, it appears his efforts to repeal and defund ESSA remain a primary focus.

## EXPLORING RECENT BUDGET PROPOSALS & REPORTS

The next section provides the methods used as we analyzed the recent budget proposals and reports. We begin with our analysis of funding within ESSA related to PD and follow that with funding found within IDEA. There is no explicit reference to inclusion as a priority in any of the programmatic initiatives included in the ESSA law. When layered on top of the President's proposed cuts to inclusive programmes and lack of rhyme or reason for Congress's allocations of funds, the inclusion of students with disabilities is in need of immediate assistance.

*ESSA Funding*

As we attempted to tease out the ways in which inclusion is supported by the federal government, we began with an examination of the President's budgets from the most recent five years. The current five year period was selected as it encompasses the current Presidential term. These documents contained descriptions of programmes and prior allocations and proposed changes under ESSA. We then dug deeper to examine publicly available reports from (or about) the programmes which were put on the chopping block. Within these reports and websites, we sought to identify activities that related to the professional development (PD) of teachers and more specifically, PD related to instruction and inclusion of students with disabilities as well as other under-represented groups including English Language Learners (ELLs). We are interested in where recent administrations propose funding and cuts to funding as it pertains to the PD of teachers in support of inclusion. Professional development programmes, which ultimately focus on serving students with disabilities within ESSA, are challenging to identify as the descriptions of programmes do not specifically include language about inclusion. We did, however, identify programmes that mention services for students from disadvantaged or diverse backgrounds as well as students with disabilities. What follows is a discussion of two programme areas in ESSA that relate to teacher PD and which impact inclusive education.

**Funds for supporting effective instruction.** Title II of ESEA originally allocated funds for school library resources, textbooks and other instructional materials (Fiscal Year 2020 Budget of the US Government, 2019). However, as Title II evolved, two programmes were funded. The largest of these provided block funding to states. The other programme, known as the Supporting Effective Instruction (SEI) programme, included an allocation for competitive collaborative state/university projects to provide professional development supporting teacher and principal quality and reducing class size. This collaborative higher education aspect of the SEI programme was cut from the budget in 2016, with the rationale that the competitive nature was a burden to accessing the funds. However, the remaining SEI and block funding in Title II allowed states and districts to partner with universities if they so choose to provide professional development. In the 2019 budget, the President proposed to further cuts to the remaining Title II SEI programmes, stating that,

> SEI grants are poorly targeted and funds are spread too thinly to have a meaningful impact on student outcomes. In addition, there is limited evidence that teacher professional development (PD), a primary activity funded by the programme, has led to increases in student achievement. (Fiscal Year 2020 Budget of the US Government, 2019, p. 32)

However, findings from an evaluation of the outcomes of Title II in ESEA included in a 2017 report from the National Center for Education Evaluation and Regional Assistance indicated that the funds were indeed well-spent. The report demonstrates that from 2005 to 2015, proficiency rates on the National Assessment of Educational Progress (NAEP) slightly increased from 2005 to 2015 among students from disadvantaged backgrounds served by the Title II programmes (Troppe, Milanowski, Heid, Gill, & Ross, 2017). However, pertinent to understanding the impact of Title II on students with disabilities, the report notes that, while the NAEP proficiency rates grew for the majority of students during this time, growth was mixed, or not seen at all, for students with disabilities or English Language Learners (Troppe et al., 2017). They do note it is difficult to reliably report such data because students may move in or out of ELL or disability status during a given school year, and definitions for these categories often vary from state to state.

**Funds for teacher grant programmes.** Another large cut that has been proposed in recent years involves two teacher grant programmes, known as the Supporting Effective Educators Development (SEED) Grant Programme and Teacher Quality Partnership (TQP) Programme. Both programmes were created to increase the number of effective teachers in K-12 schools (Fiscal Year 2020 Budget of the US Government, 2019). According to the Fiscal Year 2020 Budget of the US Government (2019),

> The SEED programme provides competitive grants to support professional development for teachers. The TQP programme provides competitive grants to partnerships of school districts and higher education institutions to create a variety of effective pathways into teaching and increase the number of teachers effective in improving student outcomes. (p. 33)

With connections to evidence-based strategies for improving student outcomes, these programmes are meant to fund PD activities and training for classroom teachers and school leaders.

In reviewing recent budgets, these activities are still funded under the Elementary and Secondary Education Act formula grant funds under ESSA Title I (Fiscal Year 2020 Budget of the US Government, 2019). Furthermore, reasoning for the elimination of these programmes includes the idea that states should determine the best practices of teachers rather than the federal government. In justifying these cuts, the proposed budget also states,

...The Administration is pursuing a new, scalable strategy that will empower educators to select professional development that is tailored to their individual needs. Should rigorous evaluation find this strategy to be effective at increasing student outcomes, the Administration will seek to expand this strategy. (p. 33)

When worded so eloquently, it makes sense; however, we argue that the cuts to the programmes mentioned limit the funding for PD of teachers.

After examining the proposed budgets since 2016, there is an interesting trend that can be seen from 2016 and 2017 as compared to the proposed budgets of 2018 through 2020. It is important to point out that during this presidency, there was direct focus and an explicit interest in funding for PD of teachers. According to the 2017 budget, there were multiple programmes that were proposed to attract and retain highly effective teachers. One such programme included a proposed

$100 million for Supporting Effective Educator Development to support nonprofits that provide evidence-based professional development activities and prepare teachers and principals from nontraditional preparation and certification routes to serve in high-need LEAs. (U. S. Department of Education, 2016c, p. 5)

The RESPECT: Best Job in the World Programme was another programme recommended with a one-time, $1 billion investment to

...support a nationwide effort to attract and retain effective teachers in high-need schools by increasing compensation and paths for advancement, implementing teacher-led development opportunities to improve instruction, and creating working conditions and school climates conducive to student success. (U. S. Department of Education, 2016c, p. 5)

Other highlights included $250 million for the Teacher and School Leader Incentive Programme, $125 million for the proposed Teacher and Principal Pathways programme and $10 million for Teach to Lead grants, all with connections to the support of the development of highly effective teachers and PD (U. S. Department of Education, 2016c). Such proposals show the former President's interest in funding programmes related to the professional development of teachers and more specifically, PD related to instruction and inclusion of students with disabilities as well as other under-represented groups.

### IDEA 2004 Funding

Similar to our examining of funding for PD in ESSA, we explore and discuss IDEA funding through an examination of publicly available budgets and reports. Five years of data were included in this analysis to ensure that a consistent period of analysis was included across the policies presented in this chapter. As previously mentioned, the current five year period was selected as it encompasses the current Presidential term. While procedures were consistent across ESSA and IDEA, reports related to IDEA are not readily available for some data related to this discussion. As such, when data for 2018 and 2019 were not available, data from 2012 and 2013 were included to ensure five years of data were analyzed and considered in our discussion.

IDEA 2004 is composed of and funded in four parts: General Provisions (Part A), Assistance for Education of all Children with Disabilities (Part B), Infants and Toddlers with Disabilities (Part C) and National Activities to Improve Education of Children with Disabilities (Part D) (Education of Individuals with Disabilities, 2015). Annually, IDEA 2004 receives an appropriation amount from the federal government in order to fund each part of the legislation. Under each budget, Part B, which includes Section 611 (for students age 3–21) and 619 (for students age 3–5), receives the largest percentage of the annual appropriation, as this is the largest component of the policy (Dragoo, 2019). According to the U. S. Department of Education, funds provided under Part B may be used for 'support and direct services; technical assistance and personnel preparation; assisting LEAs in providing positive behavioural interventions and supports; and improving the use of technology in the classroom' (2016a). While Part B is the largest component of IDEA 2004 and receives the largest amount of funding for services and supports for children age 3 to 21, Part C is also crucial in providing support and services to children as this section outlines support and services for infants and their families. As such, Part B and C both directly impact the support and services provided to students with disabilities in the US education system.

Delving into funding for IDEA 2004, documents analyzed included U.S. Department of Education State Funding History Tables for formula-allocated and selected student aid programmes as well as justifications for the 2019 fiscal year budget. U.S. Department of Education State Funding History Tables for formula-allocated and selected student aid programmes indicate the exact amount the government spent to fund Part B and C of IDEA. Currently, U.S. Department of Education State Funding History Tables for formula-allocated and selected student aid programmes are published through 2017. Funding of Part D is not reported under these reports as this section includes National Activities to Improve Education of Children with Disabilities. As such, funding for Part D is analyzed through the 2019 proposed budget justification document. In analyzing and discussing findings from all reports, it is imperative to note allocations provide the amount of funds the government requested for a given year and may not be indicative of the total sum the government spent or will spend.

Table 1 highlights the funding trends for Part B and Part C of IDEA 2004 from 2012 to 2017. These trends appear to indicate that funding has, and continues to be, fluctuated with minimal overall growth from year to year. These figures alone appear to show the funding system for students with disabilities is stable; however, these numbers fall short of the promises made by the federal government and the funding necessary to support students' access to a free and appropriate education (Free Appropriate Public Education, 2017) in the least restrictive environment (LRE Requirements, 2017) as mandated by IDEA. Specifically, Congress committed the federal government to pay up to 40% of the added cost associated with educating a student with a disability, which is known as the average per pupil expenditure (APPE). When the federal government meets the 40% commitment, IDEA is considered to have full funding (National

***Table 1.*** Percentage of APPE Funded 2012–2017.

| Fiscal Year | Percentage of APPE Funded |
| --- | --- |
| 2012 | 16% |
| 2013 | 15% |
| 2014 | 16% |
| 2015 | 16% |
| 2016 | 16% |
| 2017 | 16% |

*Note:* Data from U.S. Department of Education (2016b).

Education Association, 2018). Table 2 outlines the percentage of APPE funded by the federal government from 2012 to 2017. These percentages indicate that the federal government is funding 24–25% less of the APPE for students than the congressional commitment. The National Education Association (NEA) estimates this discrepancy resulted in a -$21,543.6 million dollar gap in funding for the 2017–2018 school year (National Education Association, 2018).

In understanding the federal government's commitment to funding 40% of the APPE and the reality that the government funds an estimated 16% of the APPE, it is imperative that the proposed 2019 budget is viewed through a critical lens. According to the U. S. Department of Education (2018), the federal government requested $12,002,848,000 to support grants to states under Part B section 611 for the 2019 fiscal year. Additionally, the budget includes $368,238,000 for section 619, Special Education Preschool Grants. Grants for Infants and Families include a requested amount of $458,556,000. In total, the proposed budget for Part B and C is $12,829,642,000. This proposed budget provides a slight increase of $34,885 for Part B and C, which indicates the federal government continues to fund less than half of the 40% APPE funding commitment to support the education of students with disabilities under IDEA 2004.

Aforementioned, funding for Part D of IDEA 2004 supports National Activities to Improve Education of Children with Disabilities. National activities under this section relevant to inclusion and professional development include Subpart 1, State Personnel Development (SPD) and Subpart 2, Personnel Preparation (section 661 and 662). According to the U. S. Department of Education (2018),

> The SPD programme provides funding for professional development to improve the knowledge and skills of special education and regular education teachers serving children with disabilities. Specifically, SPD funds are used to provide training in effective interventions. Examples include positive behavioural interventions and supports to improve student behaviour in the classroom, scientifically based reading instruction, early and appropriate interventions to identify and help children with disabilities, effective instruction for children with low incidence disabilities and strategies for successful transitioning to postsecondary opportunities. (p. H-61)

While the SPD programme focuses on personnel development for certified special and general educators in effective interventions that may support

*Table 2.* IDEA 2004 State, Preschool, and Infants and Families Grant Funding (Part B and C).

| | 2012 | 2013 | 2014 | 2015 | 2016 | 2017 |
|---|---|---|---|---|---|---|
| Special Education Grants to States | $11,577,855,236 | $10,974,865,803 | $11,472,848,000 | $11,497,848,000 | $11,912,848,000 | $12,002,813,115 |
| Special Education Preschool Grants | $372,645,367 | $353,237,522 | $353,238,000 | $353,238,000 | $368,238,000 | $368,238,000 |
| Grants for Infants and Families | $442,709,694 | $419,652,810 | $438,498,000 | $438,556,000 | $458,556,000 | $458,556,000 |
| Total Amount Funded | $12,393,210,297 | $11,747,756,135 | $12,264,584,000 | $12,289,642,000 | $12,739,642,000 | $12,829,607,115 |

*Note:* Data from U.S. Department of Education (2019).

*Table 3.* IDEA 2004 State Personnel and Preparation Grant Funding.

|                                | 2014 | 2015 | 2016 | 2017 | 2018 | 2019 |
|--------------------------------|------|------|------|------|------|------|
| State personnel development    | $41,630,000 | $41,630,000 | $41,630,000 | $38,630,000 | $38,368,000 | $38,630,000 |
| Personnel preparation          | $83,700,000 | $83,700,000 | $83,700,000 | $83,700,000 | $83,132,000 | $83,700,000 |

*Note:* Data from U.S. Department of Education (2018). 2019 totals represent the requested budget and may not be representative of actual funding total.

inclusion, the Personnel Preparation programme focuses on preparing both special and general education teachers to enter the profession. Specifically, the Personnel Preparation programme aims to support states in training individuals to become certified general education teachers, special education teachers, related service providers and early intervention providers who are prepared to meet the needs of children with disabilities. Further, activities funded under Subpart 2, Personnel Preparation, must 'ensure regular education teachers have the necessary knowledge and skills to provide instruction to students with disabilities in regular education classrooms' (U. S. Department of Education, 2018, p. H-78).

As noted in the current President's budget rationale for the 2019 IDEA budget, teacher shortages are prevalent across the United States, especially in the area of special education (U. S. Department of Education, 2018). Despite shortages, funding under IDEA Part D for SPD continues to decline. In fact, as shown in Table 3, the SPD programme experienced a $3,000,000 decrease between 2016 and 2017. While the programme received a slight increase of $8,000 in 2018, the 2019 budget indicates a decrease by the same $8,000. In addition, the Subpart 2, Personnel Preparation programme has maintained relatively constant; however, the programme experienced a $568,000 dip in funding during the 2018 year.

Holistically, IDEA 2004 is, at best, inconsistently funded. While funding may be inconsistent from year to year in Part B, C, and D, it is clear that the federal government is not meeting their commitment to fully fund IDEA 2004. This is somewhat parallel to what we found when examining ESSA. Inclusion is not a priority and when paired with Congress's inconsistent allocations of funds, the inclusion of students with disabilities is at risk of failure.

## REFLECTIONS ON IMPLICATIONS OF BUDGETS

Upon examination of the proposed budgets from the current US presidency, there are extensive proposed cuts to funding for programmes tied to PD of teachers. Justification for the cutting of funds for PD is loosely tied to a lack of evidence indicating student outcomes. Furthermore, there has not been any explicit reference to inclusion as a priority in any of the programmatic initiatives included in the ESSA law. The President's proposed cuts to inclusive programmes and lack of consistency for Congress's allocations of funds send the message that the inclusion of students with disabilities is not important. Notably, the President's budget rationale recognizes that these funds are not sufficient in addressing teacher shortages and the number of qualified personnel in the school system. Specifically, the rationale states,

> While the funds available through this programme are by no means sufficient to resolve ongoing shortages in special education nationwide, they have played a critical role in increasing the supply of personnel in specific areas where the demand for additional staff are especially critical, such as in the area of low incidence disabilities at both the postsecondary and K-12 levels. (U. S. Department of Education, 2018, p. H-81)

We assert that developing such an ideal inclusive educational system requires not only significant policy changes (such as the merger of educational legislation) but also increased funding for teacher PD explicitly focused on inclusion. Further, we believe the contemporary reforms noted by Spaulding and Pratt (2015) and advancements in inclusive education are at risk, given an evolving neoliberal approach to education and intolerant societal attitudes, which are re-emerging in America today, and these influences are reflected in the budgetary priorities of the current administration (Baynton, 2013; Spaulding & Pratt, 2015).

## CONCLUSION

In recent Presidential budgets, justification for the cutting of funds for PD is justified by a lack of evidence indicating student outcomes. Within the field, it is well known that linking student outcomes to PD is complex and often problematic (Guskey, 2016). This is particularly problematic, given funding levels have consistently been low or have decreased over time. Evidence from student outcomes should not be the main measure of the value of PD – a tool that is prioritized in virtually every other professional field.

The role of inclusive programmes, more specifically PD of teachers, is vital to the success of students with disabilities. Through an exploratory analysis of recent budget proposals, we see a need for the prioritization of funding on the preparation and PD of teachers in order to improve the educational experiences of students across the country. To be clear, this is not a true, critical assessment or economic analysis, rather a group of concerned special educators looking to better understand how funding is allocated when it comes to PD of teachers for inclusive programming. When looking into the Council of Exceptional Children's (CEC) State of The Special Education Profession Survey Report, we continue to see a call for more equipped teachers capable of meeting the diverse needs of their learners (Fowler, Coleman, & Bogdan, 2019). According to Fowler et al. (2019), 'Only half [of them] rated their skills in using culturally relevant strategies for assessment (51%) and culturally responsive strategies for discipline (53%) as very high' (p. 18). Further, '...this finding requires attention and should be highlighted in ongoing professional development and in recruitment of a more diverse teaching force' (Fowler et al., 2019, p. 18). Without the support of funding specifically aimed at providing inclusion-focused professional development to prepare, recruit and retain high quality teachers and teacher candidates in PK-12 education, we run the risk of repeating the same mistakes we have made in the past.

# REFERENCES

Baynton, D. C. (2013). Disability and the justification of inequality in American history. In L. J. Davis (Ed.), *The disability studies reader*. (4th ed., pp. 12–33). New York, NY: Routledge.

Berry, A. B., Petrin, R. A., Gravelle, M. L., & Farmer, T. W. (2012). Issues in special education teacher recruitment, retention, and professional development: Considerations in supporting rural teachers. *Rural Special Education Quarterly*, *30*(4), 3–11.

Darling-Hammond, L. (2017). Education for sale? *The Nation*, *304*(10), 16–20.

Dragoo, K. E. (2019). The individuals with disabilities education act (IDEA) funding: A primer. Retrieved from https://www.everycrsreport.com/files/20190829_R44624_c85f49a0d2b1c25913 346932a5bf6b9c30831c8d.pdf

Education of Individuals with Disabilities. (2015). Education of individuals with disabilities. 20 U.S.C. § 1400–1482. Retrieved from https://sites.ed.gov/idea/statute-chapter-33/subchapter-i/1400

Free Appropriate Public Education (FAPE). (2017). Free Appropriate Public Education (FAPE), 34 CFR § 300.101. Retrieved from https://sites.ed.gov/idea/regs/b/b/300.101

Faraclas, K. L. (2018). A professional development training model for improving Co-teaching performance. *International Journal of Special Education*, *33*(3), 524–540.

Fiscal Year 2020 Budget of the US Government. (2019). A budget for a better America: Major savings and reforms. Retrieved from https://www.govinfo.gov/content/pkg/BUDGET-2020-MSV/pdf/ BUDGET-2020-MSV.pdf

Fowler, S., Coleman, M. R., & Bogdan, W. (2019). The state of the special education profession survey report. *Council for Exceptional Children*, *52*(1), 1–29. doi:10.1177/0040059919875703

Goldstein, D. (2017). Obama education rules are swept aside by Congress. *New York Times*, March 9. Retrieved from https://www.nytimes.com/2017/03/09/us/every-student-succeeds-act-essa-congress.html?_r=0

Guskey, T. R. (2016). Gauge impact with 5 levels of data. *Journal of Staff Development*, *37*(1), 32–37.

Kitzmiller, E. M. (2019). Public schools, private dollars: An education arms race. *Phi Kappa Phi Forum*, *99*(1), 14–17.

Lowrey, K. A., & Smith, S. J. (2018). Including individuals with disabilities in UDL framework implementation: Insights from administrators: Administrator insights on UDL. *Inclusion*, *6*(2), 127–142. doi:10.1352/2326-6988-6.2.127

Lowrey, K. A., Hollingshead, A., Howery, K., & Bishop, J. B. (2017). More than one way: Stories of UDL and inclusive classrooms. *Research and Practice for Persons with Severe Disabilities*, *42*(4), 225–242. doi:10.1177/1540796917711668

LRE Requirements. (2017). LRE requirements, 34 CFR § 300.114. Retrieved from https://sites.ed.gov/ idea/regs/b/b/300.114/a

Musgrove, M. (2017). Education policy's critical role in improving the futures of individuals with disabilities. *Inclusion*, *5*(2), 136–148.

National Education Association. (2018). IDEA funding gap. Retrieved from https://www.nea.org/ assets/docs/IDEA-Funding-Gap-FY2017-with-State-Table.pdf

Quirk, C., Lea Ryndak, D., & Taub, D. (2017). Research and evidence-based practices to promote membership and learning in general education for students with extensive support needs. *Inclusion*, *5*(2), 94–109. doi:10.1352/2326-6988-5.2.94

Schuh, M. C., Knackstedt, K. M., Cornett, J., Choi, J. H., Pollitt, D. T., & Satter, A. L. (2018). All means all: Connecting federal education policy and local implementation practice through evidence and equity. *Inclusion*, *6*(1), 45–59. doi:10.1352/2326-6988-6.1.45

Sharp, L. A. (2016). ESEA reauthorization: An overview. *Texas Journal of Literacy Education*, *4*(1), 9–13. Retrieved from http://www.texasreaders.org/journal.html

Shepherd, K. G., Fowler, S., McCormick, J., Wilson, C. L., & Morgan, D. (2016). The search for role clarity: Challenges and implications for special education teacher preparation. *Teacher Education and Special Education, 39*(2), 83–97.

Smith, D. D. & Tyler, N. C. (2011). Effective inclusive education: Equipping education professionals with necessary skills and knowledge. *Prospects, 41*, 323. doi:10.1007/s11125-011

Spaulding, L. S., & Pratt, S. M. (2015). A review and analysis of the history of special education and disability advocacy in the United States. *American Educational History Journal, 42*(1/2), 91–109.

Troppe, P., Milanowski, A. T., Heid, C., Gill, B., & Ross, C. (2017). Implementation of title I and title II-A program initiatives: Results from 2013-14. NCEE 2017-4015. Retrieved from https://ies.ed.gov/ncee/pubs/20174014

U. S. Department of Education, Individuals with Disabilities Education Act. (2004). Sec. 300.114 lre requirements. Retrieved from http://sites.ed.gov/idea/regs/b/b/300.114

U. S. Department of Education. (2016a). Special education: Grants to states. Retrieved from https://www2.ed.gov/programs/osepgts/index.html

U. S. Department of Education. (2016b). Special education: Fiscal year 2017 budget request. Retrieved from https://www2.ed.gov/about/overview/budget/budget17/justifications/h-specialed.pdf

U. S. Department of Education. (2016c). Budget factsheet. Retrieved from https://www2.ed.gov/about/overview/budget/budget17/budget-factsheet.pdf

U. S. Department of Education. (2018). Special education: Fiscal year 2019 budget request. Retrieved from https://www2.ed.gov/about/overview/budget/budget19/justifications/h-specialed.pdf

U. S. Department of Education. (2019). Budget history tables. Retrieved from https://www2.ed.gov/about/overview/budget/history/index.html

United States Government Accountability Office. (2009). *Teacher quality [electronic resource]: Survey results of state officials on efforts to coordinate teacher quality initiatives (GAO-09-594SP, July 2009), an e-supplement to GAO-09-593/U.S Government Accountability Office.* US Government Accountability Office, Washington, DC.

Weiss, J., & McGuinn, P. (2016). States as change agents under ESSA. *Kappan Magazine, 8*(97), 28–33.

Woodcock, S., & Hardy, I. (2017). Probing and problematizing teacher professional development for inclusion. *International Journal of Educational Research, 83*, 43–54.

Woolf, S. B. (2019). Critical skills for special educator effectiveness: Which ones matter most, and to whom? *Teacher Education and Special Education, 42*(2), 132.

# GLOBAL TRENDS IN THE FUNDING OF INCLUSIVE EDUCATION: A NARRATIVE REVIEW

Umesh Sharma and Samantha Vlcek

## ABSTRACT

*This chapter reports on how funding is used in general education schools around the world to facilitate inclusive education. While research has established the importance of inclusive education and investigated the diverse funding models employed in different global regions, this narrative review reports on how funding is operationalized at the school and classroom level to achieve the goals of inclusive education. Results indicate funding is commonly allocated to in-service professional learning programmes, resource acquisition, and purposefully tailored supplementary programmes for students with specific educational needs. This chapter outlines recommendations for researchers and policymakers in developing new ways of funding inclusive practices.*

**Keywords**: Funding; inclusive education; funding models; considerations; resourcing; inclusion

International research into provisions for and methods of funding inclusive education has increased in recent years (see, for example, Graham, 2015; Meijer & Watkins, 2019; Mitchell, 2010; Sharma, Furlonger, & Forlin, 2019). This increase is likely attributed to the extensive research supporting the benefits of inclusive education. Students educated in school settings that successfully promote inclusive principles have greater academic and social outcomes compared with peers in segregated settings (Boyle, Scriven, Durning, & Downes, 2011). Inclusive settings have further been linked to increased student engagement, academic outcomes and the development of appropriate interpersonal skills

Resourcing Inclusive Education
International Perspectives on Inclusive Education, Volume 15, 51–65
ISSN: 1479-3636/doi:10.1108/S1479-363620210000015006

(Chandler-Olcott & Kluth, 2009; Farrington et al., 2012, pp. 1–106; Katz, 2013). Despite the reported benefits inclusive education offers all students, the historical relationship between inclusive education and special education remains a prominent focus in recent literature on inclusive education and funding (Haug, 2017).

The expense of providing appropriate resources to educate a student with a disability in a mainstream school varies across OECD countries; however, the cost is generally increased two to four times compared with a student without disability (Evans, 2004). This cost further increases by approximately 20% when education is provided in a segregated special school setting (Evans, 2004). These statistics may, at least in part, explain the continued association between inclusive education and students with a disability where inclusive education and funding is concerned. As Johnstone, Lazarus, Lazetic, and Nikolic (2018) pointed out, increased funding for marginalized students does not necessarily intend to label certain students, nor remove the relevance of inclusive education for all students; however, it does recognize that understanding where funds are needed and how they are allocated is an important aspect of reforming funding mechanisms that have historically underserved specific populations. Irrespective of the link between funding and disability, current processes for supporting the education of all students in inclusive settings are needed. Beyond financial provisions, the underproductive use of resources also impacts the capacity of inclusive education to be implemented effectively (Slee, 2007). Loreman (2014) has further identified the need for appropriate resource provisions and allocation in inclusive settings, as well as guidance for how to use resources to their full potential. These points further emphasize the purpose and value of examining how funding for inclusive education is currently influencing practice in schools and classrooms around the world.

Beyond provisions for and models of funding inclusive education, global trends regarding the types of services and supports financed under these systems, particularly at the school and classroom level, have not been addressed in literature to date. As Haug (2017) has argued, student placement is often over-emphasized in inclusive education discourse and less attention is given to the processes and practices needed to support students and schools to achieve the intention of truly inclusive settings. This review intended to guide future research and policy relating to how funding is directed and employed to support inclusive education for all students at the school and classroom level. This chapter begins with a brief overview of inclusive education internationally and how some countries have attempted to fund inclusive education. It then presents the method used to undertake the review and discuss key considerations on how this information can be used to improve research and policy into this aspect of education.

## INTERNATIONAL RESPONSES TO INCLUSIVE EDUCATION

Commitment to inclusive education has been an international priority for decades. A fundamental move towards inclusive education came with the release of the Salamanca Statement (UNESCO, 1994), where 92 countries committed to working towards providing inclusive, accessible and effective educational settings for all students. More recently, Sustainable Development Goal 4 (SDG) (United Nations General Assembly, 2015) emphasized inclusive education as a global necessity. The Goal forms part of SDG's larger blueprint for targeting global inequities and strengthening development and sustainability by 2030. Despite widespread commitment to Salamanca and SDG, policy and practice of inclusive education, and opportunities for students to access an advantageous mainstream education, varies significantly across global regions.

Approaches to inclusive education in countries largely operating from a social justice model of education, such as Australia, the United States and the United Kingdom, emphasize the rights of students to be included and supported in general education settings. Each of these three nations further provides the option for families to elect to enrol their child with a disability in a special education setting or programme if specific enrolment criteria is met (Konza, 2008). Policy and provisions for inclusive education frequently differ in countries operating from a psychomedical model of education. For instance, Kazakhstan's developing inclusive education policies regulate educational enrolment options for students with a disability (OECD/The World Bank, 2015). In saying this, recent advances in national policy have recognized opportunities for students with a disability to be accommodated in general education settings when institutional facilities are deemed appropriate (OECD/The World Bank, 2015). Dissimilar to these approaches, Italy has a predominantly singular educational structure, *integrazione scholastic*, which anticipates all schools accommodate students irrespective of need or disability; however, segregated educational settings continue to operate for students with a disability determined as being too severe for mainstream school enrolment (Anastasiou, Kauffman, & Di Nuovo, 2015; D'Alessio, 2011). While policies and provisions relating to school enrolment options for students with a disability are typically accessible in the public domain, less is known about the way inclusive education is resourced to support inclusive practices to meet all students' educational needs.

## FUNDING INCLUSIVE EDUCATION

Although inclusive education is more than the provision of support for students with a disability (see, for example, Florian, 2008; Norwich, 2014; Thomas, 2013), funding for inclusive education is often inextricably linked to students with diagnosed or imputed disability. A recent narrative review of international funding models and their impact on the education of students with autism spectrum disorder found many funding models sought to finance supports based on the level of a student's needs (Sharma et al., 2019). Funding in this instance was not related to a specific disability or categorization of disability, instead, students deemed to have mild needs were typically provided for under general funding models, and students with more prominent needs received support within additional funding schemes. Globally, three funding models emerged from the findings: input funding, throughput funding, and output funding. Input funding finances individual students or an educational institution based on individual disability categorization. Throughput funding is less reliant on the demographics of the student population, and additional monies are distributed according to the services a school is expected to provide to meet the needs of the school population. Output funding is outcome-driven and bases the allocation of additional funds on the achievement of particular output criteria (Sharma et al., 2019).

Meijer and Watkins (2019) recently reviewed funding provisions for students with additional needs in Europe. Their research compared the results of two studies conducted by the European Agency into financing inclusive education across 17 different European countries: the first in 1999 and the second in 2016. Meijer and Watkins (2019) found many of the underpinning constraints and needs for funding inclusive education remained consistent across this time span. While different funding approaches had been initiated, at the core of the support is the need to balance the needs of an entire school environment (throughput funding) and the additional supports needed to ensure a virtuous education for students with specific educational needs (input funding). The study reemphasized equity, effectiveness, and efficiency as the three core underpinning principles of prosperous inclusive education systems. Funding programmes that aim to meet the needs of all students, irrespective of diagnosed disability or quantifiable disadvantage, and allow educational institutions to successfully implement appropriate practices competently are needed to achieve the goals of inclusive education. The authors argued productive funding structures should be targeted towards the needs of all students, focus on building the capacity of educators, ensure flexible learning environments, and are developed upon regulatory frameworks that anticipate accountability and improvement at the school and classroom level for this to occur. They concluded financing remains a critical aspect of achieving these ideals and developing successful inclusive education systems across different regions (Meijer & Watkins, 2019).

Globally, different regions have attempted to achieve these objectives through the development and implementation of specific funding structures to target whole-school and individual student needs. In Australia, the Nationally Consistent Collection of Data on School Students with Disability (NCCD) finances the needs of individual students with a disability based on the level of adjustments provided by an educational provider in addition to the amount allocated on a per capita basis from both federal and state government funds (Australian Government Department of Education, Skills and Development (DESD), 2020). The initial level, Quality Differentiated Teaching Practice, anticipates educators provide adjustments commensurate with the standard monitoring and supports expected to be provided to all students in Australia and attracts no additional funds. The second level, Supplementary, recognizes the additional adjustments required for some students and the minor financial impact of providing these adjustments on educational providers; therefore, in 2020, $4,934 has been allocated for eligible students enrolled in primary schools, and $4,871 for those in secondary schools. Students requiring more consistent adjustments across a school day are considered to require Substantial adjustments. At this level, $17,151 has been allocated for each eligible student enrolled in primary school, and $17,123 for each student enrolled in secondary school. The highest level, Extensive, recognizes the significant and constant adjustments required to educate some students and attracts a considerable loading ($36,651 for primary school students and $36,607 for students enrolled in secondary school) to ensure each student is provided the necessary supports to receive an education on the same basis of a student without disability (DESD, 2020); in line with Australian Commonwealth law (Commonwealth of Australia [COA], 2006)).

Since its inception, the NCCD programme has been adopted by various private and public regional educational authorities as their primary funding mechanism for students with a disability. The programme is founded upon Australian disability and educational law (Australian Government, 1992; COA, 2006), whereby each student with a disability has the right to receive an education on the same basis as a student without disability. The NCCD has four funding levels based on evidence of assessed need, evidence of adjustments provided and monitoring and reviewing of adjustments. Each funding level is tied to the level of the specific adjustments provided to each student with a diagnosed or imputed disability. While each educational institution funded under the NCCD has unilateral discretion for how their budget is managed, the programme requires educational providers to demonstrate how they have met their legal obligations (such as consultation with parents and caregivers) and how the funds are inextricably tied to the level of adjustments a student has received. The data provided by each school form a national body of evidence to further inform policy and guide the supports required by schools to ensure each student with a disability is best supported to achieve equitable educational opportunities.

In contrast, funding for students with additional needs in the United States is significantly more complex. Despite multiple legal bases (i.e., American with Disabilities Act of 1990, No Child Left, Every Student Succeeds Act, and Individuals with Disabilities Education Act, etc.), funding assigned to support students with a disability is distributed through various models based on locality and additional qualifying criteria. Educational institutions are supported through federal, state, local and discretionary educational funding programmes, as well as through the national medical service program, Medicaid. Each revenue source has different qualification criteria (both related to individual student needs and the economic arrangement of the locality), lists of permissible expenditures and other formulaic considerations aimed at equalizing the supports afforded to students (Hill, Warren, Murphy, Ugo, & Pathak, 2016; McCann, 2014). When student support cannot be provided at the school level, students might be eligible for support through a voucher programme to gain access to permissible therapies outside of the school setting.

Despite variability in the way inclusive education is funded, consistent areas of concern are noted by teachers and school providers around the world. Within the literature there has been an international trend for educators to suggest increased funding, resources and education and training is needed to better support students with a disability to achieve a truly inclusive education (see, for example, Cambridge-Johnson, Hunter-Johnson, & Newton, 2014; Lindsay, Proulx, Thomson, & Scott, 2013; St Leger, 2014). Watson (2009) has further reported on systematic issues with resourcing to support educator preparedness to appropriately meet the educational needs of students with a disability. This chapter reports on a review of recent research into how funding is operationalized to enhance inclusive educational practices in schools around the world. The review intended to inform how funding it currently employed and what can be learnt from existing practices.

## METHOD: REVIEWING INCLUSIVE EDUCATION FUNDING

A narrative approach was selected to best summarize the subject given the diversity in funding models employed to finance inclusive education in different contexts (Sharma et al., 2019). Unlike a systematic review, a narrative review provided an integrated overview of the focus area (Baumeister & Leary, 1997). Contextual differences relating to definitions and terminology of inclusive education, as well as identification and categorization of students with a disability, precluded the option of a comparative review in this instance (D'Alessio & Watkins, 2009). A narrative review was determined to be the most suitable method given the interrelationship between educational policy, funding provisions and individual school priorities in diverse geographical locations. It was anticipated that the review would provide researchers and policymakers with a deepened understanding for how funding is employed to support inclusive education in different regions in order to inform opportunities for further research and policy analysis.

Each journal article was published in English between 2004 and 2019, with the full text available online. The search was conducted through ERIC and EBSCO databases, and included two search terms: 'funding' and 'inclusive education'. While there remains no consistent definition of inclusive education across jurisdictions (UNESCO, 2015), for the purpose of this article inclusive education was defined as the provisions and supports provided to students that enable them to attend and participate in educational programmes on an equitable basis. The scope of the review was further limited to educational settings generally accessible to all students (i.e., 'mainstream' or 'general' education settings). This methodological choice provided a consistent basis to explore the types of resources and supports in similarly organized educational settings around the world.

## RESULTS

Sixty-two articles were located in the initial search. Of these, 57 were discarded as they did not meet the qualifying criteria; particularly the requirement each article be based on an empirical study. A total of five empirical articles specifically examined the relationship between funding and the supports or services acquired. Funding allocation within these studies is presented in Table 1. References marked with an asterisk indicate studies included in the analysis.

*Table 1.* Funding Allocation.

| | Region | Professional Development | | | Personnel | Resourcing | | Programming | |
|---|---|---|---|---|---|---|---|---|---|
| | | All Educational Staff | Teaching Staff | Educational Support Staff | | Physical/ Environmental Resources | Consumables | All Students | Profiled Students |
| Anastasiou and Kauffman (2009) | United States | | | | | X | | | |
| Deluca and Stillings (2008) | International | | | | X | X | | | X |
| Frederickson, Simmonds, Evans, and Soulsby (2007) | United Kingdom | | X | | | X | | | |
| Kaelin et al. (2019) | Switzerland | | | | X | | | | |
| Abawi and Oliver (2013) | Australia | X | | | X | | X | X | X |

## RESOURCING

One of the most common themes for resourcing amongst the articles reviewed was the need for specific human resources to support inclusive education; however, the types of personnel engaged differed amongst each study. Two studies discussed additional classroom teachers and teacher aides (Abawi & Oliver, 2013; Deluca & Stillings, 2008), and one other reported on OTs in the school setting (Kaelin et al., 2019). Beyond personnel, two studies reported further on resourcing as a means to provide distinct educational environment options (i.e., mainstream schools and special schools) (Anastasiou et al., 2015; Deluca & Stillings, 2008), and one other reported on the procurement of consumables; however, this categorization was not elaborated on further.

## PROFESSIONAL DEVELOPMENT AND CAPACITY BUILDING

Two articles reviewed in this study cited the allocation of funds as a means to increase student support through educator professional development and capacity building opportunities. While both studies reported on different benefits of training and development, the primary focus remained on increasing an educator's capacity to provide inclusive settings for the students in their care. Abawi and Oliver's (2013) study focussed generally on supporting educators to respond to all students' needs and to work within collegial teams to increase the support they were able to provide to students. Increasing the understanding and capacity of teachers to respond to the unique social and affective needs of students transitioning to a mainstream school from specialist settings was explored by Frederickson et al. (2007).

## SPECIFIC EDUCATIONAL PROGRAMMES

Within the empirical studies reviewed, two articles reported on funding specific educational programmes to support student inclusion and achievement. The programmes discussed responded to a diverse range of student needs and were delivered at a whole-school or classroom level dependant on the needs of the target cohort. The school at the centre of Abawi and Oliver's (2013) case study provided both individualized support programmes for students with specific educational needs and a social skills programme included within the weekly curriculum of each class across the whole school. The more general discussion provided within Deluca and Stillings' comparative review indicated funding was used by schools in some nations to provide after school programmes for students with additional support requirements on an as-needed basis; however, qualifying criteria and the specific programmes offered were not discussed in detail.

## DISCUSSION AND CONSIDERATIONS

The findings of this review have demonstrated funding for inclusive education purposes generally applied to three primary categories: resource acquisition, educator professional development and the inclusion of specific educational programmes to support student needs. These categories are further examined within this discussion, as well as additional research into these areas of education. Alongside discussion and empirical evidence regarding how funds are implemented to support inclusive education within schools and classrooms internationally, the limited number of articles reported on within this review underscore a significant problem with this area of research, and educational funding in general. Recently, there has been an increase in studies into the varied models of funding inclusive education (see, for example, Banks, Frawley, & McCoy, 2015; Johnstone et al., 2018; Meijer & Watkins, 2019; Sharma et al., 2019). This research explores the vital mechanisms for enabling policymakers to distribute funds with the intention of supporting schools to achieve the goals of inclusive education. Unfortunately, without a clear understanding of how this allocation is used at the school or classroom level, it is unclear whether these funds do, or are even able to, achieve their intended purpose. The way inclusive education is supported at the school and classroom level requires further examination to ensure allocated funds are able to achieve their objective. We provide four considerations for how this can be addressed moving forward to support targeted research and inform potential policies into this vital aspect of education.

### *Consideration 1: Interpreting Inclusive Education*

As discussed throughout this chapter, there is no universally accepted definition of inclusive education. The absence of a single definition of this field creates the opportunity for inconsistent interpretations at the district and school level.

Each of the five articles reviewed approached inclusive education from a different perspective. While four articles reported on the needs of students with additional educational needs, the characteristics of each study differed. For example, Kaelin et al. (2019) addressed inclusive education in the context of supporting students across a variety of diagnostic groups, including developmental coordination disorder, whereas Anastasiou and Kauffman (2009), Deluca and Stillings (2008) and Frederickson et al. (2007) approached inclusive education in relation to students with additional educational needs more generally. Abawi and Oliver's (2013) study was the only article reviewed that did not limit their exploration to a specific student population, instead choosing to explore their case study school's approach to inclusive education.

Amongst the dialogue surrounding the overemphasis of special education within inclusive education, Haug (2017) has argued that on one hand, quality teaching practice relies on an understanding of various conditions and specialized services to tailor appropriate programmes and supports for students with additional learning needs. On the other hand, inclusive education is simply 'good teaching' and irrespective of student diagnoses or label, high-effect teaching is about meeting the needs of all learners, and all learners require individualized programmes and supports (Haug, 2017). In reconciling these points, the authors of this chapter acknowledge inclusive education is a major component of quality teaching practice; however, teachers' knowledge of and access to specialized supports is also necessary to aid the identification and implementation of appropriate adjustments to meet the individual needs of all students. For this to occur, it is also necessary that school leaders and teachers are aware of the primary needs of students when attempting to cultivate inclusive schools and classrooms. Six items have been identified as critical to achieving comprehensive inclusive education for students with a disability: presence (i.e., student attending the school regularly), participation across school activities, acceptance of the student by the members of the school community, achievement of the student, having a positive sense of belongingness, as well as a degree of happiness of attending a particular school (Schwab, Sharma, & Loreman, 2018).

### Consideration 2: Increased Autonomy and Accountability

Leaders of educational institutions are in the best position to determine the most appropriate supports needed within their schools to ensure the conception and maintenance of inclusive environments for all students (Cheng, Ko, & Lee, 2016). Through a greater level of financial reporting on how funds dedicated to achieving the goals of inclusive education are spent, policymakers would be better positioned to assess the value of current models, and to determine the overarching needs of the community to address current and long-term funding needs. As addressed earlier in this chapter, there are concerns for how resources are used in inclusive settings (Loreman, 2014; Slee, 2007), and whether further support is needed at the school level to achieve the best outcome of additional funds. Additional measures to gauge how funds are used at the school level is likely to inform the professional development needs of teachers and school leaders alike.

Interestingly, Falkmer, Anderson, Joosten, and Falkmer's (2015) narrative review on parental perspectives of inclusive education for their children with autism spectrum conditions enrolled in mainstream schools found only five articles between 1990 and 2011 referenced funding as an influential aspect of inclusive education. This suggests that unless parents are aware of the specific funds allocated to a school based on their child's needs, they are likely to observe the outcomes of any financial injection instead of the costs attributed to providing the specific resources or programmes at the basis of the support. Increased reporting measures for how additional funds are being spent have the potential to inform the multiple and varied ways student needs are targeted at the classroom level to a range of different stakeholders.

While it is beyond the scope of this chapter to discuss parental involvement and awareness of funding provided on the basis of a child's specific needs, it is prudent to suggest further research into the potential benefits for schools and institutions to report on the expenditure of these funds is necessary. In the case of Australia's NCCD funding program, the funds attributed to each of the four funding levels are made publicly available. There is no requirement for schools to release the details of the funding level assigned to students; however, before applying for NCCD funding schools are obligated to formally consult with each student's parent/s or an associate (COA, 2006), which anticipates some caregivers might request this information. It appears beneficial to consider the potential community benefits of greater transparency from schools, within Australia and internationally, to report on and justify how these funds are being spent to ensure funds promote appropriate and evidence-based adjustments to meet the individual needs of the student population.

### Consideration 3: Explicit vs Implicit Funding Reported in Research

The current review provided a lens to examine recent research into how funding is specifically operationalized to advance inclusive education in different global regions; however, the scope only permitted articles which explicitly connected funding and the supports acquired. The nature of many empirical studies on inclusive education as an examination into the utilization and/or benefit of different educational supports (e.g., value and deployment of evidence-based practices or the specific needs of a particulars student population) suggests funding would play a role in the acquisition and implementation of certain programmes. Despite this, operational expense is rarely explicitly discussed beyond evaluation of appropriate funding structures.

The variability in funding structures and intended outcomes of those funds, from both macro (i.e., national policy and federal government department commitments) and micro (i.e., individual district and school priorities) levels, is an important consideration in inclusive education research. A greater emphasis on consolidating these areas and exploring how funds are specifically used in practice is needed to ensure the ideals of inclusive education are influencing classroom practice in different regions around the world. Given this, there should be clear mechanisms to determine what impact the increased funds have on schools, educational staff and, in turn, the students the funds are directed towards supporting.

### Consideration 4: Funding Sources

Kaelin et al.'s (2019) examination of the role, responsibilities and perceived benefit of school-based OTs working alongside educational staff and students in schools in Switzerland highlighted a concern with the way student needs are met. The results of the study found OTs were most commonly engaged to support students with diagnosed conditions, rather than support the general population of students. As cited by the authors, this finding might be directly related to the separation between educational and medical funding in Switzerland. Of the 302 recorded results, only four OTs ($n = 1\%$) reported being funded directly by schools. The remaining participants responded that their services were paid for through insurance programmes, privately by parents, or other community initiatives (Kaelin et al., 2019).

Similar bilateral funding structures are present in other nations, and may be impacting IE more generally. Students with a disability in Australia have the potential to receive support from multiple funding programmes. While the

NCCD provides educational funding for Australian students with a disability, school-aged children might also receive support from the national medical program, the National Disability Insurance Scheme (NDIS) (National Disability Insurance Agency [NDIA], 2019). Eligibility for each programme differs, with the major distinctions being the definition and acceptance of disability, as well as how funds are managed. The NCCD supports students with both diagnosed and imputed disability based on the level of adjustments a student is provided in the school setting, whereas the NDIS restricts programme enrolment to individuals with diagnosed disability and additional qualifying criteria. Under the NDIS parents have more discretion for how a child's allocated budget is used; however, the separation between educational support (NCCD) and medical support (NDIS) restricts NDIS monies being used directly for educational purposes or to enhance an educator's professional knowledge for how to support the child in the school setting (NDIA, 2014).

## LIMITATIONS AND DIRECTIONS FOR FUTURE RESEARCH

The small quantity of empirical studies that discussed how funding is specifically used to achieve the intentions of inclusive education has implications for the findings of this chapter. While there is a plethora of studies on the types of resources and supports suggested to increase IE, a significant barrier to understanding how funding is used to achieve inclusive education is the omission of the explicit relationship between allocated funds and the programmes or supports commissioned through that funding. Despite this, we suggest this presents an opportunity for researchers and policymakers to deepen their understanding of how allocated funds are targeting individual students and schools.

On an administrative level, clear parameters around school and institution accountability and reporting of the use of funding should also be considered. If funds are assigned to achieve inclusive environments, it is reasonable to expect transparent reports on how allocated monies are targeting individual student needs, as well as inclusive education across the environment as a whole. Further, achieving inclusive environments relies on governmental support to increase teacher capacity and general resourcing targeting all students, rather than isolating funds to students with specific educational needs alone. Evaluations into pre-service and in-service teacher professional knowledge of inclusive education strategies and supports should also be ongoing to ensure teachers can equitably meet the needs of all students in their care.

## CONCLUSION

This chapter has presented a varied discussion on the benefits and limitations of previous research into how funding is operationalized to support inclusive education. Specific funding provisions have been cited as an essential component of creating inclusive education in schools and classrooms around the world. Despite this, empirical research into how funds are currently being spent and whether allocated monies are truly achieving their intended targets is sparse. This chapter has addressed some of the pivotal considerations for advancing knowledge and practice in this area through answering the research question, 'How is funding for inclusive educational purposes being used around the world?' More funding is unlikely to result in better outcomes unless clear mechanisms are in place to identify how funds will be used to support teachers and resource schools. Continued research into funding for inclusive education is needed to ensure policy and funding schemes appropriately equip school leaders and teachers with the necessary knowledge, supports and resources to create truly inclusive educational settings.

# REFERENCES

References marked with an asterisk indicate studies included in the meta-analysis.

*Abawi, L., & Oliver, M. (2013). Shared pedagogical understandings: Schoolwide inclusion practices supporting learner needs. *Improving Schools*, *16*(2), 159–174.

*Anastasiou, D., & Kauffman, J. M. (2009). When special education goes to the marketplace: The case of vouchers. *Exceptionality*, *17*(4), 205–222. doi:10.1080/09362830903232109

Anastasiou, D., Kauffman, J. M., & Di Nuovo, S. (2015). Inclusive education in Italy: Description and reflections on full inclusion. *European Journal of Special Needs Education*, *30*(4), 429–443. doi: 10.1080/08856257.2015.1060075

Australian Government Department of Education, Skills and Development. (2020). What is the Australian Government doing to support students with disability in schools? Retrieved from https://www.education.gov.au/what-australian-government-doing-support-students-disability-schools

Australian Government. (1992). *The Disability Discrimination Act.* Retrieved from https://www.legislation.gov.au/Details/C2016C00763

Banks, J., Frawley, D., & McCoy, S. (2015). Achieving inclusion? Effective resourcing of students with special educational needs. *International Journal of Inclusive Education*, *19*(9), 926–943. doi: 10.1080/13603116.2015.1018344

Baumeister, R. F., & Leary, M. R. (1997). Writing narrative style literature reviews. *Review of General Psychology*, *1*(3), 311–320. doi:10.1179/2047480615z.000000000329

Boyle, C., Scriven, B., Durning, S., & Downes, C. (2011). Facilitating the learning of all students: The "professional positive" of inclusive practice in Australian primary schools. *Support for Learning*, *26*(2), 72–78. doi:10.1111/j.1467-9604.2011.01480.x

Cambridge-Johnson, J., Hunter-Johnson, Y., & Newton, N. G. L. (2014). Breaking the silence of mainstream teachers' attitude towards inclusive education in the Bahamas: High school teachers' perceptions. *Qualitative Report*, *19*(42), 1–20.

Chandler-Olcott, K., & Kluth, P. (2009). Why everyone benefits from including students with autism in literacy classrooms. *The Reading Teacher*, *62*(7), 548–557. doi:10.1598/rt.62.7.1

Cheng, Y. C., Ko, J., & Lee, T. T. H. (2016). School autonomy, leadership and learning: A reconceptualisation. *International Journal of Educational Management*, *30*(2), 177–196.

Commonwealth of Australia. (2006). Disability standards for education 2005: Plus guidance notes. Retrieved from https://docs.education.gov.au/system/files/doc/other/disability_standards_for_education_2005_plus_guidance_notes.pdf.

D'Alessio, S., & Watkins, A. (2009). International comparisons of inclusive policy and practice: Are we talking about the same thing? *Research in Comparative and International Education*, *4*(3), 233–249. doi:10.2304/rcie.2009.4.3.233

D'Alessio, S. (2011). *Inclusive education in Italy: A critical analysis of the policy of integrazione scholastica.* Rotterdam, NL: Sense.

*Deluca, M., & Stillings, C. (2008). Targeting resources to students with special educational needs: National differences in policy and practice. *European Educational Research Journal, 7*(3), 371–385.

Evans, P. (2004). Educating students with special needs: A comparison of inclusion practices in OECD countries. *Education Canada, 44*(1), 1–4.

Falkmer, M., Anderson, K., Joosten, A., & Falkmer, T. (2015). Parents' perspectives on inclusive schools for children with autism spectrum conditions. *International Journal of Disability, Development and Education, 62*(1), 1–23. doi:10.1080/1034912X.2014.984589

Farrington, C. A., Roderick, M., Allensworth, E., Nagaoka, J., Keyes, T. S., Johnson, D. W., & Beechum, N. O. (2012, June). *Teaching adolescents to become learners: The role of noncognitive factors in shaping school performance: A critical literature review.* Chicago, IL: University of Chicago Consortium on Chicago School Research.

Florian, L. (2008). Special or inclusive education: Future trends. *British Journal of Special Education, 35*(4)202. doi:10.1111/j.1467-8578.2008.00402.x

*Frederickson, N., Simmonds, E., Evans, L., & Soulsby, C. (2007). Assessing the social and affective outcomes of inclusion. *British Journal of Special Education, 34*(2), 105–115. doi:10.1111/j.1467-8578.2007.00463.x

Graham, L. J. (2015). A little learning is a dangerous thing: Factors influencing the increased identification of special educational needs from the perspective of education policy-makers and school practitioners. *International Journal of Disability, Development and Education, 62*(1), 116–132. doi:10.1080/1034912X.2014.955791

Haug, P. (2017). Understanding inclusive education: Ideals and reality. *Scandinavian Journal of Disability Research, 19*(3), 206–217. doi:10.1080/15017419.2016.1224778

Hill, L., Warren, P., Murphy, P., Ugo, I., & Pathak, A. (2016). *Special education finance in California.* San Francisco, CA: Public Policy Institute of California.

Johnstone, C., Lazarus, S., Lazetic, P., & Nikolic, G. (2018). Resourcing inclusion: Introducing finance perspectives to inclusive education policy rhetoric. *Prospects, 47*(4), 1–21. doi:10.1007/s11125-018-9432-2

*Kaelin, V. C., Ray-Kaeser, S., Moioli, S., Kocher Stalder, C., Santinelli, L., Echsel, A., & Schulze, C. (2019). Occupational therapy practice in mainstream schools: Results from an online survey in Switzerland. *Occupational Therapy International, 2019*, 9. doi:10.1155/2019/3647397

Katz, J. (2013). The three block model of universal design for learning (UDL): Engaging students in inclusive education. *Canadian Journal of Education, 36*(1), 153–194.

Konza, D. (2008). Inclusion of students with disabilities in new times: Responding to the challenge. In P. Kell, W. Vialle, D. Konza, & G. Vogl (Eds.), *Learning and the learner: Exploring learning for new times* (pp. 39–64). Wollongong: Faculty of Education, University of Wollongong.

Lindsay, S., Proulx, M., Thomson, N., & Scott, H. (2013). Educators' challenges of including children with autism spectrum disorder in mainstream classrooms. *International Journal of Disability, Development and Education, 60*(4), 347–362. doi:10.1080/1034912X.2013.846470

Loreman, T. (2014). Measuring inclusive education outcomes in Alberta, Canada. *International Journal of Inclusive Education, 18*(5), 459–483. doi:10.1080/13603116.2013.788223

McCann, C. (2014). *Federal funding for students with disabilities: The evolution of federal special education finance in the United States.* Washington, DC: New America Foundation.

Meijer, C. J. W., & Watkins, A. (2019). Financing special needs and inclusive education: From Salamanca to the present. *International Journal of Inclusive Education, 23*(7–8), 705–721. doi: 10.1080/13603116.2019.1623330

Mitchell, D. (2010). *Education that fits: Review of international trends in the education of students with special educational needs.* Wellington.

National Disability Insurance Agency. (2014). Fact sheet: Supports the NDIS will fund in relation to education. Retrieved from https://www.ndis.gov.au/document/factsheet-supports-ndis-will-fund

National Disability Insurance Agency. (2019). What is the NDIS?. Retrieved from https://www.ndis.gov.au/understanding/what-ndis

Norwich, B. (2014). Recognising value tensions that underlie problems in inclusive education. *Cambridge Journal of Education, 44*(4), 495–510. doi:10.1080/0305764X.2014.963027

OECD/The World Bank. (2015). *OECD reviews of school resources: Kazakhstan 2015.* Paris: OECD. doi:10.1787/9789264245891-en

Schwab, S., Sharma, U., & Loreman, T. (2018). Are we included? Secondary students' perception of inclusion climate in their schools. *Teaching and Teacher Education, 75*, 31–39. doi:10.1016/j.tate.2018.05.016

Sharma, U., Furlonger, B., & Forlin, C. (2019). The impact of funding models on the education of students with autism spectrum disorder. *Australasian Journal of Special and Inclusive Education, 43*(1), 1–11. doi:10.1017/jsi.2019.1

Slee, R. (2007). Inclusive schooling as a means and end of education? In L. Florian (Ed.), *The SAGE handbook of special education* (pp. 160–170). London: SAGE Publications.

St Leger, P. (2014). Practice of supporting young people with chronic health conditions in hospital and schools. *International Journal of Inclusive Education, 18*(3), 253–269. doi:10.1080/13603116.2012.679320

Thomas, G. (2013). A review of thinking and research about inclusive education policy, with suggestions for a new kind of inclusive thinking. *British Educational Research Journal, 39*(3), 473–490.

UNESCO. (1994). *The Salamanca statement and framework for action on special needs education.* Paris: Author.

UNESCO. (2015). *Education for all 2000–2015: Achievements and challenges.* Paris: Education for All Global Monitoring Report.

United Nations General Assembly. (2015). *Transforming our world: The 2030 agenda For sustainable development.* New York, NY: UN Publishing.

Watson, S. F. (2009). Barriers to inclusive education in Ireland: The case for pupils with a diagnosis of intellectual and/or pervasive developmental disabilities. *British Journal of Learning Disabilities, 37*(4), 277–284. doi:10.1111/j.1468-3156.2009.00583.x

# RESOURCES FOR INCLUSIVE EDUCATION IN AUSTRIA: AN INSIGHT INTO THE PERCEPTION OF TEACHERS

Marie Gitschthaler, Julia Kast, Rupert Corazza and Susanne Schwab

## ABSTRACT

*Even though the progress in creating inclusive learning environments varies across different countries, the implementation of inclusive education systems can clearly be considered a European shared policy goal. However, there is still a lack of both a clear definition of inclusive education and indicators on the provision of necessary resources in order to implement a high-quality inclusive school system. In the presented study, we aimed to shed light on how teachers who work at different schools in Austria perceive the resources provided to them in order to realize high-quality inclusive education. Furthermore, the study searched for factors, which influence teachers' subjective perception of resources, like years of work experience or the number of students in a classroom. To assess teachers' perception of resources, a revised version of the Perception of Resources Questionnaire (PRQ) developed by Goldan and Schwab (2018) was used focussing on three dimensions: human resources, material resources and spatial resources. The results generally indicate that teachers feel ambivalent or have a somewhat positive perception of available resources. In line with the Organization for Economic Cooperation and Development (OECD) principles of inclusive education 'each according to his needs', we argue that it is not possible to clarify what 'adequate resources' might be. The creation of an inclusive learning environment requires considerable effort, and the degree of pedagogical support*

Resourcing Inclusive Education
International Perspectives on Inclusive Education, Volume 15, 67–88
Copyright © 2021 by Emerald Publishing Limited.
All rights of reproduction in any form reserved
ISSN: 1479-3636/doi:10.1108/S1479-363620210000015007

*should be decisive for the allocation of resources. This can only be evaluated if*
*the main learning barriers for each student are identified.*

**Keywords**: Teachers' perception of resources; attitude towards inclusion;
index-based resource allocation; empirical study; perception of resources
questionnaire (PRQ); special educational needs (SEN)

# INTRODUCTION

Recently, inclusive education for all students has become an important topic in
political and scientific discourse within Europe. Although each European country
has its own national laws regulating their school systems, all of them are moving
to or at least profess to be moving towards inclusive education. Even though the
progress in creating inclusive learning environments varies across different
countries, the implementation of inclusive education systems can clearly be
considered a European 'shared policy goal' (see e.g. Schwab, 2020). However,
inclusion still remains a 'fuzzy concept' due to the fact that there is no universal
definition, neither in policy nor in research (Schwab, 2020). Furthermore, there is
a lack of indicators on the provision of necessary resources in order to implement
a high-quality inclusive school system – although evidence from international
research clearly indicates the importance of sufficient resources. For example,
Monsen, Ewing, and Kwoka (2014) show in their study that teachers who do not
feel sufficiently supported are less likely to have a positive attitude towards the
inclusion of students with special educational needs (SEN) and are less willing to
adapt the learning environment according to the students' needs. The authors
point out that there is an urgent need to provide all teachers with adequate
internal and external resources to realize high-quality inclusive education (see
also e.g. Aichele & Kroworsch, 2017; Goldan & Schwab, 2018; Vorapanya &
Dunlap, 2014). Furthermore, Forlin and Chambers (2011), who examined the
biggest worries of pre-service teachers, showed that participants were concerned
about insufficient skills, increased workload and not being able to give enough
attention to all students in integrative classrooms. However, most of all, they
were worried about inadequate resources and lack of support staff. Boyle,
Topping, and Jindal-Snape (2013) are more critical about the positive effect of
resources on teachers' attitudes towards inclusion. In their study, they show that
even those teachers who are positive about inclusion express concerns about the
practicalities of implementation and fear, a negative impact on their teaching.
The authors emphasize the importance of these findings as fundamental to the
philosophy of inclusion because no matter how many resources are invested,
inclusion will be difficult to realize when teachers have a negative attitude (see
also Loreman, 2014). As already mentioned, neither education economics nor
policy can currently answer the question of how to optimally equip schools with
resources. Even the ICF-CY (International Classification of Functioning,
Disability and Health for Children and Youth, WHO, 2007), which can currently
be considered as the international state of the art concept on how to create

inclusive learning environments does not provide information on the attribution of resources.

In line with the principles of inclusive education 'each according to his needs' (OECD 1999, p. 28), we argue that the degree of pedagogical support should be decisive for the allocation of resources. This can only be evaluated if the main learning barriers for each student are identified. As pointed out by Goldan and Schwab (2018), it is not about setting objective standards; moreover, it is necessary to consider the subjective view of the individuals concerned and if they perceive the provided resources as sufficient. In this chapter, we focus on how teachers perceive the resources provided to them in order to realize inclusive education.

In the first section, a broad overview of the Austrian education system is given, followed by significant recent developments in making Austria's school system more inclusive. Section 2 first presents a new, more precisely determined rate of students with SEN, which is based on administrative data. The section continues with a focus on resources for students who have special educational or other needs ('anderer Förderbedarf') and finishes with the situation of students, who do not speak the language of instruction. Section 3 provides insights into the subjective perspectives of Austrian school principals and teachers regarding resources provided to them gained from TALIS (Teaching and Learning International Survey). Section 4 presents the results of the empirical study on the perceptions of teachers regarding resources for facilitating inclusive education. The study aimed to investigate how teachers, who work at different schools in three federal states in Austria, perceive the resources that are provided in order to meet the needs of all students, with a special focus on students who do not have German as a first language. Furthermore, the study searched for factors, which influence teachers' subjective perception of resources, like years of work experience or the number of students in a classroom. To assess this perception of resources, a revised version of the Perception of Resources Questionnaire (PRQ) developed by Goldan and Schwab (2018) was used (PRQ, 2.0, see Goldan & Schwab, 2019). The PRQ 2.0 consists of 10 items and distinguishes between three dimensions: human resources (1), material resources (2) and spatial resources (3). For the present study, an additional item was added, which refers to the inclusion of students, whose native language is not German.

# SIGNIFICANT DEVELOPMENTS IN CREATING A SCHOOL SYSTEM, THAT IS MORE INCLUSIVE IN AUSTRIA

Many transitions and hierarchies between the different pathways that exist through schooling and beyond characterize the Austrian education system. A characteristic feature is that, unlike many other European countries, Austria has never implemented a comprehensive secondary school system and still sticks to its strongly segregated system, that tracks ten-year-old students, either into academic secondary schools ('Gymnasium' respectively 'allgemeinbildende höhere Schule') or middle schools ('Mittelschulen'). The school choice, parents have to make after four years of primary schooling, is a burden for everyone involved, pupils, parents and teachers alike. This systemic transition into lower-secondary school is based on strict educational laws and strongly influenced by socioeconomic status and migration background, as emphasised by research (e.g. Oberwimmer et al., 2016; OECD, 2017). The 'Gymnasium' offers an attractive opportunity for students from more privileged backgrounds to distinguish themselves from students from low socioeconomic backgrounds. Therefore, in general, Austria does not have a strong private school system.

Over the last two decades, the average proportion of students in private primary schools increased from 4% (school year 1996/97) to 6% (school year 2016/17). In metropolitan areas, this contributes slightly to the social and ethnical segregation between schools. In the city of Vienna, for example, 16.2% of students attended a private primary school in 2016/17 (Lassnigg, Mayrhofer, Baumegger, Vogtenhuber, et al., 2019, p. 78), which is more than double of that in rural areas. However, the 'Gymnasium' remains the main catalyst for social and ethnical segregation within the Austrian school system.

At upper-secondary level, there are four main parallel routes, which are hierarchically ordered and entitle entrance into different further educational and vocational programmes: academic secondary schools (upper level), full-time vocational education and training (VET) colleges, full-time intermediate VET schools and the apprenticeship system. Students at academic secondary schools and VET colleges attain an upper-secondary school-leaving certificate that entitles them to enter the tertiary education system. Hence, these certificates are hierarchically of a higher level compared to the certificates acquired from other school types.

In the school year 2018/19, a total of 1,135,143 pupils were enrolled at both public and private Austrian schools (Statistik Austria, 2019a). According to official data, 29,127 (~3%) of these students were assessed as having SEN (Statistik Austria, 2019b). School attendance for students with SEN is regulated in the Austrian law, and parents have a right to choose which school their child attends. However, this regulation is rather vaguely formulated, which is problematic for both schools and parents. A deeper analysis of the respective law shows the actual problems: The first option is a choice between a special school and a regular school with integration classes. However, this only applies if the respective schools can meet the needs of the child. If the school cannot provide adequate support, the school board is responsible for facilitating inclusion. If the school board cannot fulfil this task, the child has to attend a special school, which has neither consequence for schools nor for the school boards.

> School-age children with special educational needs (§ 8(1)) are entitled to attend compulsory school either in a special school or special class suitable for them or in a primary school, secondary school, pre-vocational school, lower level of an academic secondary school or one-year school for vocational education and training which meets their special educational needs, provided that such schools (classes) are available (...) (Compulsory education law (§ 8a. (1); effective date: 01/01/2019; authors' translation, original text see Appendix 1).

This analysis shows that parents and their children with SEN depend on bureaucratic decisions regarding access to regular schools.

Looking back, the first models for integrative school settings were successfully implemented in Austria in 1984 – as a result of high engagement of concerned parents. Until 1984, it was common practice to teach students with SEN separately in special schools (Feyerer, 2013).

However, aside from single models, it took almost 10 years until integrative schooling in primary and lower-secondary schools (grade 1–8) was legally anchored as a parents' right to choose, as far as the school boards were able to arrange it.

Firstly, an amendment to the Compulsory Schooling Act 1985 (see amendments to the Compulsory Schooling Act 1985: BGBl. Nr. 513/1993) in 1993 opened up the possibility for parents to send their children to integrative classes at primary schools (grades 1–4), as an additional offer for children eligible for special educational support. In 1996, a further amendment to the Compulsory Schooling Act 1985 (Amendments to the Compulsory Schooling Act 1985: BGBl. Nr. 768/1996) extended this option to middle schools and academic secondary schools (lower level). However, in academic secondary schools, this has always been a rather theoretical option. Parents often complain about the low chance of getting a suitable place for their child in academic secondary schools. This is especially true for students labeled with learning disabilities. For students with physical or sensory impairments, or with autism, the chance of getting a place in an academic secondary school is better. However, there is no official data on the number of these students.

In 2008, Austria ratified the United Nations Convention on the Rights of Persons with Disabilities (UNCRPD), which was passed by the UN General Assembly in 2006 and came into force in 2008. Austria, thus, committed itself at an international level to implement an inclusive education system at all levels, i.e. covering all school types. A particularly relevant national document in this regard is the National Action Plan on Disability 2012–2020 (Bundesministerium für Arbeit, Soziales, Gesundheit und Konsumentenschutz, 2012). It significantly contributed to a stronger public focus on the concept of inclusion and stipulated a structural change in the education system and the implementation of model initiatives for inclusive education by 2020. These targets have been further confirmed in the work programme of the Austrian Federal Government 2013–2018 (Bundeskanzleramt Österreich, 2013). The most significant impact, to be seen, is in the completely new system of teacher education and training, whereby all students must be prepared for teaching in inclusive settings.

In contradiction to the UNCRPD, the National Disability Action Plan 2012–2020 and the work programme of the Austrian Federal Government 2013–2018, the legal situation for students with SEN regarding their participation in further education and training has hardly changed since the expansion of integrative schooling to include lower secondary schools. Although a legal basis for integrative schooling for the last year of compulsory schooling (grade 9) was established in 2012, it is restricted to pre-vocational schools (one-year schools for vocational education and training) and academic secondary schools (lower level).

With regard to further education and training, students with SEN formally have the right to attend any upper-secondary school; however, this depends on the 'good will' of individual schools – a fact that has been criticized in a recent audit report on the implementation of an inclusive education system in Austria by the Court of Auditors (see Rechnungshof, 2019). Students with SEN are only able to continue their school career after compulsory schooling at VET colleges if the school is part of a pilot project that offers an adapted curriculum. Their exclusion from academic secondary schools (upper level) contradicts Austria's binding declaration to introduce an inclusive school system at all levels (Rechnungshof, 2019, p. 34). Regarding the parents' right to choose integrative schooling for their children at academic secondary schools, Corazza (2019) speaks of a 'dead law'. Furthermore, he points out that in the school year 2015/16, only nine integration classes were available at academic secondary schools (lower level), while middle schools offered around 340 integration classes.

Finally, the Court of Audit critically noted that an overall strategy to implement inclusive education at all education levels, as is required in the UNCRPD, is missing (Rechnungshof, 2019, p. 10). Without doubt, this state-ment would be confirmed by almost all of the stakeholders, who are involved in the field of special education.

While the UNCRPD refers to the inclusion of people with disabilities, the Agenda 2030 for Sustainable Development, which was adopted by the UN General Assembly on 25 September 2015, follows a more comprehensive understanding of inclusion, taking into account other diversity dimensions such as age, gender, migration background, ethnicity and social background. The 193 member states have committed themselves:

> ...to providing inclusive and equitable quality education at all levels – early childhood, primary, secondary, tertiary, technical and vocational training. All people, irrespective of sex, age, race or ethnicity, and persons with disabilities, migrants, indigenous peoples, children and youth, especially those in vulnerable situations, should have access to lifelong learning opportunities (…). (United Nations, 2015, p. 11).

In January 2016, Austria confirmed that it would make an appropriate effort to realizing this agenda and, thus, once again committed itself at an international level to implement inclusive education in all school types (see Bundeskanzleramt Österreich, 2017). However, an analysis of the Federal Finance Act 2019 (Bundesministerium für Finanzen, 2019), which sets out the key objectives for the implementation of impact-oriented governance measures for public institutions, shows that the goal of inclusive education is not anchored in the impact goals of the Federal Ministry of Education, Science and Research (Corazza, 2019).

## RESOURCES FOR THE IMPLEMENTATION OF INCLUSIVE EDUCATION

Since the introduction of the Board of Education Organization Act §5 (4) in Austria, in general, the following applies regarding the allocation of teacher posts:

The allocation of resources for teaching staff must be based, in any case, on the number of students, the educational offer, the socio-economic background, the students' need for support and assistance as well as the language used in their everyday life and regional needs. (Version from 31/08/2020; authors' translation, original text see Appendix 2).

It becomes obvious that several factors should be considered when allocating teacher posts at compulsory schooling (primary, lower-secondary, pre-vocational and special schools), especially the degree of support students need. However, a more detailed explanation of 'need for support' is required from the law. Currently, most of the federal states in Austria focus on students with SEN, although it is clear that students' needs cannot be restricted to the need for special education.

It is common practice that a certain number of teacher posts are provided for students who need special or other support, according to the guidelines for planning teacher posts by the Federal Government – more precisely by the Ministry of Finance in cooperation with the Ministry of Education on the basis of the Financial Equalisation Act §4 (FAG 2017; §4, version of 5.1.2020). The federal states are responsible for ensuring that these resources are adequately allocated. Hence, they have a certain flexibility for the autonomous and needs-based use of teacher posts. Therefore, it is incomprehensible that resources are allocated to schools in Austria without explicitly considering the composition of the student population according to socio-economic status, i.e. according to the 'scattergun principle' (Bacher, 2017, p. 29). Furthermore, it is also worth noting that the Federal Government has never evaluated the adequate allocation of these resources.

Nonetheless, this does not apply to the field of special education, where resources for the provision of special needs and inclusive education are not allocated uniformly to all school locations, but rather according to the demands schools submit to the Board of Education (Corazza, 2017, p. 37). This approach thus strengthens the implementation of index-based resource allocation in the field of special education. However, for the last 15 years, there has been an ongoing debate about the appropriate number of permanent teacher posts for the special education system, as will be outlined in the following two sections.

### *Numbers and Figures on Students with Special Educational Needs*

In Austria, the main official source for all statistical data is Statistik Austria. However, many necessary adaptations concerning the determination of data regarding students with SEN or other needs are missing. Consequently, official data on special education provide reliable information neither about the number of children with SEN nor about the need for resources to adequately educate these children. Hence, the official data, while not fundamentally wrong, are still under-determined. The main reason is that only students at compulsory schools (i.e. schools with no access restrictions = primary, middle, pre-vocational and special schools) are included in the total student population. Students at federal schools, i.e. schools with restricted access, (grades 1–9) are not taken into account. In the metropolitan area of Vienna, more than half of the students

*Table 1.* Number of Students with SEN and SEN Rate for the City of Vienna.

| School Type | Number of Students in Vienna (Grades 1–9) | Number of Students with SEN in Vienna (Grades 1–9) | SEN Rate for Vienna |
|---|---|---|---|
| Compulsory schools | 109,980 | | |
| Federal schools | 55,678 | | |
| Total population of students | 165,658 | | |
| | | 6,252 | |
| | | | 3.8% |

*Source:* Authors' own calculation.

attend an academic secondary school (= federal school). Hence, any determination that does not consider students at federal schools is strongly distorted. Table 1 shows the SEN rates published by the Board of Education for Vienna.

Except the number of students at federal schools, all figures provided in the table are based on administrative data.

Official data (Statistik Austria, 2019b) show that half of these students attend integrative classes at primary, middle and pre-vocational schools. The remaining students are educated segregatively at special schools according to the regulations of the respective federal states. This means that not all special schools are uniformly organized. Some special schools provide on-site regular classes, which can also be attended by students without SEN. Other special schools work closely with regular schools. It is worth noting that the mere fact that a child with SEN attends a regular school does not give reliable information about the degree of his or her inclusion. Usually, there are five to six students with SEN in an integration class together with about 17 'typical' students. Still, it is often common practice that these students receive special treatment in an extra room, obvious to all other students, and are stigmatized as so called 'integration children'. There is empirical evidence (e.g. Koster, Pijl, Nakken, & Van Houten, 2010; Schwab, 2018a) that students with SEN in integrative school settings feel less socially included and have fewer stable friendships and fewer interactions with their classmates. Furthermore, they are less often chosen by peers for joint activities compared to their peers without SEN. In Austria, these results are underpinned by several studies (Gebhardt, 2013; Schwab, 2014, 2015; Venetz, Zurbriggen, & Schwab, 2019). These results show that integration classes can be discriminating if attitudes and guidance of teachers and other personnel are not adequate. Therefore, Kozleski (2015) refers to the importance of considering the whole education system and its interdependences. These are relevant pedagogical aspects that cannot be reflected in official statistics on the degree of inclusion of students with SEN.

### Resources for Students with Special Educational Needs

At first glance, the question whether students with SEN require additional resources is almost reflexively only associated with an increase in permanent teacher posts. A closer examination shows that the situation is much more complex.

In Austria, there is the controversially discussed situation that resources provided by the Federal Government in the form of approved teacher posts are determined independently of the number of children actually entitled to special educational support. More specifically, this means that for each federal province, a uniform rate of 2.7% of the total number of students (grades 1–9) is assumed to be students with SEN.

The implementation of integrative schooling of children with SEN in elementary schools in addition to special schools in 1993 resulted in a parallel system. In order to obtain the approval of the Ministry of Finance for the financing of this system, the Ministry of Education ensured that the number of children with SEN would not increase above 2.7% nationwide, in order to contain the forecasted higher costs (*Source:* provisional list of teacher posts 1995 from 31.8.1995, signed by Dr Gullner, commissioned by the Ministry of Education). The assumption, also made by particularly strong proponents of inclusion, that the parallel system is significantly more cost-intensive is fundamentally wrong. Both settings require approximately the same resources in the form of teaching hours for educating students with SEN. However, calculations using a rigid childcare ratio are not appropriate because, in principle, the degree of pedagogical support is decisive for the allocation of resources. This leads to an imbalance between special schools and integration classes at regular schools because the severity of the impairment of a child determines the extent of resources required and the greater the probability that he or she will be educated in a special school.

The cap of 2.7% was first applied to approve teacher posts for the school year 1995/1996. In the years before (1985–1994), each federal state was granted a contingent of teacher posts according to demand. Even though the 2.7% cap became effective for all federal states in the same year, metropolitan areas were at least considered as aggravating factors in the allocation of teacher posts until 2001. Finally, from the 2001/2002 school year onwards, the teacher–student ratio was also standardised for all federal states and set from originally 1:2.7 at 1:3.2 in a stepwise implementation until 2004/2005 (important note: a coincidence that the former teacher–student ratio is equivalent to the cap of 2.7%). This means that one teacher is responsible for 3.2 children with SEN. Three federal states, most of all Vienna, followed by Carinthia and Vorarlberg, lost teacher posts, while the remaining six states gained additional posts.

The limitation of the share of students with SEN to 2.7% and the ratio of teachers to students set at 1:3.2 have led to an ongoing debate among the educational directors in the Federal Boards of Education as to whether there is an undersupply of teacher posts or not. However, no objective statement can be made with certainty in this matter. Nevertheless, it can be observed that the number of children with diagnoses has been increasing slowly, but steadily for years. Also, the demand for individualised teaching and 'leaving no child behind' is always associated with a higher number of lessons by teachers. Furthermore, inclusion can only be realized by providing human resources, especially when care and support staff are not available.

Some federal states of Austria, such as Vienna, have clearly documented their requirements for additional teacher posts and showed that the cap on the arbitrary value of 2.7% does not meet the real demand. The increased need for resources has been reported to the Federal Government since the school year 2004/2005 but has been consistently rejected. To understand why this criticism by the federal states has not led to a change in the practice during fiscal equalization negotiations between the Federal Government and the federal states would require further investigation and cannot be answered here. Moreover, even though the federal states feel strongly disadvantaged by this regulation, they have regularly approved the fiscal equalization law.

In addition to the lack of teacher posts, the lack of clear legal provisions on the responsibility for funding of care and support staff in schools for children with SEN is an aggravating factor. With reference to the 15th School Organisation Act and the Compulsory School Maintenance Basic Law (§10), the Federal Government takes the legal view that care and support personnel must be financed by the municipalities. However, this regulation does not refer to care and support personnel for children with special needs (Rechnungshof, 2019, p. 108). Due to this ambiguous formulation, the municipalities see a clear responsibility of the Federal Government in this regard. The ambiguities relate to the group of recipients, the type of benefit, the amount of cost coverage and the qualifications of the staff. The unclear legal situation has resulted in the fact that the financing of care and support personnel is currently regulated differently in all nine federal states (Rechnungshof, 2019, p. 109), a fact that makes sensible comparisons of resources rather impossible within the Austrian education system.

## Resources for Students Who Need 'Other Support'

As already mentioned, resources to ensure the inclusion of students are not provided solely for students with a SEN diagnosis. Children and youths with functional impairments, who are able to achieve learning targets through provision of adequate support and compensatory measures because of disabilities or disadvantages ('Nachteilsausgleich'), should not receive a SEN diagnosis. However, this occurs in practice. According to the Board of Education Organization Act § 19 (2) (see 'Bundesgesetz über die Einrichtung von Bildungsdirektionen in den Ländern', 2020), 'other support' ('sonstiger Förderbedarf') is provided for these students and has to be covered by the schools, in line with the budget for inclusive pedagogical measures. Currently, the provision of other support is primarily in the realm of learning difficulties; this is done by providing the possibility to achieve differentiated educational targets within the regular curriculum ('lernzieldifferenter Unterricht'). Other fields of application include autism spectrum disorder and socio-emotional impairments; the latter is especially relevant in Vienna. The Board of Education for Vienna has decided to stop diagnosing students with severe social and emotional behavioural problems in as SEN students. These students are now deemed as needing 'other support' by specially trained teacher staff ('Beratungslehrer') and attend classes with a smaller number of students.

The numerous differing regulations across the federal states have been symptomatic of the Austrian education system since the beginning of integrative actions. Currently, there are no data available on the number of students receiving 'other support', and this regulation is rarely implemented. However, it serves as a step towards overcoming the 'labelling resource dilemma' in Austria in the future.

*Resources to Support Students, Who Do not Have German as a First Language*

Within the Austrian school system 'The language of instruction is German' (Schulunterrichtsgesetz § 16 (1)). This regulation makes clear that the use of German language is the key to a successful educational career and that Austria adheres to the traditional model of monolingual school instruction, despite social multilingualism. In this context, the recently introduced German language support classes and courses to support students with insufficient skills in the German language (Bundesministerium für Bildung, Wissenschaft und Forschung, 2019) are politically charged. These students are taught in separate classrooms for up to 20 hours a week in order to learn the German language as quickly as possible, as this is a key prerequisite for participation in education. All students with a migrant background or who have deficits in their German language skills are assessed through a standardised test ('MIKA-D Test') when they enrol at school. Based on this assessment of their German language skills, one of the following three scenarios is possible:

- Students with sufficient language skills (= 'ordentlicher SchülerIn') attend regular classes.
- Students with elementary language skills (= 'außerordentlicher SchülerIn') attend regular classes and receive additional language tuition and support for six hours a week in a pull-out course.
- Students with beginner-level language skills (= 'außerordentlicher SchülerIn') attend German language support classes for 15 hours a week in primary school or 20 hours in middle schools, respectively.

The language support measures are valid for one semester and can be extended, if necessary, for further three semesters. At the end of each semester, the student has to be tested again (Bundesministerium für Bildung, Wissenschaft und Forschung, 2019). The reliability, objectivity and validity of the 'MIKA-D Test' quickly came under criticism. Before the introduction of this new regulation, it was common practice to support students with difficulties in German language on an individual basis for 12 hours a week. Due to the recent implementation, there are currently insufficient data on the effects of these measures. First data, however, show that only 17.5% of students who attended a German language tuition and support class in the school year 2018/2019 managed the transition into regular school classes by the end of the school year (Bundesministerium für Bildung, Wissenschaft und Forschung, 2019, p. 7).

The equation of language and German, which becomes clear in the act and the associated exclusion of other first languages, is strongly criticized by researchers from various disciplines such as education, migration and linguistics (e.g. Döll, 2019; Müller & Schweiger, 2018), as well as key actors in the field of education. Furthermore, teaching multilingual students in separate educational settings bears a high risk of further putting students with a migrant background at a disadvantage, due to strong segregation and homogenization within German language support classes.

## SUBJECTIVE PERCEPTIONS OF RESOURCES

School principals' and teachers' perceptions of the resources available to them have been evaluated by TALIS (see Schmich & Itzlinger-Bruneforth, 2019), which is an international comparative OECD study on the conditions of teaching and learning in lower-secondary schools. The results on educational impairments due to a lack of both personnel and material resources show that Austria, compared to the other participating European Union (EU) countries, is somewhere in the middle. While educational impairments due to a lack of qualified teachers are considered as a minor problem in Austria, a shortage of support personnel, however, is seen as the major barrier for the provision of high-quality education by 47% of participating schools in the survey (EU-average: 30%) (Wallner-Paschon, Suchań, & Oberwimmer, 2019, p. 30). On average, the ratio of teachers to support staff is at 19:1, much higher in Austria compared to the EU-average (8:1). Regarding administrative support, the situation is similar: A single staff member administratively supports 15 teachers (EU-average: 1:7). The second most frequently perceived barrier (26% of schools) is a lack of adequate classrooms (EU-average: 24%). A comparison between school types shows that a lack of classrooms is perceived at a significantly higher level by principals at academic secondary schools (~42%), compared to middle schools (~20%) (Wallner-Paschon et al., 2019, p. 30). Despite below the EU-average perception of the shortage of qualified teachers supporting students with SEN, low SES or who are multilingual, middle schools report more problems offering adequate support for disadvantaged students, compared to academic secondary schools (Wallner-Paschon et al., 2019, p. 30).

## EMPIRICAL STUDY ON HOW TEACHERS
## PERCEIVE RESOURCES

The results presented in this chapter are the outcome of the research project 'In-service teachers', pre-service teachers' and parents' attitudes towards the development of pupils with another first language than German in German language support classes and courses', which was carried out in spring/summer

2019 in Vienna (Austria's capital city) and two federal states of Austria (Lower Austria and Burgenland). This contribution focuses on the sample of teachers, who work at different schools in Vienna, Lower Austria and Burgenland (i.e. 'in-service' teachers). Schools and teachers were selected randomly and asked for their participation. Data were collected using a paper-pencil version of the questionnaire, which was delivered to schools and re-collected personally (special thanks to Amina Alagic, Julia Daneczek, Nina Leyer and Christina Popp who collected and entered the data).

## RESEARCH QUESTIONS

The study aimed to investigate how teachers, who work at different schools within the Austrian education system, perceive the resources for realizing inclusion in general and in particular for students, who do not have German as a first language. It further searches for factors which influence teachers' subjective perception of resources. The study was particularly driven by the following research questions:

(1) Do teachers have rather neutral, positive or negative perceptions of resources that are provided to their schools?
(2) Do teachers perceive the provided resources for the inclusion of students, who do not have German as a first language as rather neutral, positive or negative?
(3) Which factors (years of work experience, number of students in class, number of school grades in class (dummy-coded: one or more levels) and number of students in class, who do not have German as first language) influence teachers' general perception of resources?

### Sample

The sample consisted of 221 teachers (188 female and 33 male) from three federal states in Austria: 57.7% from Vienna, 30.5% from Lower Austria and 11.8% from Burgenland. The age of the teachers varied from 24 to 63 years (M = 42.43, SD = 11.9), and the years of work experience varied from 2 months to 43 years. Furthermore, 37.6% of the participants worked in primary schools, 18.6% in middle schools, 19% in academic secondary schools, 15.4% in VET collages, 4.1% in pre-vocational schools and 3.2% in special schools and 2.1% in other types of schools.

Furthermore, 72.4% taught students of the same school grade in their class, while 27.6% taught students of different school grades in one classroom. In addition, 92.4% of the participants taught in regular classes, 3.9% in German language support courses and 1.5% in German and support classes.

*Measures*

To assess the perception of resources of the teachers in this study, a revised version of the PRQ (Goldan & Schwab, 2018) was used (PRQ, 2.0, see Goldan & Schwab, 2019). The PRQ 2.0 consists of 10 items and distinguishes between three dimensions: (1) human resources ('In class, all students get the help they need') (2) material resources ('We have all the materials we need for our lessons') and (3) spatial resources ('In our classrooms, all students have enough space to learn'). The PRQ 2.0 focuses on the teachers' general perception of resources provided in their school to realize inclusive education. For the present study, we added an additional item, which refers especially to the inclusion of students, who do not have German as a first language: 'In my school there are enough classrooms to support students, who do not have German as a first language (German language support classes/courses)'. All 11 items are rated on a four-point Likert scale ranging from not at all true (1) to certainly true (4).

Factor analysis with varimax rotation of the 10 items of the PRQ 2.0 showed two factors with eigenvalues greater than one (according to the Kaiser–Guttman criterion: factor I: Eigenvalue = 2.58, explained variance = 32.3%, factor II: Eigenvalue = 2.28, explained variance = 28.5%). The first factor includes items 1–4 ('personnel resources'), and the second factor includes items 5–8 ('material and spatial resources'). Goldan and Schwab's questionnaire (2019) showed a high internal consistency (Cronbach's alpha = 0.84). The reliability of the 10 items for the present sample was also high (Cronbach's alpha = 0.856).

To evaluate the perception of resources of the teachers, the sum score of the items was computed, divided by the number of items. Since a 4-point Likert scale was used, the theoretical mean of the scale is 2.5. According to Schwab (2018b), a rule of thumb was used: subjective perceptions that were 2.0 or lower were defined as negative and values from 3.0 upwards were defined as positively perceived resources.

*Results*

Calculations were done separately for the 10 items of the original PRQ 2.0 (*General perception of resources*) and the additional item which refers to the inclusion of students, who do not have German as a first language (*Perception of resources regarding students, who do not have German as a first language*).

*Perception of Resources*

*General Perception of Resources.* In general, results showed that teachers have a rather neutral to somewhat positive perception of resources (M = 2.9, SD = 0.53). Furthermore, this was found to be true for female teachers (M = 2.9, SD = 0.55) compared to male teachers (M = 3, SD = 0.44).

Further, descriptive statistics showed that teachers from middle schools have a more positive perception of resources. Whereas, teachers who worked in the other types of schools had a more neutral perception of the provision of resources (see Table 2).

***Table 2.*** Mean Scores of the General Perception of Resources.

| School Type | M | SD |
|---|---|---|
| Elementary school | 2.9 | 0.49 |
| Middle school | 3.15 | 0.53 |
| Academic secondary school | 2.9 | 0.44 |
| VET colleges | 2.8 | 0.6 |

***Table 3.*** Mean Scores of the Preception of Resources in Connection with Students, Who Do not Have German as First Language.

| School Type | M | SD |
|---|---|---|
| Elementary school | 2.4 | 0.97 |
| Middle school | 2.85 | 1.00 |
| Academic secondary school | 2.4 | 0.76 |
| VET colleges | 1.89 | 0.92 |

*Perception of Resources Regarding Students, Who Do not Have German as a First Language.* Teachers tend to perceive the resources to teach students, who do not have German as a first language neutrally (M = 2.4, SD = 0.98). Regarding differences between the genders, the results indicate that both female and male teachers perceive the resources neutrally (female: M = 2.4, SD = 0.99; male: M = 2.7, SD = 0.84).

Looking at the different school types, descriptive statistics showed that teachers who work in VET colleges have a rather negative perception of their resources, while teachers who work in other school types tend to perceive the resources more neutrally (see Table 3).

*Factors That Influence Teachers' Perception of Resources*
*Factors within the General Perception of Resources.* To examine which variables influence teachers' perception of resources, a stepwise multiple linear regression was computed. The following predictors were included: years of work experience, number of students in class, number of school grades in class (dummy-coded: one or more levels) and number of students in class, who do not have German as a first language. The results of the stepwise regressions indicated the number of students, who do not have German as a first language as first predictor ($\beta = -0.332$, $p < 0.001$) and the number of school grades within one classroom as second predictor ($\beta = 0.175$, $p < 0.001$). 12.8% of the variance of the teachers' subjective perception of resources can be explained by these two variables ($F_2 = 11.388$, $p < 0.001$). The years of work experience ($\beta = 0.05$ n.s.) as well as the number of students in class ($\beta = 0.096$ und n.s.) did not significantly influence the teachers' perception of resources.

# SUMMARY AND DISCUSSION

Martha Nussbaum postulates that no individual person should have to rely on case-specific decisions of institutions or public spaces (Nussbaum, 2007, p. 167). Austria committed itself on both national and international levels to facilitate inclusive education at all school levels. However, the widely shared assumption that parents have a right to choose which school their child attends is not true in those federal states that are not part of the inclusive model regions in Austria. Parents and their children with SEN depend upon bureaucratic decisions regarding access to regular schools. A child can only attend a specific school of choice, if the school or the school board is able to create a learning environment that meets the needs of that child. Furthermore, the law is restricted to compulsory schooling. With regard to further education at upper-secondary level, students with SEN can only attend VET colleges *if* a pilot project with an adapted curriculum is offered. Students with SEN are virtually excluded from attending academic secondary schools (upper level). These regulations contradict Austria's binding declaration to implement an inclusive education system at all levels, i.e. covering all school types, which has been strongly criticized in a recent report by the Austrian Court of Audit. Furthermore, the Court of Audit critically noted that an overall strategy to implement inclusive education at all educational levels, as is required in the UNCRPD, is still lacking. Due to the federal system in Austria, numerous differing regulations currently exist across the federal states.

The creation of an inclusive learning environment requires considerable effort. From an economic point of view, it is practically impossible to clarify what 'adequate resources' might be. At least it can be concluded, as far as Austria is concerned, that the available figures and data on students with special or other education needs are strongly biased and inconclusive. This has been exemplified by the fact that there is a cap of 2.7% for students who are eligible for special educational support and a rigid childcare ratio set at 1:3.2. Neither of these regulations are appropriate in objectively determining the necessary resources. Regarding the subjective perspective of teachers and head teachers, the OECD study TALIS provides evidence that in Austria a shortage of support personnel is perceived as a major barrier to the provision of high-quality education for all students. In general, one may ask critically if an increase in the number of support staff is the best solution in order to create more inclusive learning environments. The answer to this question is ambiguous. If, as a consequence, teachers do not feel responsible or care about inclusion and depend on special personnel, then this cannot be considered to be the best solution. Furthermore, being supported by special staff can lead to a child being isolated from classmates, as has been seen in integration classes. The ideal scenario would be that it should not make any difference to teachers whether a student has impairments or not. This would require teachers to perceive themselves as 'inclusive education coordinators' and 'agents of change' instead of simply using unsuitable approaches.

However, even if all students needing special or other support received a specific amount of resources, this would still not be adequate, as the group of students with SEN or other needs is very heterogeneous. The degree of pedagogical support should be the deciding factor for the allocation of resources, and this can only be evaluated if the main learning barriers for each student are identified (e.g. investigating the students' personal environment, the school environment, the students' strengths and weaknesses, the teachers' strength and weaknesses). This process would be a prerequisite to estimating required resources, but even within this scenario constant monitoring of the development of the student's progress would be necessary as the situation may change over time.

The results of the study presented in this contribution generally indicate that teachers feel ambivalent or have a somewhat positive perception of available resources. Interestingly, teachers working at different school types (e.g. middle schools, academic secondary schools) feel relatively similar about the levels of resources. The lack of significant differences between the groups is interesting given the high academic heterogeneity between students at the respective school types.

In comparison, the resources available to teach students, who do not have German as a first language, are perceived more negatively, compared to teachers' general perception of resources at school. Those who work at VET colleges, in particular, perceive a lack of resources. This result can be seen in the lower number of resources made available to VET colleges compared to those in compulsory schools. A further possible explanation can be seen in the differing institutional self-image of this school type, compared to compulsory schools. VET colleges consider themselves as 'elite institutions' that prepare students for entry into the tertiary education system. Hence, mastery of the German language may be considered as a prerequisite for attending schools of this type.

Furthermore, results indicate that the higher the number of students, who do not have German as a first language, the stronger the feeling is that resources are lacking. Therefore, the number of students, who do not have German as a first language, strongly influences how teachers perceive available resources. It has to be considered that the majority of teachers in the sample teach at schools in the city of Vienna, which has the highest number of students, who do not have German as a first language.

Interestingly, the overall number of students in class as well as the number of years of work experience are not linked with teachers' perception of resources. The latter might be explained by the fact that more experienced teachers are not able to utilise resources efficiently. On the other hand, schools do not give teachers the opportunity to use resources flexibly – so personal characteristics or variables of teachers do not have any impact on their perceptions of resources.

The findings show that the allocation of human resources and the method of distribution of children across different types of schools are important when evaluating the inclusive movement in Austrian education. Without doubt, the perception of the transformation progress is being critically and constantly observed by teachers and parents. The fear of hidden reduction of resources, although law guarantees stability, makes all those involved highly sensitive towards all change processes.

A limitation of recent research, which also applies to this study, is that teachers' subjective perception of resources is not linked with an objective perception of the available resources, such as budget or personnel. This gap needs to be addressed in further studies as it has to be ensured that resources are allocated according to real demands. This requires not only a specific amount of money but also the efficient and flexible use of resources (see e.g. Schwab, 2020).

The question of a whole concept of inclusion in the Austrian education system is very difficult to answer. Government programs do not contain clear targets. As a result, during an extensive education reform in 2017, the responsible persons for education in the ministries created a new diversity management system, which covers a range of new aspects and indicates in which direction the education system should develop:

- Independent diversity managers have the competence to assess students who might have special needs and allocate resources in cooperation with school boards. Furthermore, they are the central contact persons for schools with regard to requests concerning learning support.
- The issue of inclusive education has been implemented in teacher education and training; all pre-service teachers now get basic instruction in teaching students with impairments.
- Inclusive education is now included in the curricula for all types of schools.

An internal report from the Ministry of Education 'Dimensions of Diversity' ('Dimensionen von Diversität'; Bundesministerium für Bildung, Wissenschaft und Forschung 2019c) summarized the idea behind the Austrian method of implementing an inclusive education system and formulated the following target in the foreword:

> School has the fundamental task of enabling all children and young people to develop optimally (…) regardless of social background, gender, talent, migration background, first language or even a disability or impairment.

Based on this target, it is guaranteed by law that human resources must not be reduced in future and that key actors in the field of education have to respect the individual needs, which is not restricted to students with impairments, but covers all students, who need support. Recalling the recent report of the Austrian Court of Auditors on the implementation of inclusive education in Austria, we conclude that there is still 'a long way to go'.

# REFERENCES

Aichele, V., & Kroworsch, S. (2017). *Inklusive Bildung ist ein Menschenrecht*. Berlin: Deutsches Institut für Menschenrechte.

Bacher, J. (2017). Chancenausgleich durch sozialindex-basierte Mittelvergabe. In E. Feyerer, W. Prammer, & R. Wimberger (Eds.), *Inklusion Dokumentation. Flexible und bedarfsgerechte Ressourcenzuteilung für inklusive Schulen* (pp. 27–33). Linz: BZIB.

Boyle, Ch, Topping, K., & Jindal-Snape, D. (2013). Teachers' attitudes towards inclusion in high schools. *Teachers and Teaching: Theory and Practice, 19*(5), 527–542.

Bundesgesetz über die Einrichtung von Bildungsdirektionen in den Ländern (Bildungsdirektionen-Einrichtungsgesetz – BD-EG). (2020). Retreived from https://www.ris.bka.gv.at/Geltende Fassung.wxe?Abfrage=Bundesnormen&Gesetzesnummer=20009982&FassungVom=2020-08-31

Bundeskanzleramt Österreich. (2013). Arbeitsprogramm der österreichischen Bundesregierung 2013 – 2018. Retreieved from https://www.justiz.gv.at/file/2c94848642ec5e0d0142fac7f7b9019a.de.0/regprogramm.pdf

Bundeskanzleramt Österreich. (2017). Beiträge der Bundesministerien zur Umsetzung der Agenda 2030 für nachhaltige Entwicklung durch Österreich. Retreieved from https://www.bundeskanzleramt.gv.at/themen/nachhaltige-entwicklung-agenda-2030

Bundesministerium für Arbeit, Soziales, Gesundheit und Konsumentenschutz. (2012). Nationaler Aktionsplan Behinderung 2012–2020. Strategie der österreichischen Bundesregierung zur Umsetzung der UN-Behindertenrechtskonvention: Inklusion als Menschenrecht und Auftrag. Retreieved from https://broschuerenservice.sozialministerium.at/Home/Download?publicationId=165

Bundesministerium für Bildung, Wissenschaft und Forschung. (2019a). Deutschförderklassen und Deutschförderkurse Leitfaden für Schulleiterinnen und Schulleiter. Retreieved from https://www.bmbwf.gv.at/Themen/schule/schulpraxis/ba/sprabi/dfk.html

Bundesministerium für Bildung, Wissenschaft und Forschung. (2019b). Schriftliche parlamentarische anfrage nr. 3087/J-NR/2019 betreffend sprachfortschritte in den deutschförderklassen.

Bundesministerium für Bildung, Wissenschaft und Forschung. (2019c). "Dimensionen von Diversität". Internal document.

Bundesministerium für Finanzen. (2019). Bundesgesetz über die Bewilligung des Bundesvoranschlages für das Jahr 2019. (Bundesfinanzgesetz 2019). Retreieved from https://service.bmf.gv.at/BUDGET/Budgets/2018_2019/bfg2019/Bundesfinanzgesetz_2019.pdf

Corazza, R. (2017). Indexbasierte ressourcenzuteilung in der Wiener inklusionspädagogik. In E. Feyerer, W. Prammer, & R. Wimberger (Eds.), *Inklusion Dokumentation. Flexible und bedarfsgerechte Ressourcenzuteilung für inklusive Schulen* (pp. 34–42). Linz: BZIB.

Corazza, R. (2019). Gerecht, fair, tolerant, offen und sozial inklusive. *Schulheft, 2*, 22–44.

Döll, M. (2019). Perspektive Migrationsgesellschaft. Sprachassimilativer Habitus in Bildungsforschung, Bildungspolitik und Bildungspraxis. *ÖDaF-Mitteilungen Fachzeitschrift für Deutsch als Fremd- und Zweitsprache, 35*(1–2), 191–206.

Feyerer, E. (2013). *Inklusive Regionen in Österreich. Bildungspolitische Rahmenbedingungen zur Umsetzung der UN-Konvention.* Working Paper. Retreieved from http://bidok.uibk.ac.at/library/feyerer-regionen.html

Forlin, Ch., & Chambers, D. (2011). Teacher preparation for inclusive education: Increasing knowledge but raising concerns. *Asia-Pacific Journal of Teacher Education, 39*(1), 17–32.

Gebhardt, M. (2013). *Integration und schulische Leistungen in Grazer Sekundarstufenklassen. Eine empirische Pilotstudie.* Berlin: Lit Verlag.

Goldan, J., & Schwab, S. (2018). Measuring students' and teachers' perceptions of resources in inclusive education – validation of a newly developed instrument. *International Journal of Inclusive Education, 14*(1), 1–14.

Goldan, J., & Schwab, S. (2019). PRQ 2.0 - perception of resources questionnaire. doi:10.13140/RG.2.2.35304.11522.

Koster, M., Pijl, S. J., Nakken, H., & Van Houten, E. J. (2010). Social participation of students with special needs in regular primary education in The Netherlands. *International Journal of Disability, Development and Education, 57*, 59–75.

Kozleski, E. (2015). Inklusive Pädagogik: Lehrer/innenbildung durch die Brille der Bildungsgerechtigkeit. In G. Biewer (Ed.), *Inklusive pädagogik in der Sekundarstufe* (pp. 149–163). Stuttgart: Kohlhammer Verlag.

Lassnigg, L., Mayrhofer, L., Baumegger, D., Vogtenhuber, St., Weber, Ch., Aspetsberger, R., … Oberwimmer, K. (2019). B: Input – personelle und finanzielle Ressourcen. B3.6 Privatschulen in der Primar- und Sekundarstufe I. In K. Oberwimmer, St. Vogtenhuber, L. Lassnigg, & C. Schreiner (Eds.), *Nationaler bildungsbericht Österreich 2018. Band 1, Das Schulsystem im Spiegel von Daten und Indikatoren* (pp. 78–79). Graz: Leykam.

Loreman, T. (2014). Measuring inclusive education outcomes in Alberta, Canada. *International Journal of Inclusive Education, 18*(5), 459–483.

Monsen, J. J., Ewing, D. L., & Kwoka, M. (2014). Teachers' attitudes towards inclusion, perceived adequacy of support and classroom learning environment. *Learning Environments Research*, *17*, 113–126.

Müller, B., & Schweiger, H. (2018). Stellungnahme von Forschenden und Lehrenden des Bereichs Deutsch als Zweitsprache der Universitäten Graz, Innsbruck, Salzburg und Wien zum Bildungsprogramm 2017 bis 2022 der österreichischen Bundesregierung. Retreieved from https://www.univie.ac.at/germanistik/wp-content/uploads/2018/02/-daz-stellungnahme-bildungsprogramm-20180206.pdf

Nussbaum, M. (2007). *Frontiers of justice*. Cambridge, MA: Harvard University Press.

Oberwimmer, K., Bruneforth, M., Siegle, T., Vogtenhuber, St., Lassnigg, L., Schmich, J., . . . Trenkwelder, K. (2016). Indikatoren D: Output – ergebnisse des Schulsystems: Früher Bildungsabbruch. In M. Bruneforth, L. Lassnig, S. Vogtenhuber, C. Schreiner, & S. Breit (Eds.), *Nationaler Bildungsbericht Österreich 2015, Band 1. Das Schulsystem im Spiegel von Daten und Indikatoren* (pp. 134–139). Graz: Leykam.

OECD. (1999). *Inclusive education at work: Including students with disabilities in mainstream schools*. Paris: OECD Publishing.

OECD. (2017). *Education at a glance 2017: OECD indicators*. Paris: OECD Publishing.

Rechnungshof. (2019). Bericht des Rechnungshofes: Inklusiver Unterricht: Was leistet Österreichs Schulsystem? Retreieved from https://www.parlament.gv.at/PAKT/VHG/XXVI/III/III_00242/imfname_736329.pdf

Schmich, J., & Itzlinger-Bruneforth, U. (2019). *TALIS 2018 (Band 1). Rahmenbedingungen des schulischen Lehrens und Lernens aus Sicht von Lehrkräften und Schulleitungen im internationalen Vergleich. Bundesinstitut für Bildungsforschung, Innovation & Entwicklung (Bife)*. Graz: Leykam. doi:10.17888/talis2018-1.

Schwab, S. (2014). *Schulische Integration, soziale Partizipation und emotionales Wohlbefinden in der Schule - ergebnisse einer empirischen Längsschnittstudie*. Wien: Lit. Verlag.

Schwab, S. (2015). Social dimensions of inclusion in education of 4th and 7th grade pupils in inclusive and regular classes: Outcomes from Austria. *Research in Developmental Disabilities*, *43–44*, 72–79.

Schwab, S. (2018a). Peer-relations of students with special educational needs in inclusive education. In S. Polenghi, M. Fiorucci, & L. Agostinetto (Eds.), *Diritti cittadinanza inclusione* (pp. 15–24). Rovato: Pensa MultiMedia.

Schwab, S. (2018b). *Attitudes towards inclusive schooling. A study on students', teachers' and parents' attitudes*. Münster: Waxmann Verlag.

Schwab, S. (2020). *Inclusive and special education in Europe. Oxford research encyclopedia of education*. Oxford: Oxford University Press. doi:10.1093/acrefore/9780190264093.013.1230

Statistik Austria. (2019a). Schülerinnen und Schüler an öffentlichen und privaten Schulen 1923/24 bis 2018/19. Retreieved from https://www.statistik.at/wcm/idc/idcplg?IdcService=GET_PDF_FILE&RevisionSelectionMethod=LatestReleased&dDocName=020951

Statistik Austria. (2019b). Schülerinnen und Schüler mit sonderpädagogischem Förderbedarf 2018/19. Retreieved from https://www.statistik.at/web_de/statistiken/menschen_und_gesellschaft/bildung/schulen/schulbesuch/029658.html

United Nations. (2015). Transforming our world. The 2030 agenda for sustainable development. Retreieved from https://sustainabledevelopment.un.org/content/documents/21252030%20Agenda%20for%20Sustainable%20Development%20web.pdf

Venetz, M., Zurbriggen, C. L. A., & Schwab, S. (2019). What do teachers think about their students' inclusion? Consistency of students' self-reports and teacher ratings. *Frontiers in Psychology*, *10*, Article 1637. doi:10.3389/fpsyg.2019.01637

Vorapanya, S., & Dunlap, D. (2014). Inclusive education in Thailand: Practices and challenges. *International Journal of Inclusive Education*, *18*(10), 1014–1028.

Wallner-Paschon, Ch., Suchań, B., & Oberwimmer, K. (2019). Profil der Lehrkräfte und Schulen der Sekundarstufe. In J. Schmich, & U. Itzlinger-Bruneforth (Eds.), *TALIS 2018 (Band 1). Rahmenbedingungen des schulischen Lehrens und Lernens aus Sicht von Lehrkräften und Schulleitungen im internationalen Vergleich* (pp. 17–38). Graz: Leykam.

World Health Organization. (2007). *International classification of functioning, disability, and Health: Children & youth version: ICF-CY*. Geneva: World Health Organization.

# APPENDICES

## APPENDIX 1

**Schulpflichtgesetz § 8a (1).**
"Schulpflichtige Kinder mit sonderpädagogischem Förderbedarf (§ 8 Abs. 1) sind berechtigt, die allgemeine Schulpflicht entweder in einer für sie geeigneten Sonderschule oder Sonderschulklasse oder in einer den sonderpädagogischen Förderbedarf erfüllenden Volksschule, Mittelschule, Polytechnischen Schule, Unterstufe einer allgemein bildenden höheren Schule oder einjährigen Fachschule für wirtschaftliche Berufe zu erfüllen, soweit solche Schulen (Klassen) vorhanden sind und der Schulweg den Kindern zumutbar oder der Schulbesuch auf Grund der mit Zustimmung der Eltern oder sonstigen Erziehungsberechtigten des Kindes erfolgten Unterbringung in einem der Schule angegliederten oder sonst geeigneten Schülerheim möglich ist." (Effective date: 01/01/2019).

## APPENDIX 2

**Bildungsdirektionen-Einrichtungsgesetz § 5 (4).**
"Die Bewirtschaftung der Lehrpersonalressourcen hat sich jedenfalls an der Zahl der Schülerinnen und Schüler, am Bildungsangebot, am sozio-ökonomischen Hintergrund, am Förderbedarf der Schülerinnen und Schüler sowie an deren im Alltag gebrauchter Sprache und an den regionalen Bedürfnissen zu orientieren. Das zuständige Mitglied der Bundesregierung kann zur Berücksichtigung des sozio-ökonomischen Hintergrunds der Schülerinnen und Schüler durch Verordnung entsprechende Kriterien festlegen. Zu diesem Zweck kann das zuständige Mitglied der Bundesregierung auch Daten heranziehen, die vom BIFIE im Rahmen der Überprüfungen der Bildungsstandards erhoben wurden, soweit diese nicht bereits aus Datenbeständen der Bundesanstalt Statistik Österreich verfügbar sind. Der Bereich Pädagogischer Dienst hat bei der Bewirtschaftung der Lehrpersonalressourcen mitzuwirken." (Version from 31/08/2020).

## APPENDIX 3

Items of the PRQ 2.0 (Goldan & Schwab, 2019) and their relating factors (P = personnel resources; S + M = spatial and material resources).

In the following we would like to know how you perceive the provision of resources at your school. Please indicate to what extent you agree with the statements.

|    |                                                                              | Relating Factors | Not at all True | Somewhat not True | Somewhat True | Certainly True |
|----|------------------------------------------------------------------------------|------------------|-----------------|-------------------|---------------|----------------|
| 1  | In class, all students get the help they need.                               | P                |                 |                   |               |                |
| 2  | I have enough time for my students.                                          | P                |                 |                   |               |                |
| 3  | When my students have a problem, there is always someone at school to help them. | P            |                 |                   |               |                |
| 4  | In class, all students get the support they need to learn.                   | P                |                 |                   |               |                |
| 5  | In our classrooms, all students have enough space to learn.                  | S + M            |                 |                   |               |                |
| 6  | We have all the materials we need for our lessons.                           | S + M            |                 |                   |               |                |
| 7  | In the classroom, we have many different materials for learning.             | S + M            |                 |                   |               |                |
| 8  | Our classrooms are designed so that the students feel comfortable.           | S + M            |                 |                   |               |                |
| 9  | We have enough professionals to consult when I need them.                    | S + M            |                 |                   |               |                |
| 10 | I have enough support in class.                                              | S + M            |                 |                   |               |                |

# APPENDIX 4

Schule hat die grundsätzliche Aufgabe, allen Kindern und Jugendlichen eine optimale Entwicklung zu ermöglichen. Alle sollen in der Schule unabhängig von sozialer Herkunft, Geschlecht, Begabung, Migrationshintergrund, Erstsprache oder auch einer Behinderung bzw. Beeinträchtigung ihre Potenziale bestmöglich entfalten und ihre Bildungsziele erreichen können. Dies ist ein Kinderrecht und liegt im persönlichen Interesse des Einzelnen ebenso wie im Interesse der Gesellschaft. (Bundesministerium für Bildung, Wissenschaft und Forschung, 2019c, foreword; internal report).

# A MATTER OF RESOURCES? – STUDENTS' ACADEMIC SELF-CONCEPT, SOCIAL INCLUSION AND SCHOOL WELL-BEING IN INCLUSIVE EDUCATION

Janka Goldan, Lisa Hoffmann and Susanne Schwab

## ABSTRACT

*According to the literature, a lack of resources is seen as a major barrier of implementing inclusive education. Previous studies, which have mostly been limited to the perspective of teachers, show that the perception of resources has a considerable influence on teachers' self-efficacy and in particular on their attitude towards inclusive education. The 'Perception of Resources Questionnaire' (PRQ) by Goldan and Schwab (2018) is the first instrument to assess the perspective of students. The PRQ was applied in the present study comprising N = 701 students from lower-secondary level in Germany. It is aimed to explore whether the perception of resources has an effect on relevant dimensions on the side of the students. Results of multilevel regression analyses show that students' perception of resources is a significant predictor of their well-being in school, academic self-concept and social inclusion. Finally, the results are discussed with regard to practical implications.*

**Keywords**: Resource perception; inclusive education; school well-being; social inclusion; academic self-concept; students with special needs; inclusive education

With the ratification of the United Nations convention on the rights of persons with disabilities (UN CRPD) (United Nations, 2006) in 2009, the Federal

Resourcing Inclusive Education
International Perspectives on Inclusive Education, Volume 15, 89–100
Copyright © 2021 by Emerald Publishing Limited.
All rights of reproduction in any form reserved
ISSN: 1479-3636/doi:10.1108/S1479-363620210000015008

Republic of Germany has committed itself to a school system in which students with and without special educational needs (SEN) and disabilities are generally taught in joint classes. In implementing an inclusive school system, Germany meets particular challenges especially because its school system is among the most segregated ones in the world (Biermann & Powell, 2014; Powell, 2011). In addition, Germany is characterized by a federal structure, giving the right to frame the education system almost exclusively to the federal states. Hence, in most of the federal states, the UN Convention has been adopted differently and with reservations.

One of the main restrictions is that the attendance of students with SEN in regular schools is subject to available resources, which is not in accordance with the UN CRPD. Article 24, 2c of the CRPD states (United Nations, 2006): 'In realizing this right, States Parties shall ensure that [...] reasonable accommodation of the individual's requirements is provided'. Although various people have argued that an inclusive school system is more cost-efficient than a segregated system of special schools and general schools (Peters, 2004; UNESCO, 2009), the transition phase undoubtedly requires additional provision and costs. These resources, namely material, spatial and particularly personnel resources, are considered a critical factor in the successful implementation of inclusive education (Schwab, 2018a; UNESCO, 2009).

In this context, recent studies indicate that not only the amount of the resources actually provided is relevant but also whether the provision is *perceived* as sufficient by the stakeholders, e.g., teachers and students.

To assess perceptions of resources, Goldan and Schwab (2018) have developed the 'Perception of Resources Questionnaire' (PRQ), an instrument for both students and teachers. While for teachers it has already been shown that perceptions of resources have significant effects on their attitudes towards inclusion and self-efficacy beliefs (Avramidis & Norwich, 2002; Chiner & Cardona, 2013), no studies have yet been conducted for students that show similar correlations. This chapter aims to explore whether the perception of resources has an influence on inclusion-related dimensions on the part of students.

## RESOURCES

According to the literature, a lack of resources is seen as a major barrier of implementing inclusive education (Armstrong, Armstrong, & Spandagou, 2011; UNESCO, 2009). Previous studies on the perception of resources in inclusive education have mostly been limited to the perspective of teachers (Goldan & Schwab, 2018). The results consistently show that the perception of resources has a considerable influence on the teachers' self-efficacy (Avramidis & Norwich, 2002) and in particular on the attitude towards inclusive education (Avramidis & Norwich, 2002). The more resources a teacher perceives, the more positive the attitude towards inclusion, as several studies have found. Although Article 24 of the UN CRPD specifies that the provision of schools – i.e., resources – must be adapted to the needs of the students (United Nations, 2006), there has so far been no instrument available which measures the perception of resources from the students' perspective. The PRQ by Goldan and Schwab (2018) is the first instrument to assess the perspective of both teachers and students.

Qualitative studies asking teachers or parents about inclusive education clearly pointed out that inclusive education requires adequate resourcing (see e.g., Schwab, 2018a). In most of the countries all over the world, additional resources to support students with SEN in inclusive classrooms are provided, whereas the different modes of allocation differ (Goldan, 2019). The question of how much resources are needed or are sufficient, however, is still unanswered. In this respect, the UN CRPD (United Nations, 2006) stresses that states have to ensure adequate resourcing to support the individual needs of all learners. Consequently, it is important to assess the students' perspective, i.e., all the students, and not limited to those with SEN, in inclusive education research (De Leeuw, de Boer, & Minnaert, 2018), also regarding their view on accommodation in schools. As proposed by Giangreco, Edelman, Broer, and Doyle (2001), 'We need to spend more time listening to and trying to understand the perspectives of self-advocates' (p. 59).

To date, the research on students' perceptions of resources is scarce. Goldan and Schwab (2018) developed the PRQ to assess the perspective of the students. Interestingly, when comparing the study of Goldan and Schwab (2018) with the results from another study by Schwab, Alnahdi, Goldan, and Elhadi (2020), which focused on primary school students, the results indicate that primary school students experience a higher level of resources compared to secondary school students. Furthermore, an international comparison between Germany and Saudi Arabia indicated that German students perceive a higher level of resources compared with Saudi Arabians (Schwab et al., 2020). Moreover, within this study, the high impact of resources for inclusive education was stressed as the authors showed that a higher level of resource perception is positively linked to the teachers' use of inclusive teaching practices (such as individualization or personalization of instruction).

## SOCIAL INCLUSION, SCHOOL WELL-BEING AND ACADEMIC SELF-CONCEPT

The success of inclusive education is evaluated not only by the development of student performance but also, for example, by the extent of students' social inclusion, their well-being in school and their academic self-concept. Venetz, Zurbriggen, and Eckhart (2014) describe three dimensions that should reflect the quality of inclusion by capturing (a) being integrated in the sense of positive well-being at school, (b) being socially included in the sense of relationships with peers and (c) being academically integrated in the sense of trust in one's own academic performance (academic self-concept).

Students' social inclusion and students' well-being in school can be seen as both determinants but also outcome variables of inclusive education (Hascher, 2017). Especially, the argument that some students with SEN should not be socially excluded by being taught in a special school was used as a strong argument for inclusive education. For inclusive education, however, the empirical evidence indicated that students with SEN are at risk of lower social inclusion compared to their peers without SEN (Bossaert, Colpin, Pijl, & Petry, 2013; Koster, Nakken, Pijl, & van Houten, 2009; Schwab, 2018b). Similarly, for students with migration background, it was found that they have a lower level of social inclusion compared to peers without migration background (Graham, Taylor, & Ho, 2009; Krull, Wilbert, & Hennemann, 2018; Plenty & Jonsson, 2017).

For students' well-being in school, previous studies sometimes indicated that students with SEN perceive lower levels compared to their peers (e.g., McCoy, Banks, & Shevlin, 2012; McCoy & Banks, 2017; Skrzypiec, Askell-Williams, Slee, & Rudzinski, 2016) while other studies found no differences between these groups (e.g., Schwab et al., 2015). Similarly, having both SEN and a migration background might put students into a risk according to their well-being in school. For instance, the Organization for Economic Co-operation and Development (OECD, 2018) reported a lower sense of school belonging for students with migration background. Also Hughes, Im, and Allee (2015) found differences in school belonging across ethnic groups; however their results have been inconsistent (see also Scorgie & Forlin, 2019).

Students' academic self-concept has also been extensively researched in the context of inclusive education and has been consistently shown that students with SEN have a lower level of academic self-concept compared to students without SEN (Bear, Minke, & Manning, 2002; Cambra & Silvestre, 2003). According to migration background, the results of Cokley and Patel (2007) indicate that there might be a difference as they found a negative relation between academic self-concept and adherence to Asian values while this effect was positive for adherence to European American values.

Personnel support has been linked with social inclusion and school well-being. For instance, results from Schwab (2017) demonstrated that students, who feel better supported by the collaboration of two teachers, also feel higher levels of social inclusion and school well-being. To expand on this, we investigated further if students' school well-being, social inclusion and academic self-concept are also related to availability of resources.

## RESEARCH QUESTIONS

Based on studies with teachers, it can be assumed that perceptions of resources also have an influence on different dimensions that are considered essential for inclusive education on the side of the students. In the following, it will be analyzed from the students' perspective to what extent their perception of resources has an impact on their school well-being, social integration and academic self-concept.

With regard to their resource perception, it will be explored whether this differs depending on the grade level. To determine the effect on school well-being, social inclusion and the academic self-concept, three multi-level regression models are estimated with the respective construct as a dependent variable. At the individual level, gender, SEN status and migration background are included in the model as control variables. On class level, the grade level, the type of school, the class size (number of students in the class) and the weekly number of hours in which a special needs teacher supports the class are included.

The following questions are examined:

(1) How do students in inclusive education perceive the provision of (personnel, material, spatial) resources? What is the level of the students' school well-being, social inclusion and academic self-concept? Are there significant differences between the groups of students with and without SEN?
(2) Does the perception of available resources differ depending on the grade level?
(3) When controlling for potential confounders (e.g., gender, SEN status, migration background, grade level, class size and number of hours in which a special education teacher supports the class), does the perception of resources have a significant effect on students' school well-being, social inclusion and academic self-concept?

## METHODOLOGY

### Sample

The sample is based on the study RESE (Resources and Self-Efficacy in Inclusive Education), for which data were collected in autumn 2017 from a total of 42 classes of lower secondary education in North Rhine-Westphalia, Germany. A total of $N = 701$ students from 16 schools participated in the paper-pencil survey, 52.8% of whom were boys. The students in the sample are distributed relatively equally over five different grade levels (grades 5–9). The lowest proportion is in grade 9 with 15.9%, and the highest is in grade 7 with 23.4% of all participating students. The other students are distributed among the grades five (17.29%), six (20.71%) and eight (22.71%). Of the 701 students in the sample, 94 had a SEN (13.4%) and 161 (23.6%) indicated that they spoke a first language other than German (indicating a migration background).

As some teachers did not complete the questionnaires at class level, information on special needs teachers is sometimes missing. For the multi-level regression analyses, the sample size is reduced accordingly to 31 classes and 483 students for which complete data are available. The classrooms in the study have an average size of 24.7 (SD = 3.4) students per class. The smallest class has only 17 students, whereas the largest class consists of 31 students. The average weekly number of hours in which a special education teacher supports the class amounts to 4.4 hours. However, with a standard deviation of 3.2, the distribution varies considerably. The minimum is 0, i.e., there is no special educational support at all and the maximum is 12 hours per week. The secondary level is a suitable place to examine the research questions in so far as – particularly with regard to personnel resources – a greater variety of resources can be assumed (Goldan, 2019).

*Instruments*

To minimize the cognitive strain on the students, the answer format within the battery of questionnaires was kept identical. The items and scales described below were all to be answered on a four-level Likert scale (1 = 'not at all true', 2 = 'somewhat not true', 3 = 'somewhat true to 4 = 'certainly true').

**PRQ** – Students were asked to indicate whether they perceived the resources available in their school or classroom to be sufficient/adequate. The questions were asked with regard to personnel resources ('There are enough teachers at our school'), spatial resources ('The classrooms at our school are big enough') and material resources ('In class there are many different materials for the students to learn'). Despite the heterogeneity of the items, the scale has a single factor structure and an acceptable reliability (Cronbach's alpha = 0.67; see Goldan & Schwab, 2018).

**PIQ (Perceptions of Inclusion Questionnaire)** – School well-being, social inclusion and academic self-concept were assessed by using the three subscales of the PIQ (Venetz et al., 2014; Venetz, Zurbriggen, Eckhart, Schwab, & Hessels, 2015). The three subscales comprise school well-being (e.g., 'I like going to school'), social inclusion (e.g., 'I have a lot of friends at school') and academic self-concept (e.g., 'I am a fast learner'). All three subscales show a high psychometric quality: Cronbach's α for school well-being is 0.90, for social inclusion 0.83 and for academic self-concept 0.79 (see Zurbriggen, Venetz, Schwab, & Hessels, 2017).

## RESULTS

Referring to the first research question, the descriptive results in Table 1 show the descriptive statistics of the different constructs. The mean values were calculated for the students when at least half of the answers were obtained, i.e., the deviations in sample size occur when individual students refused more than half of the answers or, in some cases, refused all answers.

The values indicate that the average perception of the students is consistently above the theoretical average of the four-level scales. The level of resource provision is similarly perceived by both students with SEN (MW = 2.91, SD = 0.44) and students without SEN (MW = 2.90; SD = 0.48). Due to the occurrence of variance heterogeneity, the Welch's t-test showed that the small mean difference was not significant ($t_{114}$ = 0.15, n.s.).

The social inclusion is rated highest by the students (Mean = 3.37; SD = 0.55). In accordance with the current state of research, this study also showed a somewhat less positive rating for students with SEN (Mean = 3.16; SD = 0.69). The lower mean value compared to students without SEN is significant ($t_{694}$ = 3.96,

**Table 1.** Means, Standard Deviations and Results of *t*-tests for Students' PRQ, Social Inclusion, School Well-Being and Academic Self-Concept.

|  |  | *N* | Mean | SD | Diff$_M$ No SEN – SEN | *p* Value |
|---|---|---|---|---|---|---|
| Perception of resources (PRQ) | No SEN | 590 | 2.91 | 0.44 | −0.01 | 0.883 |
|  | SEN | 91 | 2.90 | 0.48 |  |  |
|  | Total | 681 | 2.91 | 0.44 |  |  |
| Social inclusion (PIQ) | No SEN | 604 | 3.40 | 0.52 | −0.24 | 0.000 |
|  | SEN | 92 | 3.16 | 0.69 |  |  |
|  | Total | 696 | 3.37 | 0.55 |  |  |
| School well-being (PIQ) | No SEN | 603 | 2.90 | 0.76 | −0.14 | 0.176 |
|  | SEN | 92 | 2.76 | 0.84 |  |  |
|  | Total | 695 | 2.87 | 0.77 |  |  |
| Academic self-concept (PIQ) | No SEN | 603 | 2.95 | 0.53 | −0.42 | 0.000 |
|  | SEN | 92 | 2.53 | 0.62 |  |  |
|  | Total | 695 | 2.89 | 0.56 |  |  |

**Table 2.** Perception of Resources Differentiated by Grade Level.

|  | *N* | Mean | SD |
|---|---|---|---|
| Grade 5 | 114 | 3.15 | 0.41 |
| Grade 6 | 140 | 2.94 | 0.41 |
| Grade 7 | 161 | 2.91 | 0.41 |
| Grade 8 | 156 | 2.80 | 0.42 |
| Grade 9 | 109 | 2.77 | 0.47 |
| Total | 680 | 2.91 | 0.44 |

$p < 0.001$). With regard to school well-being, a Welch's t-test showed no significant group difference ($t_{114} = 1.36$; n.s.). On average, the students tend to feel quite well at school (Mean = 2.87; SD = 0.77), with the relatively large standard deviation indicating a wide variation. The students' academic self-concept also shows values above the theoretical mean (Mean = 2.89; SD = 0.56). While students without SEN even show values that are above the overall mean (Mean = 2.95; SD = 0.53), students with SEN show a lower academic self-concept (Mean = 2.53; SD = 0.62). A t-test for independent samples showed that the difference is significant ($t_{693} = 6.99$; $p < 0.001$).

To test the second research question, namely whether students perceive the provision of resources differently depending on the grade level, a single factor ANOVA (analysis of variance) and a post hoc test according to Scheffé were calculated. The descriptive results of resource perception differentiated by grade level are shown in Table 2. It can be seen that the average level of resource perception continuously decreases with increasing grade level. The highest value can be found for students in grade 5 (Mean = 3.15; SD = 0.41) and the lowest for grade 9 (Mean = 2.77; SD = 0.47).

The result of the F-test shows that the grade level has a significant influence on resource perception ($F_{4,675}$ = 14,75, $p < 0.000$, $Eta^2$ = 0.08). The Scheffé test showed that grade five differs significantly from all other grades. Grade six also differed significantly from grade nine, and all other pairwise comparisons were not significant.

***Table 3.*** Multi-Level Regression Model for Predicting Students' School Well-Being, Social Inclusion and Academic Self-Concept.

| | School well-being | Social inclusion | Academic self-concept |
|---|---|---|---|
| Intercept | 0.42** | −0.45** | −0.57* |
| Level 1 | | | |
| Perception of Resources | 0.1178** | 0.1882** | 0.1726*** |
| | (0.43) | (0.07) | (0.05) |
| Social Inclusion | 0.2831*** | | |
| | (0.05) | | |
| Boys (Reference category) | | | |
| Girls | 0.1988 | −0.0420 | −0.0869 |
| | (0.10) | (0.12) | (0.06) |
| Students with SEN (Reference category) | | | |
| Students without SEN | −0.1010 | 0.4682*** | 0.8852*** |
| | (0.11) | (0.09) | (0.11) |
| First language German (Reference category) | | | |
| First language other than German | −0.0293 | 0.0431 | −0.0566 |
| | (0.10) | (0.07) | (0.12) |
| Level 2 | | | |
| Grade 5 (Reference category) | | | |
| Grade 6 | −0.8497*** | 0.3531 | −0.3405 |
| | (0.18) | (0.26) | (0.24) |
| Grade 7 | −0.4106* | 0.1539 | −0.1626 |
| | (0.16) | (0.21) | (0.23) |
| Grade 8 | −0.5253*** | 0.1393 | −0.1054 |
| | (0.13) | (0.20) | (0.29) |
| Grade 9 | −0.5598*** | −0.2705** | −0.1410 |
| | (0.12) | (0.10) | (0.17) |
| Number of students in class | −0.0535 | 0.0740 | −0.0291 |
| | (0.04) | (0.05) | (0.45) |
| Number of hours in which a special education teacher supports the class | −0.0802 | 0.0049 | −0.0528 |
| | (0.06) | (0.02) | (0.04) |
| Residual variance on individual level | 0.7806 | 0.8592 | 0.8632 |
| | (0.07) | (0.02) | (0.06) |
| Residual variance on class level | 0.0299 | 0.0170 | 0.0002 |
| | (0.03) | (0.02) | (0.02) |

*$p < 0.05$, **$p < 0.01$, ***$p < 0.001$.
*Notes:* 1. clustered standard errors were calculated for all models at school level; 2. the dependent variables and all metric independent variables were *z*-standardized at the Grand Mean.

To answer the third research question, three multi-level regression models were calculated (see Table 3). Multi-level models were indicated because students are nested in classes (level 2). In addition, a random intercept model, which is used here, also allows the introduction of explanatory variables at the second level.

First, the empty models were calculated without predictors. Here, the variance components were shown to be lower on level 2 – the level of the class. For school well-being 11.1%, for social inclusion 6.2% and for academic self-concept 2.1% of the variance can be explained on class level.

Subsequently, independent variables have been included in the model with predictors. At the student level, the PRQ mean was added to determine the effect on the dependent variable, gender (reference: boy), SEN (yes/no; reference: students with SEN), grade level (reference: grade 5) and a proxy for the migration background (here: the question of whether the first language is German; reference: first language German). For the model to explain school well-being, social inclusion was additionally included as a predictor, since it is assumed that it can have a significant influence on both the perception of resources (e.g., by peer support) and well-being, and, thus, confounds the effect.

On class level ($N = 31$), the following variables were included: the grade level, the number of students per class and the number of weekly hours in which a special education teacher supports the lessons. The dependent variable and all metric independent variables were z-standardized on the Grand Mean before calculation. The standard errors were clustered at school level.

The results in Table 3 illustrate that the students' perception of resources is a significant predictor in all of the three models. Students' resource perception shows a positive relationship with school well-being as well as social inclusion and academic self-concept. The strongest relation can be observed for social inclusion and accordingly means that with each standard deviation in the perception of resources, the experienced social inclusion increases by 0.188 standard deviations on average (keeping all other variables constant).

In line with the findings from other studies, we also find significant differences in academic self-concept and social inclusion for students without SEN compared to students with SEN, i.e., the academic self-concept of students without SEN is 0.88 standard deviations higher (or 0.47 standard deviations in the case of social inclusion) compared to their peers with SEN.

It is also noteworthy that the variables on Level 2 have no significant influence on the dependent variables. Only for the grade level, significant effects on school well-being are evident.

## DISCUSSION

The present study investigated whether students' resource perceptions were related to important dimensions of inclusive education outcomes of school well-being, academic self-concept and social inclusion. According to Hascher (2017), these constructs must be considered when evaluating the success of inclusive education. In this context, a lack of resources, particularly personnel resources, is seen as a major barrier to the successful implementation of the school reform (Goldan & Schwab, 2018). For teachers, it was shown that the perception of resources, i.e., whether they are perceived as sufficient, has a significant influence on other success factors; it influences both the attitudes towards inclusive education and the teachers' self-efficacy beliefs (Avramidis & Norwich, 2002). The purpose of this study was to explore whether students' perception of resources also has significant effects on central outcome dimensions.

Referring to the first research questions, it is found that on average students are rather satisfied with the available amount of resources, i.e., they showed values above the theoretical mean, and that the perceptions of students with and without SEN do not differ significantly. This is remarkable because it could be assumed that the demands on resources are very different between these two groups. Hence, the results may indicate that different needs are met in different ways, leading to overall satisfaction.

Similar results were found for the three constructs examined. With regard to social inclusion, school well-being and academic self-concept, all students show relatively high values on the different scales. Nevertheless, it was evident for students with SEN that they perceive significantly lower levels of social inclusion compared to their peers without SEN. This finding is in line with the current state of research, which points to the risk of lower social participation for students with SEN (Schwab, 2018b). As expected, the academic self-concept also shows that students with SEN have lower scores, which is critical since it is empirically related to school performance (Marsh & Martin, 2011). In terms of school well-being, studies come to diverging results for students with SEN. In the study at hand, the average level of well-being is high. The groups of students with and without SEN do not differ significantly from each other.

The results of research question (2) show that the perception of resources declines with rising grade levels. Further research is needed to investigate whether this is a random finding or whether it is associated, for example, with well-being, which is also known to decrease with rising grade levels. In addition, it should be examined whether the resources provided are actually reduced over the years or whether there are individual, student-related, reasons why the perception of students becomes more critical in higher grade levels.

The main focus of this chapter was whether the perception of resources has an impact on students' social inclusion, school well-being and academic self-concept of students in inclusive schools. For all three constructs, significant effects were found. Furthermore, it is noteworthy that the amount of personnel resources, i.e., hours in which a special education teacher supports the class, does not reveal a significant correlation with the constructs. This can be interpreted as an indication that the *perception* of resources plays an important role in the effective implementation of inclusive education. Also, a very important factor seems to be how the resources are processed (Loreman, 2014), i.e., whether they are used efficiently and effectively. Future research needs to examine *how* (scarce) resources can be used efficiently and the extent to which resources provided actually make a difference in certain outcome dimensions at the teacher and student level. Ultimately, however, it can be assumed that input only, i.e., the quantity of resources, does not directly affect the outcomes and that the perception of resources is a crucial factor in the successful implementation of inclusive education.

# REFERENCES

Armstrong, D., Armstrong, A. C., & Spandagou, I. (2011). Inclusion: By choice or by chance?. *International Journal of Inclusive Education, 15*(1), 29–39. doi: 10.1080/13603116.2010.496192.

Avramidis, E., & Norwich, B. (2002). Teachers' attitudes towards integration/inclusion: A review of the literature. *European Journal of Special Needs Education, 17*(2), 129–147.

Bear, G. G., Minke, K. M., & Manning, M. A. (2002). Self-concept of students with learning disabilities: A meta-analysis. *School Psychology Review, 31*, 405–427.

Biermann, J., & Powell, J. J. W. (2014). Institutionelle Dimensionen inklusiver Schulbildung - herausforderungen der UN-Behindertenrechtskonvention für Deutschland, Island und Schweden im Vergleich. [Institutional dimensions of inclusive schooling: comparing the challenge of the UN Convention on the Rights of Persons with Disabilities in Germany, Iceland and Sweden]. *Zeitschrift für Erziehungswissenschaft, 17*(4), 679–700. doi: 10.1007/s11618-014-0588-0.

Bossaert, G., Colpin, H., Pijl, S. J., & Petry, K. (2013). Truly included? A literature study focusing on the social dimension of inclusion in education. *International Journal of Inclusive Education, 17*(1), 60–79.

Cambra, C., & Silvestre, N. (2003). Students with special educational needs in the inclusive classroom: Social integration and self-concept. *European Journal of Special Needs Education, 18*, 197–208.

Chiner, E., & Cardona, M. C. (2013). Inclusive education in Spain: How do skills, resources, and supports affect regular education teachers' perceptions of inclusion?. *International Journal of Inclusive Education, 17*(5), 526–541.

Cokley, K., & Patel, N. (2007). A psychometric investigation of the academic self-concept of Asian American college students. *Educational and Psychological Measurement, 67*(1), 88–99.

De Leeuw, R. R., de Boer, A., & Minnaert, A. E. M. G. (2018). Student voices on social exclusion in general primary schools. *European Journal of Special Needs Education, 33*, 166–186.

Giangreco, M., Edelman, S., Broer, S., & Doyle, M. B. (2001). Paraprofessional support of students with disabilities: Literature from the past decade. *Exceptional Children, 68*(1), 45–63.

Goldan, J. (2019). Demand-oriented and fair allocation of special needs teacher resources for inclusive education – assessment of a newly implemented funding model in North Rhine-Westphalia, Germany. *International Journal of Inclusive Education.* doi: 10.1080/13603116.2019.1568598.

Goldan, J., & Schwab, S. (2018). Measuring students' and teachers' perceptions of resources in inclusive education – validation of a newly developed instrument. *International Journal of Inclusive Education, 14*(2), 1326–1339. doi: 10.1080/13603116.2018.1515270.

Graham, S., Taylor, A. Z., & Ho, A. Y. (2009). Race and ethnicity in peer relations research. In K. H. Rubin, W. M. Bukowski, & B. Laursen (Eds.), *Social, emotional, and personality development in context. Handbook of peer interactions, relationships, and groups* (pp. 394–413). New York, NY: Guilford Press.

Hascher, T. (2017). Die Bedeutung von Wohlbefinden und Sozialklima für Inklusion. In B. Lütje-Klose, S. Miller, S. Schwab, & B. Streese (Hrsg.), *Inklusion: Profile für die Schul- und Unterrichtsentwicklung in Deutschland, Österreich und der Schweiz. Band II in der Reihe "Beiträge der Bildungsforschung" der Österreichischen Gesellschaft für Forschung und Entwicklung im Bildungswesen (ÖFEB)* (pp. 65–75). Münster: Waxmann.

Hughes, J. N., Im, M. H., & Allee, P. J. (2015). Effect of school belonging trajectories in grades 6–8 on achievement: Gender and ethnic differences. *Journal of School Psychology, 53*(6), 493–507.

Koster, M., Nakken, H., Pijl, S. J., & van Houten, E. (2009). Being part of the peer group: A literature study focusing on the social dimension of inclusion in education. *International Journal of Inclusive Education, 13*, 117–140.

Krull, J., Wilbert, J., & Hennemann, T. (2018). Does social exclusion by classmates lead to behaviour problems and learning difficulties or vice versa? A cross-lagged panel analysis. *European Journal of Special Needs Education*, *33*(2), 235–253. doi: 10.1080/08856257.2018.1424780.

Loreman, T. (2014). Measuring inclusive education outcomes in Alberta, Canada. *International Journal of Inclusive Education*, *18*(5), 459–483. doi: 10.1080/13603116.2013.788223.

Marsh, H. W., & Martin, A. J. (2011). Academic self-concept and academic achievement: Relations and causal ordering. *British Journal of Educational Psychology*, *81*(1), 59–77.

McCoy, S., & Banks, J. (2017). Simply academic? Why children with special educational needs don't like school. *European Journal of Special Needs Education*, *27*, 81–97.

McCoy, S., Banks, J., & Shevlin, M. (2012). School matters: How context influences the identification of different types of special educational needs. *Irish Educational Studies*, *31*(2), 119–138.

OECD. (2018). *The resilience of students with an immigrant background: Factors that shape well-being, OECD reviews of migrant education*. Paris: OECD Publishing. doi: 10.1787/9789264292093-en.

Peters, S. J. (2004). *Inclusive education. An EFA strategy for all children*. Washington, DC: Disability Group, World Bank.

Plenty, S., & Jonsson, J. O. (2017). Social exclusion among peers: The role of immigrant status and classroom immigrant density. *Journal of Youth and Adolescence*, *46*(6), 1275–1288.

Powell, J. J. W. (2011). *Barriers to inclusion. Special education in the United States and Germany*. Boulder, CO: Paradigm Publishing.

Schwab, S. (2017). Interprofessionelle Lehrkraftkooperation im inklusiven Unterricht aus der Perspektive der Schülerinnen und Schüler. *Unterrichtswissenschaft*, *45*, 262–279. doi: 10.3262/UW1704262.

Schwab, S. (2018a). *Attitudes towards inclusive schooling: A study on students', teachers' and parents' attitudes*. Münster: Waxmann Verlag.

Schwab, S. (2018b). Peer-relations of students with special educational needs in inclusive education. In S. Polenghi, M. Fiorucci, & L. Agostinetto (Eds.), *Diritti cittadinanza inclusione* (pp. 15–24). Rovato: Pensa MultiMedia. Retrieved from https://www.siped.it/wp-content/uploads/2018/10/2018-Roma-Atti.pdf. Accessed on May 18, 2020.

Schwab, S., Alnahdi, G., Goldan, J., & Elhadi, A. (2020). Assessing perceptions of resources and inclusive teaching practices: A cross-country study between German and Saudi students in inclusive schools. *Studies in Educational Evaluation*, *65*:100849. doi: 10.1016/j.stueduc.2020.100849.

Schwab, S., Rossmann, P., Tanzer, N., Hagn, J., Oitzinger, S., Thurner, V., & Wimberger, T. (2015). Schulisches wohlbefinden von schülerInnen mit und ohne sonderpädagogischem förderbedarf: Integrations- und regelklassen im vergleich [school well-being of students with and without special educational needs: A comparison of students in inclusive and regular classes]. *Zeitschrift für Kinder- und Jugendpsychiatrie und Psychotherapie*, *43*(4), 265–274.

Scorgie, K., & Forlin, C. (2019). *Promoting social inclusion: Co-creating environments that foster equity and belonging* (Vol. 13). Series Editor C. Forlin. Bingley: Emerald.

Skrzypiec, G., Askell-Williams, H., Slee, P., & Rudzinski, A. (2016). Students with self-identified special educational needs and disabilities (si-SEND): Flourishing or languishing!. *International Journal of Disability, Development and Education*, *63*(1), 7–26.

UNESCO. (2009). *Policy guidelines on inclusion in education*. Paris: UNESCO.

United Nations. (2006). *Convention on the rights of persons with disabilities*. New York, NY: United Nations. Retrieved from http://www.un.org/disabilities/documents/convention/convoptprot-e.pdf. Accessed on May 18, 2020.

Venetz, M., Zurbriggen, C., & Eckhart, M. (2014). Entwicklung und erste Validierung einer Kurzversion des Fragebogens zur Erfassung von Dimensionen der Integration von Schülern (FDI 4-6) von Haeberlin, Moser, Bless & Klaghofer. *Empirische Sonderpädagogik*, *6*(2), 99–113.

Venetz, M., Zurbriggen, C. A. L., Eckhart, M., Schwab, S., & Hessels, M. G. P. (2015). The perceptions of inclusion questionnaire (PIQ). Retrieved from www.piqinfo.ch. Accessed on May 18, 2020.

Zurbriggen, C. L. A., Venetz, M., Schwab, S., & Hessels, M. G. P. (2017). A psychometric analysis of the student version of the Perceptions of Inclusion Questionnaire (PIQ). *European Journal of Psychological Assessment*, *35*, 641–649. doi: 10.1027/1015-5759/a000443

# SECTION 2

# PROFESSIONAL DEVELOPMENT FOR INCLUSIVE EDUCATION

# TRANSITIONING FROM SEGREGATION TO INCLUSION: AN EFFECTIVE AND SUSTAINABLE MODEL TO PROMOTE INCLUSION, THROUGH INTERNAL STAFFING ADJUSTMENTS, AND ROLE REDEFINITION

Sheila Bennett, Tiffany L. Gallagher, Monique Somma, Rebecca White and Kathy Wlodarczyk

## ABSTRACT

*This work explores the effectiveness of an innovative inclusion model that is based on the development and operationalization of the inclusion coach (IC) role in one school district (in Ontario, generally referred to as a 'board'). This model has implications for school systems that desire a change in practice but may perceive challenges to this change in their local capacity. In this model, internal school district funding and existing structures were reallocated to convert teaching positions into IC positions. This staffing change was designed to support the desegregation of stand-alone special education classes at the elementary and secondary levels within that school district. While significantly decreasing the number of segregated settings, the intervention was not without its challenges. Challenges and successes will be examined through the perspectives of school principals, ICs and classroom teachers. This school district created an effective and sustainable model to promote inclusion, through internal staffing adjustments, and role redefinition. Utilizing a shared focus*

Resourcing Inclusive Education
International Perspectives on Inclusive Education, Volume 15, 103–116
Copyright © 2021 by Emerald Publishing Limited.
ISSN: 1479-3636/doi:10.1108/S1479-363620210000015009

*and support for staff, this school district was successfully able to transition beliefs and practices from segregated special education to full inclusion for students with special education needs.*

**Keywords**: Inclusion; coaching; special education; schooling; school district; transformation

## INTRODUCTION

This work examines the use of existing school district funding and structures to accomplish inclusion through the development and implementation of an inclusion coach (IC) role. This model has the potential to create successful, long-term inclusive practice through the redistribution of existing funding and structures. The IC role was created internally through school district leadership. The successes and potential challenges of the IC and transition process are highlighted through the perceptions of the school-based principals, ICs, and classroom teachers. This chapter presents a service delivery model that accomplished the successful desegregation of self-contained special education classes and developed an inclusive system, which can be adopted in a variety of school contexts.

## THE POSSIBILITY OF CHANGE

Within an educational milieu, autonomy and decision-making can be seemingly restrictive – particularly when funding is government-dependent. As with many bureaucratically created and dependent systems, guidelines, procedures and what can be commonly referred to as 'red tape' can serve to stifle innovation. Within such parameters, it is not unusual for schools and school systems to maintain the status quo and, thus, fail to innovate. As the field of inclusion moves forward, school systems can be caught between the desire to respond to the changing ethos of disability rights and their own inability to shift practice. Literature on inclusive practices indicates clearly that educators desire to include children (Bennett, 2009; Mulholland & O'Connor, 2016); however, practical realities often serve as a barrier to implementation (Woodcock & Woolfson, 2019). It is also clear that leadership matters. Mindset, experiences, and expertise can all play a role in a leader's ability to promote and sustain good inclusive practice (Irvine, Lupart, Loreman, & McGhie-Richmond, 2010; Lupart & Porath, 2009).

In the presence of evolving knowledge and belief systems, transformation can be inhibited and systems can seem unresponsive. Despite the reality of inherent inertia and within seemingly strict parameters, change is possible and can be accomplished. This chapter tells the story of one such change. Utilizing existing resources, personnel and funding one school district transitioned a service delivery for students with disabilities from a segregated to an inclusive model. Within the context of this change process, inclusion was broadly defined. Certainly, the first priority was to desegregate stand-alone special education classes, but in addition to this the focus of inclusion was much broader than physical space. Academic, social and access opportunities to broaden interaction and create meaningful relationships were essential goals for success.

# ONTARIO SPECIAL EDUCATION SERVICES AND FUNDING: A CONTEXT

The vast majority of school districts in Ontario are administered by the provincial government through the Ontario Ministry of Education. The Ministry is responsible for policy, curriculum, funding and direction schools in the province. Groups of schools, often defined by geography and population, are managed by school districts. Each school district has local representatives, called trustees, who are elected to represent the interests of the general public. Employees of school districts are usually led by a director, then often superintendents, consultants and any number of support people who are responsible for specific functions. School districts oversee how dollars are spent, staffing, programming and ensuring that the district adhere to provincial regulations. While the Ministry sets direction and policy, each school district in the province has a considerable amount of decision-making autonomy related to service delivery. The legal mandate for students with special education needs was introduced in 1980 with the introduction of the Educational Amendment Act. Until then, the decision to allow students with special needs into local schools was optional. Initially, many of these settings were segregated, and over the last number of decades, individual school boards have maintained segregated practices while others have embraced inclusion.

Public school educational funding models in Canada are, almost exclusively, funded at the provincial and territorial governmental levels. Data reported from the Fraser Institute indicate that from 2006 to 2016, educational funding in Canada increased per pupil spending from $10,901 to $12,791 (MacLeod & Emes, 2019). Analysis of costs indicates that factors such as salary, pension as well as capital costs are the primary drivers for overall spending increases.

Within the province of Ontario, government spending for student need is based on a per pupil amount referred to as a Foundation Grant. In addition to the Foundation Grant, Special Purpose Grants are designed to allow school district funds to meet the unique needs of students within their jurisdiction and allow for flexible and nuanced spending (Bennett, Dworet, Gallagher, & Somma, 2019). Special Education Grants allow school districts to have autonomy within the parameters of their districts' particular special education services framework, though funds must remain within a protected fund.

These dollar amounts are shared among 72 school districts and 10 school authorities across the province. While a majority of the funding is predetermined in relation to population size, a percentage of the more specialized funding is provided based on need, which is determined via an application process.

Though funding models are provincially based, the decision on how that money is spent is school district specific as service delivery is flexible. Lacking direct mandates for inclusion from the Ministry of Education, school districts can choose the programming path that their students take. Fully segregated service delivery co-exists with neighbouring schools that are fully inclusive.

## COACHING AS A MODEL FOR INCLUSIVE PRACTICE

Although few studies have explored education coaching in Canada (Hardy, 2009; Lynch & Ferguson, 2010), coaching models of professional learning have been recommended for over a decade (Kise, 2006; Knight, 2011). Coaching is premised on collegial collaboration which can enhance teachers' pedagogical knowledge through engaging in critical reflection and goal-directed, self-regulated learning (Stephens & Mills, 2014; Toll, 2007; Walpole & McKenna, 2012). Coaching is an opportunity to further enhance teachers' inclusive practices, build their repertoire of skills and co-construct practical solutions that foster increased student learning (Elish-Piper & L'Allier, 2011). Yet, facilitating the professional growth of teachers is a complex process. Critical reflection, new knowledge and efficacy are required to promote such growth (Guskey, 2002). In addition, professional support with goal-directed, self-regulated learning is important (Stephens & Mills, 2014; Walpole & McKenna, 2012). Research has also documented the importance of building on teachers' existing professional knowledge and working collaboratively to build capacity for self-directed professional growth (Stover, Kissel, Haag, & Shoniker, 2011).

The context within which coaching is developed and the environment in which it is implemented is important for outcomes (MacDonald & Green, 2001). Stakeholders who develop the coaching model influence the social aspects of coaching, the coaching content and its delivery (Wlodarczyk, 2019). When the perspectives of the service provider agency (school district stakeholders) were aligned with the service user (schools and educators), the training of the coach and delivery of content were also aligned. When the service provider agency and the service user were not from the same institution, the alignment was more difficult to achieve. Coaches were perceived and treated as either members or visitors of the school community and this was contingent on whether the coach was hired internally (by the school board) or externally (by a service provider agency) (Wlodarczyk, 2019).

## OPERATIONALIZING AN INNOVATIVE MODEL

The desegregation of special education classes for this particular school district began as a concept inspired by a groundswell of parent dissatisfaction, a changing understanding of best practices for students with disabilities and a synchronous belief systems alignment of senior administrative leads open to a discussion for change. A decision was made to engage community members and parents in a discussion on the merits of inclusive practice. Speakers were brought in to address the parent, community and trustee groups; feedback was also solicited. The decision was made by district leadership to invite the research team as a partner group at the beginning and throughout the project. Researchers had access to coaches, principals, parents, students, teachers, community members and school board administrators. Multiple sets of data were collected through surveys, interviews, focus groups and journal entries. With momentum towards more inclusive service delivery, meetings, presentations and conversations were organized for school district level personnel and school administrators (including principals). While complete consensus was not (and would never be) reached in terms of full inclusion, feedback elicited a willingness to consider, 'a different way of doing things'. Given the mandate for change, to support the transition and educators' ongoing practice, the school district leadership created the IC role.

Over a four-year period, the school district reallocated existing funding to create and support the new role of the IC. Thirteen ICs were assigned to schools to support teachers as the transition from segregated to inclusive service delivery transpired. ICs visited assigned schools and worked with teachers weekly to develop inclusive practices for students with disabilities entering non-segregated classes for the first time. After the second implementation year, segregated classrooms were reduced by 90%. Initially, ICs experienced some resistance from staff; however, inclusive practices within their schools were developed over time through successful collaboration and support. After some exposure to the model, educators described coaching as, 'a really wonderful experience' between two 'equal partners and witnesses to success'. Furthermore, educators explained that coaching provided rich experiential learning that traditional professional development did not offer. Educator partners (i.e., teachers) valued the flexibility in collaboration (e.g., structured and unstructured conversations), the chance to observe teaching practice and student learning, as well as the opportunity to debrief and co-develop strategies. Educators appreciated never feeling 'alone' during the transition and learning processes (Wlodarczyk, 2019).

Following are the perspectives of the principals, educators and ICs as they share their insights on how the inclusion model was operationalized, facilitated and ultimately how it created an internal shift in inclusive practice. Principals (n = 10), educators (n = 21) and ICs (n = 11) are directly quoted below; however, their names and identifiers have been omitted to protect their privacy and confidentiality. The data presented provide insight and practical lessons that paint a picture of what this type of internal change process can add to the practice of inclusion.

## PRINCIPAL PERSPECTIVES

Leadership in any change initiative is an essential part of the success of that endeavour (Capper, Theoharis, & Sebastian, 2006; Ryan, 2006; Theoharis, 2007). Throughout the process of change, school principals were invited to engage in discussion and feedback. Inclusive belief factors such as training and expertise can strengthen the inclusive leadership within a school (Praisner, 2003).

Desegregation of existing special education classes was initially introduced to principals in a group professional development session focused on inclusion. Concurrent with this was an acknowledgement of growing parent advocacy, as well as professional dissatisfaction with traditional practices. It was not surprising that, when given a session about the possibility of change, the discussion that ensued was positive and proactive. While some individuals were reluctant to move to a fully inclusive model, the majority of voices in the discussion were receptive to change.

Findings from the interview data reflected the vantage point of school principals near the end of the process. At that time, all elementary and the majority of secondary self-contained classes were disbanded. With support and guidance from ICs, teachers were including students in regular classes.

School principals were positive about the change and progressive in their inclusive thinking and practices. They expressed a deep understanding of the importance of their role in the transition process.

> If the philosophy isn't coming from you and doing the hard work and recognizing the hard work that's being done, then it's not going to take root. If I didn't believe in it, or I even showed any little chink in the armour, that would be a significant setback.

When asked about an ideal school setting, principals consistently expressed the need for schools to be a positive and welcoming place. Principals identified the need for staff to be supportive of each other as a necessary element for success. They were also aware of the need for the conversation to transcend discussions on curriculum planning to include discussion on perspective taking and beliefs related to best practices.

> I think we work hard to make it a community where the differences of students are valued and seen as gifts as opposed to deficits and we work really hard at making sure that students have a sense of belonging and feel that they are part of something bigger than themselves, a part of the [school name].

In order to achieve a positive space of belonging, school principals reflected on the importance of staff engagement in shared goals. ICs were seen as an important part of that positive space.

> The supports in terms of the learning for all coach [IC], incredibly valuable in this school, in the last school I was at [school name] for two years and for one year there was a learning coach [IC] there, the relationships that are formed, the deep learning that happens for the teachers that work with that coach.

Essential to the success of the coaching model was the alignment of teaching staff and ICs.

> It is working tightly and closely with the teacher supports who are central, so inclusion coaches for example and my SERTs [special education resource teacher] and transition teachers, bringing those people together and aligning that work.

While noting that the role of the IC was important, school principals also discussed the evolution of the role as well as some challenges. Both principals and

IC were clear that in those cases where teachers were 'voluntold' (i.e., directed) to work with ICs, outcomes were often less than satisfactory.

> Some ICs were working with the staff that don't want to accept them into their class, who still see the self-contained classrooms for a fix to what they see as a problem, and convincing people to change their thinking.

The complexity of student needs as well as the level of training and support for educators were real factors that needed attention. Some principals expressed frustration with the inclusion coaching model as it was operationalized within the schools. Teacher buy-in was noted as a limiting factor for the success of the IC model.

> I think that particular initiative has not worked all that well. Just because those who need it most, aren't accessing it and that whole, if I had it my way, I would want to see that coach for a more intensive time period, not a once a week drop in because I find that space in between is too much.

School principals also predicted an evolutionary track for the role of ICs. In a transitioned model, the role of a special education or resource teacher could be redefined into a role that supports teacher planning and instruction rather than working exclusively with students.

> I think that the idea is that the coaching role will flip kind of into that resource role over time. I think that was kind of the original thinking, every school would have that expertise in the building in the form that already existed there, but just how that role has changed.

School principals embraced inclusion as a way to move forward towards a more equitable experience for students and a richer learning environment in which students could engage.

> Successful inclusion is when the question of whether a student should or shouldn't participate isn't even brought up, and we're going to automatically assume it's the standard that we include everybody, and plan things that do include everybody and that would be academically as well as socially.

The mindset and practices of the schools surrounding the delivery of services to students with disabilities clearly transitioned from deeply embedded practices about segregated education to equitable and inclusive practices.

> We thought we were doing what was right but I can see now that this is the better move. These students deserve to be around the same age peers and doing what everyone else is doing and quite frankly, we can learn a lot from anybody who is having to work through that and seeing the gains they make as well.

Leadership matters. The relationship between the school leadership and inclusive education practices can be pivotal in the success or failure of promoting inclusive practice (Reid et al., 2018; Theoharis, 2007). Leadership played a fundamental role in shifting both practice and mindset services within this district during this transition.

# EDUCATOR PERSPECTIVES

Research on teacher change suggests that several key factors should be considered when striving for sustained change in pedagogy and practice (Damianidou & Phtiaka, 2018; Gibbs, 2007; Somma, 2018). Educators must first demonstrate the desire to engage in change. If an educator deems change as important and achievable, the likelihood to engage in and make changes to pedagogy and practice is greater (Somma, 2018). Relevant and timely professional development such as support from an expert or coach is one way to promote new learning and risk-taking (Strieker, 2012). Furthermore, in order to challenge and change attitudes and beliefs about inclusion, educators need the opportunity to actively engage in and experience success using inclusive practices in their classrooms (Evans, 1996; Somma, 2018). When the overall goal is to improve the outcomes and opportunities for students with disabilities, engaging in a community of practice and collaborating with colleagues foster the development of strategies and pedagogy.

Educators shared their experiences of change and identified that IC supports were a key component to building their capacity and sense of competency in including children with disabilities into their classrooms. ICs were recognized as team members for bringing a wealth of knowledge as well as providing educators with helpful resources for their own learning.

> Inclusion coach was lovely in terms of understanding that this year was going to be overwhelming. So she would send links or, interesting sort of shorter pieces to read, or ideas, which I was always grateful for, but I wish that there was just more opportunity for the two of us to collaborate and reflect together.

Coaches were appreciated by the educators for helping them to better understand the needs of the students, assisting with program planning, providing a physical resource to support students and supporting the use of technology.

> I've worked closely over the last, I would say, three years now with the coaches to learn the technology I guess that would support their learning and their assessment and that has been a learning curve for me because I'm not very tech-savvy. So it's actually taken me two years to understand how these apps can work and it's only this year that I feel a lot more confident in doing that programming myself and using the coach as a resource and consultant, as opposed to doing it for me.

The educators reported that the ICs helped to support and shape their inclusive and professional practice, 'I have to give her credit for making me feel that what I was doing was suitable and was appropriate, which then encouraged you to do more things', which in turn allowed them to feel more autonomous in their ability to create inclusive classrooms.

The educators recognized how their own perceptions about inclusion were changing. Many felt they had developed a better understanding of what authentic inclusion is as a result of working with a coach.

> Successful inclusion means that each and every student is given the opportunity to work to the best of their ability and it means more, that's more what I believe it to mean than a place. Inclusion isn't about where you learn or the space in which you learn, inclusion means everyone has that opportunity.

Despite the support and positive outcomes including students with disabilities in their classrooms, educators identified challenges as a result of working with an IC. Educators indicated not having enough time to collaborate with an IC or wanting support even after the coach had moved on. They felt that sometimes the ICs were stretched too thin and not able to impact the long-term.

> Inclusion coaches should be there to coach and to instruct and provide us tools, but it doesn't work like that. They come and take pictures and videos of success stories that are not necessarily accurate of what actually happens and when they are here, it's interesting because they offer a kind of support, one-on-one support with the student, which is what we need and then the next day they're back to the board office or back to a different school or a different classroom and it's not sustainable.

When teachers experience authentic participation with students who have disabilities and reflect upon their practice, their perceptions about inclusion can be altered positively (Somma, 2018). For educators to successfully meet the needs of all learners, they need knowledge through skills and training, as well as favourable attitudes towards inclusion (Berry, 2011; Ivey & Reinke, 2002). When school districts and administration provide teachers with opportunities to reflect and challenge their practice and beliefs, the outcome can be changes in both rationale and behaviour around inclusive practice (Chrysostomou & Symeoni-dou, 2017; Pyhältö, Pietarinen, & Soini, 2012). An emphasis on continuing professional development and teacher growth results in a belief instilled in teachers that they will continue to improve their inclusive practice (Berry, 2011; Friend & Bursuck, 2002; McLeskey, Waldron, & Redd, 2014).

## INCLUSION COACH PERSPECTIVES

Coaching within the educational context has been shown to play an important role in supporting teachers' practices (Stover et al., 2011). Coaching models are effective in enhancing inclusive practice by assisting classroom teachers to work with students who have diverse needs (Cale, Delpino, & Myran, 2015). Within the context of this initiative, the role of IC played a pivotal part in the restructuring of service delivery from segregated class settings to an inclusive model. During the process of transitioning, ICs were asked to blog in relation to their experiences. ICs identified stages of growth in their development spanning the entirety of the transition (Gallagher & Bennett, 2018).

It was clear that ICs' mindsets in relation to inclusion were important. The hiring process allowed the school district to put in place experienced educators that shared the vision for desegregation and successful inclusion. The district then provided professional development, learning opportunities and in-group support to ensure that the ICs had opportunities to grow and feel connected to their colleagues.

> I was unsure of the specifics of my role and how I was going to help move inclusion forward within the schools where I was placed. Through professional development and learning opportunities, I have been able to expand my knowledge and understanding of coaching.

Initially, while being concerned about how they would be received by the schools in this new model, many of the ICs expressed relief at the willingness of teachers to allow them access to collaborate. An important part of this was the positive support from principals as well as implementing a policy that was based on invitation from the teachers themselves.

> I was also worried that teachers would not want to work with me. However, my experience has been completely the opposite. The teachers have been incredibly open to having me in their classrooms. I have developed strong bonds with kids I only see once a week. Administrators have been incredibly supportive.

In some cases, communication from principals to teachers about the role of the IC was not explicit, timely or respectful. When teachers were 'voluntold' (requested by their school administrator) that they needed to work with an IC, the ICs noted that the partnership was not as successful.

> I believe I was put into classrooms too fast by administration, my job was not explained well to staff and as a result there was a huge misconception and almost weariness of me amongst staff. As a result of being put into classrooms on the second day of school I ended up working with teachers who were selected by the administration and not as a result of teachers who wanted to work with a coach and improve their practice. All of these factors lead to a very slow start with teaching partners and not an in-depth collaborative inquiry.

It was clear from the ICs' perspective that relationships played an essential part in the success of this initiative. Without time spent on relationship building, collaboration and problem-solving suffered.

> Relationship continues to be my first focus. Until a teacher feels comfortable with having a professional in the classroom with them, it is impossible to move forward. Once this trusting relationship is established, we work together on some of their identified struggles and/or problem of practice.

ICs also expressed frustration with poor communication in relation to what their role actually was.

> For some of my partnerships we are working together very well. For my more negative partners I feel like I am an educational assistant or special education resource teacher in their room trying to build relationships.

ICs related this to any number of factors including messaging from senior administration and/or resistance at the school and classroom level.

While ICs believed they had a lot to share with their teachers, it became apparent to them, over time, that they also had a lot to learn; perspective taking became an essential cornerstone to the success of the inclusion model.

> I think the biggest challenge that I face is making the shift from a 'support teacher' to 'collaborative partner' for a couple of my partnerships. In some of my partnerships we have progressed into a partnership where we are doing some whole class, team planning and teaching around a problem of practice. In some of my partnerships, we have been planning more around the needs of a particular learner and I have been taking more of the lead with regard to next best steps.

Once engaged in the relationship, ICs showed growth in their ability to tailor their interactions in a way that was characterized by mutual respect and their own professional growth.

> I think I see things with a very different lens. I have always believed in inclusion but I see what it is and what it isn't very differently now. I am questioning my language, actions and reactions much more than I ever have in the past.

The role of the IC was fluid. Over time, the ICs recognized that the real change was happening in classrooms and their role was to maintain the inclusive practices and let teachers expand within each setting.

> I need to ask good questions and have courageous conversations with my partners. I feel my role is to allow teachers to be reflective about their practice in order to help them change their mindsets.

Over the course of data collection, it became apparent that enacting the inclusion coaching model was more complex than anticipated. The success of the inclusion coaching model was connected to a number of factors related to the effectiveness of the IC role: inclusive mindsets, administrative support, IC role definition, teachers' feelings of competence and willingness to collaborate, communication, relationships, school and community culture, as well as personality characteristics. All of these factors came into play when collaboration between the ICs and teachers either succeeded or failed.

## CONCLUSION

This chapter has illuminated the components that were synergistically at play during a school district's transition from segregated to inclusive practices. Not surprisingly, the impetus for the transition was driven by the vision of inclusion held by senior administrators who were willing to reallocate resources to make such a transition happen. Thereafter, the essential components that we have focused on in this chapter are the tripartite roles of school-based principals, educators and ICs.

School principals are at the core of the school's mindset related to inclusive practices (Theoharis, 2007). Valuing the diversity of students' needs and belief that all individuals belong in the school community is foundational to the administrator's role. The principal's own mindset needs to be forward-thinking, willing to change, ready to do the necessary work and prepared for resistance (Irvine et al., 2010). The role of the principal is to set the tone in the school setting and work to support all educators as they include students in the classroom community. Principals also played an essential role in the redeployment and support of displaced special education self-contained classroom teachers. Research done with some of these special education teachers indicated that overall, despite some uncertainties, they felt prepared to meet the needs of students with disabilities in inclusive classes and they identified an appreciation for the available supports such as ICs within their schools (Somma, 2018) The presence and active participation of the principal sends an implicit message of accountability and explicit message that collaboration is worth the time investment (Theoharis, 2007). School principals reflected on the importance of staff engagement in their shared goals for inclusion. Furthermore, they recognized their educators need support and resources to enhance expertise and commitment. In this school district, the dedicated time to facilitate change in teachers' practices was delivered by ICs. Clearly, there is an interconnectedness between school leadership and educators' support on the enactment of inclusive practice.

It is important that educators must first demonstrate the desire to engage in the change process. If there is a degree of self-determination to change to inclusive practice and resilience in teacher self-efficacy, then change is possible. Educators need authentic opportunities to 'test-drive' inclusive practices in their actual classrooms and then reflect on and enhance these experiences (Somma, 2018). ICs are able to support new learning from these experiences by collaborating and encouraging reflection as collegial dialogue. Educators who worked with ICs over the course of a year evaluated the IC role as key to building their own capacity and sense of competence in inclusive practices. Interestingly, educators who were supported through this change process also expressed a rich understanding of genuine belonging.

ICs acknowledged the distinctions among teachers that are committed to enhancing their inclusive practices and those that are not. Commitment in beliefs and practices is vital to successful change. When the beliefs of the educators being coached aligned with the school district priorities and beliefs about inclusion, there were fewer barriers for ICs and coaching relationships were enriched (Wlodarczyk, 2019). As such, culture and ethos within the coaching environment were important for educator participation and the effectiveness of inclusion coaching as a newly established role. ICs and educators also expressed that dedicated time to this process of collaboration and reflection is integral; the journey from segregation to inclusion does not happen overnight or in one workshop. Given the dedicated time, the coach must develop relationships with educator colleagues that are premised on mutual trust, confidence and respect.

The overview of the success of this transformation allows educators and administrators in various settings and organizational models to contemplate significant shifts in practice within existing structures utilizing the resources at hand. This transition was a significant transformation of existing segregated service delivery into a predominantly inclusive one. It demonstrates what is possible when thinking and action align and provides a template for transition towards inclusive practice.

## REFERENCES

Bennett, S. (2009). *Including students with exceptionalities*. Research monograph 16. The literacy and numeracy Secretariat, with the Ontario Association of Deans of education. Retrieved from http://www.edu.gov.on.ca/eng/literacynumeracy/inspire/research/Bennett.pdf

Bennett, S., Dworet, D., Gallagher, T., & Somma, M. (2019). *Special education in Ontario schools* (8th ed.). St. David's, ON: Highland Press.

Berry, R. (2011). Voices of experience: General education teachers on teaching students with disabilities. *International Journal of Inclusive Education, 15*(6), 627–648. doi:10.1080/13603110903278035

Cale, M., Delpino, C., & Myran, S. (2015). Instructional leadership for special education in small to mid-size urban school districts. *Advances in Educational Administration, 22*, 155–172. doi:10.1108/S1479-366020150000022018

Capper, C. A., Theoharis, G., & Sebastian, J. (2006). Toward a framework for preparing leaders for social justice. *Journal of Educational Administration, 44*(3), 209–224. doi:10.1108/09578230610664814

Chrysostomou, M., & Symeonidou, S. (2017). Education for disability equality through disabled people's life stories and narratives: Working and learning together in a school-based professional development programme for inclusion. *European Journal of Special Needs Education, 32*(4), 572–585. doi:10.1080-08856257.2017.1297574

Damianidou, E., & Phtiaka, H. (2018). Implementing inclusion in disabling settings: The role of teachers' attitudes and practices. *International Journal of Inclusive Education, 22*(10), 1078–1092. doi:10.1080/13603116.2017.1415381

Elish-Piper, L., & L'Allier, S. K. (2011). Examining the relationship between literacy coaching and student reading gains in grades K-3. *The Elementary School Journal, 112*(1), 83–106.

Evans, L. (1996). Understanding teacher morale and job satisfaction. *Teaching and Teacher Education, 13*(8), 831–845.

Friend, M., & Bursuck, W. (2002). *Including students with special needs: A practical guide for classroom teachers.* Boston, MA: Allyn & Bacon.

Gallagher, T. L., & Bennett, S. (2018). The six 'P' model: Principles of coaching for inclusion for inclusion coaches. *International Journal of Mentoring and Coaching in Education, 7*(1), 19–34.

Gibbs, S. (2007). Teachers' perceptions of efficacy: Beliefs that support inclusion or segregation. *Educational and Child Psychology, 24*(3), 47–53.

Guskey, T. (2002). Professional development and teacher change. *Teachers and Teaching, 8*(3), 381–391. doi:10.1080/135406002100000512

Hardy, I. (2009). Teacher professional development: A sociological study of senior educators' PD priorities in Ontario. *Canadian Journal of Education, 32*(3), 509–532.

Irvine, A., Lupart, J., Loreman, T., & McGhie-Richmond, D. (2010). Educational leadership to create authentic inclusive schools: The experiences of principals in a Canadian rural school district. *Exceptionality Education International, 20*(2), 70–88.

Ivey, J., & Reinke, K. (2002). Pre-service teachers attitudes towards inclusion in a non-traditional classroom. *Electronic Journal for Inclusive Education, 1*(6), 4.

Kise, J. (2006). *Differentiated coaching: A framework for helping teachers change.* Thousand Oaks, CA: Corwin Press.

Knight, J. (2011). What good coaches do. *Educational Leadership, 69*(2), 18–22.

Lupart, J. L., & Porath, M. (2009). Building a better future for Canadian students. In J. L. Lupart, A. McKeough, M. Porath, L. Phillips, & V. Timmons (Eds.), *The challenges of student diversity in Canadian schools: Essays on building a better future for exceptional children* (pp. 1–14). Markham, ON: Fitzhenry and Whiteside.

Lynch, J., & Ferguson, K. (2010). Reflections of elementary school literacy coaches on practice: Roles and perspectives. *Canadian Journal of Education, 33*(1), 199–227.

MacDonald, M. A., & Green, L. W. (2001). Reconciling concept and context: The dilemma of implementation in school-based health promotion. *Health Education & Behavior, 28*(6), 749–768. doi:10.1177/109019810102800607

MacLeod, A., & Emes, J. (2019). *Education spending in public schools in Canada.* Vancouver, BC: Fraser Institute.

McLeskey, J., Waldron, N. L., & Redd, L. (2014). A case study of a highly effective, inclusive elementary school. *The Journal of Special Education, 8*(1), 59–70. doi:10.1177/0022466912440455

Mulholland, M., & O'Connor, U. (2016). Collaborative classroom practice for inclusion: Perspectives of classroom teachers and learning support/resource teachers. *International Journal of Inclusive Education, 20*(10), 1070–1083.

Praisner, C. L. (2003). Attitudes of elementary school principals toward the inclusion of students with disabilities. *Exceptional Children, 69*(2), 135–145.

Pyhältö, K., Pietarinen, J., & Soini, T. (2012). Do comprehensive school teachers perceive themselves as active professional agents in school reforms? *Journal of Educational Change, 13*(1), 95–116. doi:10.1007/s10833-011-9171-0

Reid, L., Bennett, S., Specht, S., White, R., Somma, M., Li, X., … Patel, A. (2018). If inclusion means everyone, why not me? Retrieved from https://www.inclusiveeducationresearch.ca/docs/why-not-me.pdf

Ryan, J. (2006). Inclusive leadership and social justice for schools. *Leadership and Policy in Schools, 5*(1), 3–17. doi:10.1080/15700760500483995

Somma, M. (2018). From segregation to inclusion: Special educators' experiences of change. *International Journal of Inclusive Education, 24*(4), 381–394. doi:10.1080/13603116.2018.1464070

Stephens, D., & Mills, H. (2014). Coaching as inquiry: The South Carolina reading initiative. *Reading & Writing Quarterly, 30*(3), 190–206.

Stover, K., Kissel, B., Haag, K., & Shoniker, R. (2011). Differentiated coaching: Fostering reflection with teachers. *The Reading Teacher, 64*(7), 498–509.

Strieker, T. (2012). Effects of job-embedded professional development on inclusion of students with disabilities in content area classrooms: Results of a three-year study. *International Journal of Inclusive Education, 16*(10), 1047–1065.

Theoharis, G. (2007). Social justice educational leaders and resistance: Toward a theory of social justice leadership. *Educational Administration Quarterly, 43*(2), 221–258. doi:10.1177/0013161 X06293717

Toll, C. A. (2007). *Lenses on literacy coaching: Conceptualizations, functions and outcomes.* Norwood, MA: Christopher-Gordon Publishers.

Walpole, S., & McKenna, M. C. (2012). *The literacy coach's handbook: A guide to research-based practice.* New York, NY: Guilford Press.

Wlodarczyk, K. (2019). Developing educator capacity using job–embedded coaching: A collective case study. Unpublished Doctoral dissertation. McMaster University, Hamilton, ON.

Woodcock, S., & Woolfson, L. M. (2019). Are leaders leading the way with inclusion? Teachers' perceptions of systemic support and barriers towards inclusion. *International Journal of Educational Research, 93*, 232–242. doi:10.1016/j.ijer.2018.11.004

# SOKA EDUCATION PHILOSOPHY AS A FOUNDATION FOR TEACHER PREPARATION IN CREATING INCLUSIVE EDUCATION

Joseph Seyram Agbenyega, Kiiko Ikegami and Corine Rivalland

## ABSTRACT

*Current global shifts in education towards inclusive early childhood education are deeply engineered by the crisis of educational exclusion. In responding to exclusion, teachers have mainly utilized dominant western theories to plan and implement inclusive teaching. In this chapter, we draw on a non-western philosophy, a Nichiren Buddhist (Soka) philosophy, to provide a 'kaleidoscopic' lens through which to create inclusive educational learning spaces that engender full participation of all children. The Soka education philosophy is a humanist concept which can guide teachers when preparing to create inclusive education. The aims of this chapter are threefold: The first is an exploration of the Nichiren Buddhist (Soka) philosophy. The second aim is to highlight how this philosophy can enable teachers to unleash the unlimited potential of children in inclusive learning settings. Thirdly, we argue that grounding early childhood teacher education in this philosophy can help improve the effectiveness of inclusive educational experience for all children.*

**Keywords**: Inclusive education; Nichiren Buddhism; positive relationships; Soka education; teacher preparation; unlimited potential

## INTRODUCTION

The global shifts in education towards inclusive early childhood education are deeply engineered by the crisis of educational exclusion. Educational exclusion

Resourcing Inclusive Education
International Perspectives on Inclusive Education, Volume 15, 117–132
Copyright © 2021 by Emerald Publishing Limited
ISSN: 1479-3636/doi:10.1108/S1479-363620210000015010

goes far beyond access and involves multiple factors such as processes of teaching, acceptance, belonging, recognition and full participation of all children (Tarabini, Jacovkis, & Montes, 2018). To address the issues of exclusion in early childhood education, many countries are utilizing inclusive teaching principles in their unique contexts to promote quality education. Research suggests that the efficiency of inclusive education depends on the quality of the teachers who deliver the inclusive programs (Desimone & Garet, 2015). Teachers need a clear understanding of children's diversity and inclusive pedagogy during their initial training to support all children to learn effectively, in inclusive early childhood educational settings (Carrington et al., 2012).

In reference to teacher preparation for inclusion, Western child development and educational theories such as Vygotsky's cultural-historical theory, Rogoff's socio-cultural theory, Bronfenbrenner's bioecological theory and Piaget's cognitive theories have featured prominently in early childhood education (Boyd & Cutcher, 2015). However, little is known about the relevance of Nichiren Buddhist and Soka theoretical perspectives for preparing teachers to implement inclusive practice in early childhood educational settings. The ability of teachers to understand and integrate theory into their professional practice is considered by researchers as one of the important components in the provision of quality early childhood education (Dahlberg, Moss, & Pence, 2013). This chapter draws on key Nichiren Buddhist (Soka) philosophical concepts of happiness, value-creation, greater self, human revolution and unlimited potential to provide a 'kaleidoscopic' lens through which to create inclusive educational learning spaces that engender full participation of all children.

We used the term 'kaleidoscopic lens' as a metaphor to reflect teachers' craft or artistic work. Just as kaleidoscopes enable the visualization of colours and shapes in multiple and diverse ways, applying this concept to the Nichiren Buddhist (Soka) philosophy can assist teacher educators and teachers to reimagine their professional practice and transform the ways they perceive every child as unique and capable of learning. Again, this metaphorical conceptualization is a remarkable way to recruit intrinsic motivation, joy and wonder into teaching. Evidence suggests that theories should not be ignored, instead, they should be viewed as essential conceptual tools that support teachers to frame their teaching in ways that contribute to high-quality practices leading to enhanced learning and core developmental outcomes for all children (Chan, 2016).

## NICHIREN DAISHONIN BUDDHISM

Nichiren Buddhism espouses that 'all living beings have the potential to achieve enlightenment' (Soka Gakkai, 1999, p. 3). Enlightenment in Nichiren Buddhist philosophy refers to a condition in which one enjoys the highest wisdom, vitality, good fortune, confidence and other positive qualities of life (Soka Gakkai, 2002). The 'Lotus Sutra', which contains the most sacred writings of Nichiren Buddhism espouses that 'all people equally and without exception possess Buddha nature'. The message of the Lotus Sutra is 'to encourage people's faith in their own Buddha nature, their own inherent capacity for wisdom, courage and compassion' (Soka Gakkai International [SGI], 2014a, para. 1). Elements of these philosophical ideas relate to the notion of self-efficacy or the belief in one's capabilities. Indeed, the main belief within the Nichiren Buddhist philosophy is that the Lotus Sutra would lead people to become enlightened so that they can create happiness out of their own determination as well as through the caring support of others (Soka Gakkai, 2002; Soka Gakkai International [SGI], 2013b).

## NICHIREN BUDDHISM AND THE DEVELOPMENT OF SOKA EDUCATIONAL PHILOSOPHY

Tsunesaburo Makiguchi (18711944), Josei Toda (19001958) and Daisaku Ikeda (1928present) are regarded as key people in the development of Soka educational philosophy. Makiguchi's version of Soka educational philosophy draws heavily from Nichiren Buddhist perspectives (Ikeda, 2010) with the main ideas being 'value-creation' *Soka Kyoikugaku Taikei* (The theory of value-creating pedagogy). The concept of value-creation espouses a strong belief in the unlimited potential of every person which aligns with humanistic and holistic education (Soka Gakkai International [SGI], 2013a). Nichiren Buddhist perspective conceptualizes the relationship between teacher and students as 'mentor and disciple' where both work together, share knowledge with the mutual purpose to developing and enhancing the happiness of all to 'alleviate suffering' (Soka Gakkai International [SGI], 2017a, para. 1). In this sense, the mentor and disciple act as a key chain to pass the spirit and belief for the promotion of other people's happiness which education at any level should espouse. Being a disciple is to strive in the same manner as the mentor, through this relationship of mentor and disciple, one person can inspire others and bring out the best from them (Soka Gakkai International [SGI], 2017a).

## KALEIDOSCOPIC LENS OF SOKA EDUCATIONAL PHILOSOPHY

### *Lens 1: Indestructible Happiness*

Nichiren Buddhist Soka education theory emphasizes the pursuit of lifelong *indestructible happiness* for each child (Ikeda, 2010; Makiguchi, 2004). Ikeda (1987) elucidated that indestructible happiness is found when the individual does not easily give up in the face of challenges but overcomes difficulties and challenges irrespective of their circumstances. It is argued that the act of overcoming difficulties and challenges generates a strong spirit for success in oneself (Goulah & Ito, 2012). This kind of spirit is nurtured from within a deep reflective disposition that enables a person to view every problem as an opportunity for self-improvement or innovation (Soka Gakkai International [SGI], 2017b).

In terms of inclusive education, research internationally identified several challenges that negatively impact on teachers' practice. These include challenging behaviours (Carrington et al., 2012), lack of time, workload issues, lack of resources and inadequate funding (Desimone & Garet, 2015), and overcrowded classrooms and lack of teacher skills (de Boer, Pijl, & Minnaert, 2011). Many teachers may give up on inclusive education when they are challenged by these factors that destroy their happiness to teach. In this sense, Soka-informed philosophy for preparing teachers to teach in inclusive early childhood programs can focus on the happiness and fulfilment of the learner and teachers (Ikeda, 2010). Makiguchi (1989) argued that happiness produces a passion for individuals to persevere at things to produce long-term results. According to Rock (2009), when people are happy, there is a release of a high level of dopamine in the brain that leads to interest, joy and engagement to do difficult things, to take risks, to think deeply about issues and develop new solutions. Consequently, happiness leads to deep-level learning. Therefore, training teachers to understand the role of happiness in learning and their own teaching can help them support their students to experience positive emotions, perceive more options when trying to solve problems, solve more non-linear problems that require insight, collaborate better and generally perform better on tasks.

### Lens 2: Value Creation

In Ikeda's (2010) view, the development of a sense of happiness is based on the idea of *value creation* achieved through big and passionate goals. The notion of 'value' in Soka education is the 'positive aspects of reality that are brought forth or generated when we creatively engage with the challenges of daily life' (Soka Gakkai International [SGI], 2017c, para. 2). In the Soka tradition, 'value' is not something that exists as an outcome, instead, it is something an individual takes as their own responsibility to create. Ikeda (2010) explains that value may be considered as the relevance or impact an object or event assumed by the individual. He concluded that:

> Value arises from the relationship between the evaluating subject and the object of evaluation. If either changes, it is only obvious that the perceived value will change. The differences and shifts in ethical codes throughout history provide but one of the more outstanding proofs of the mutability of value (Ikeda, 2010, p. 16).

Therefore, such conceptualizations of 'value' are considered an integral part of teachers' competence to drive their support for children to create value within themselves. It is argued that by implementing the idea of value creation into teaching and learning, individuals can develop to become ethical global citizens (Soka Gakuen Educational Foundation, 2009). Ethical citizens are considered as educated and cultured individuals who have a profound awareness of the relationships between self, nature and society (Goulah & Ito, 2012). By fostering the concept of value creation in early childhood teacher preparation for inclusion, it is possible that first of all, teachers will identify with inclusive education as an effective means to avoid discrimination and exclusion because they would see the possibilities in every child to create and add value to society (Soriano & Hughes, 2018). Secondly, it can assist early childhood teachers to recognize inclusive education as the provision of high-quality education for all through which to enact excellence and equity. While all education levels fundamentally require the principles of inclusion to drive their practices, inclusion must start at the early childhood level.

The concept of value creation can challenge those preparing teachers to question and transform individual and societal values, enabling education reform to better respond to individual needs. Research found that when teachers 'are clear about the relationship between values and actions, that they make inclusive values explicit, and design educational activities that uphold inclusive values' (Mergler, Carrington, Kimber, & Bland, 2016, p. 21). Indeed, the notion of value creation can help teachers to develop inclusion practice as a way of life rather as appendages of education.

### Lens 3: Greater Self

The third conceptualization in Soka philosophy relates to a *greater self* as a driver in the creation of value (Soka Gakkai International [SGI], 2017b). The notion of a greater self is drawn from a Buddhist concept which describes 'a sense of self that can fully identify and empathize with the suffering of others and is thus motivated to alleviate that suffering' (Soka Gakkai International [SGI], 2017b, para. 2). Soka theory regarding greater self is the development of an individual's sense of responsibility and commitment, growth and capacities, so they can contribute to the well-being of others and their community (Soka Gakkai International [SGI], 2014b). In early childhood inclusive education, one of the fundamental requirements is teachers' ability to provide educational spaces that promote the well-being and belonging of all children (Carrington et al., 2012). Thus, the concept of greater self describes a fundamental process of inner transformation teachers can receive in training to be able to break through the constraints of a *lesser self*, bound by self-concern and ego and cater to the needs of all children.

### Lens 4: Human Revolution

Another key conceptualization in the Soka education philosophy is *human revolution* or inner transformation (Soka Gakkai International [SGI], 2014b, para. 2). In the Nichiren Buddhist perspective, this is referred to as 'changing poison into medicine':

> The process of changing poison into medicine begins when we approach difficult experiences as an opportunity to reflect on ourselves and to strengthen and develop our courage and compassion...Suffering can thus serve as a springboard for a deeper experience of happiness. From the perspective of Buddhism, inherent in all negative experiences is this profound positive potential (Soka Gakkai International [SGI], 2015, para. 67).

The concept of human revolution is a widely used term in Soka theory to describe the development of greater self. It is about transforming oneself at the very core of life by identifying and challenging difficulties that inhibit the full expression of an individual's positive potential and humanity (Soka Gakkai International [SGI], 2014b). In regards to inclusive education teachers, inner transformation is needed to foster new beliefs and dispositions that support inclusive practice (Dadvand, 2015). In self-transformation, individuals gradually expand their lives, conquer negative and destructive tendencies and ultimately attain greater self. This is accomplished by 'identifying and challenging those things which inhibit the full expression of our positive potential and humanity' (Soka Gakkai International [SGI], 2014b, para. 5).

*Lens 5: Unlimited Potential*

The concept of 'unlimited potential' in the Nichiren Buddhism perspective refers to individuals' boundless potential future development and the ability of all individuals to create new opportunities in life (Garrison, Hickman, & Ikeda, 2014). This contrasts with frequently found definitions in the literature that often refers to a level of intelligence or abilities associated with 'gifted' or 'able children' (Young & Tyre, 1995). Young and Tyre point out that this exclusive association and interpretation of human potential demands that 'all children enjoy exposure to all that is worthwhile and life-enhancing' (1995, p. 31).

Nichiren Buddhism theory argues that a Buddha nature exists in every person, and each person has potential Buddhahood (Soka Gakkai International [SGI], 2013c). It goes on to argue that an individual's 'Buddha nature' can be developed through human practice. This draws relevance to the preparation of teachers in ways that we want them to practice their craft. According to Nichiren Buddhist theory, Buddhahood is not a static condition, it is fluid and dynamic as individuals continue to develop throughout life (Soka Gakkai International [SGI], 2013c). This suggests that continuous professional development of teachers can help them discover their own unlimited potential. Teachers who identify with the concept of unlimited potential can support the development of children's unlimited potential. It is argued that the fluidity and dynamism of Buddhahood enable individuals to unleash their own 'unlimited potential' (Soka Gakkai International [SGI], 2013c). This leads to a potential not only associated with a particular group or ability rather but also it suggests that all people can create positive values and experiences to enhance each other's lives.

The question is how can the five lenses discussed in this paper inform inclusive early childhood teacher professional development in terms of program planning; theory-driven pedagogy; theory-driven assessment; and their capacity to conduct theory-driven reflections of teaching and children's learning? We present a tabular description of these aspects after which we draw conclusions based on our extrapolations.

Table 1 provides a sample framework on how to prepare early childhood teachers to draw on the five concepts identified in the Nichiren Buddhist Soka-based theory to implement the four pragmatic areas of theory-driven planning, a theory-driven pedagogy, a theory-driven assessment and a theory-driven reflection on teaching and learning in early childhood educational settings. The

*Table 1.* A Matrix of Nichiren Buddhist Soka-Based Concepts and High-Quality Inclusive Early Childhood Practice.

| | Indestructible Happiness | Human Revolution | Greater Self | Value Creation | Unlimited Potential |
|---|---|---|---|---|---|
| **Theory-driven planning** | • Activities are designed in ways that consider each child's current knowledge, ideas, culture, abilities and interests<br>• Planning focuses on building a passion for learning<br>• Planning incorporates an opportunity for children to express their ideas | • Activities are designed to stimulate children's energy<br>• Activities encourage children through the use of positive words like 'yes, you can do it'<br>• Planning incorporates activities that promote positive emotions | • A variety of materials are sourced for children to manipulate<br>• Develop children's self-efficacy<br>• Accountability<br>• Planning incorporates strategic vision and principles for self-determination<br>• Planning incorporates short and long-term goals to support children's learning | • Children's meaning-making is a central focus of planning<br>• Planning recognizes a strong link between the environment and the child's learning and development<br>• Planning provides a space for children to set their own learning goals | • Planning considers children's cultural contexts<br>• Set tough but achievable goals<br>• Planning respects each child's different skills and abilities<br>• Knowledge of each child's learning and abilities is factored into planning |
| **Theory-driven pedagogy** | • Teaching creates an opportunity for harmonious passion<br>• Teaching provides scaffolding for children's learning<br>• Observation is central to learning about children's capabilities | • Teachers are open to children's ideas<br>• Encouragement and support are used to enable children to overcome difficulties/challenges<br>• Teachers pay greater attention to children's voices, feelings and individual needs | • Teachers encourage engagement with others<br>• Children are supported to cultivate positive emotions and build positive relationships | • Teachers create greater awareness of teaching opportunities to build on children's learning<br>• Children are fostered to become active learners<br>• Teachers foster children's sense of hope | • Teachers believe that each child can be excellent<br>• Teachers encourage perseverance and foster children's sense of compassion, respect and tolerance |

*Table 1.* (*Continued*)

| | Indestructible Happiness | Human Revolution | Greater Self | Value Creation | Unlimited Potential |
|---|---|---|---|---|---|
| **Theory-driven assessment** | • Teachers provide constructive and clear feedback<br>• Children's well-being and emotional development are key to assessment | • Teachers encourage children to self-reflect on how they can improve their own learning<br>• Teachers involve children in their assessment process, such as creating a folio to record their own learning | • Teachers encourage children to self-reflect on what they do well within their learning<br>• Continuous documentation is part of the assessment process | • Teachers focus on children's self-concept and self-esteem | • Teachers provide different forms of assessment and use documentation to track children's learning and provide strategies for improvement |
| **Theory-driven reflection** | • Teachers think positively and appreciate what children have achieved<br>• Teachers foster hope and determination in oneself<br>• Teachers use continuous self-reflection on children's well-being and learning | • Teachers reflect each day on their failures and challenges and what they have learnt from children<br>• Teachers reflect on own beliefs and self-study to improve their capabilities | • Teachers set and reflect on goals to achieve quality teaching practice<br>• Teachers reflect on individual attitudes and behaviours<br>• Teachers reflect on children's holistic development | • Daily journal reflections on teaching strategies and methods are incorporated into practice<br>• Teacher reflections focus on areas to improve, grow and take responsibility | • Teachers reconfirm that each child has unlimited potential<br>• Teachers reflect on their own subjective thoughts<br>• Teachers gain professional strength through others |

relationship between theoretical concepts and practices can help teachers to see beyond their immediate classrooms and to have a deeper understanding of their practice (Dahlberg et al., 2013). Soka education perspectives encourage wisdom and passion allowing early childhood inclusive teachers to overcome challenges, transform their lives and contribute to the happiness of all children (Ikeda, 2010).

In reference to the human revolution concept, teacher training can focus on deepening teachers' concept of continuous development of the sense of self-awareness and self-reflection as well as how to take responsibility for transforming their own professional lives. This is a prerequisite for creating positive classroom practices based on compassion and respect for the dignity of all children. Ikeda (2010) elucidated that a human revolution perspective can drive teachers to support each child to bring forth their own unlimited potential from deep within themselves. This means every teacher needs to be able to implement programs that lead children to develop a disposition of life build on empathy where they are able to contribute to others' development. Ikeda (2010) argued that to create a better world, the fundamental answer can be found in people themselves. In this respect, programs and teaching that encourage the idea of human revolution is the most fundamental goal for teachers, and at the same time, the most necessary revolution for transforming inclusive education to attain high-quality levels (Soka Gakkai International [SGI], 2014b).

In reference to the matrix in Table 1, early childhood teachers must be trained to be conscious of the conditions of their educational settings to enact quality practices that add value to children's lives (Ikeda, 2010). For example, the belief in achieving a 'greater self' could potentially impact how teachers think about children and how they organize learning activities in and outside of their classrooms. Theoretical reflection, for example, can provide the tools for teachers to question their own practice in relation to each child's well-being, considering their feelings and listening to the child's voices. This process can expand and extend the lesser self of a teacher and children towards the idea of a greater self (Soka Gakkai International [SGI], 2017b).

Ikeda made use of a Buddhist metaphor to describe each individual as 'the flowering of the personality that emanates from the depths of life with the statement that each person's individuality is as unique as cherry, plum, peach or damson blossoms' (2010, p. 168). This positions every person as unique, equal, precious and full of unlimited potential and subsequently able to contribute and construct a positive functional role in society. Reflecting on such arguments, the Nichiren Buddhist view of unlimited potential is that each child can be developed to contribute to the collective good of their society in which they live.

Context is of such importance in early childhood education because of the interactions that abound. This theoretical lens can guide teachers to understand children's characteristics, the lessons being taught, conceptions of learning, beliefs about assessment and even the teacher's personal happiness (Chan, 2016). But it does not end there because other variables interact such as the curriculum materials, the socioeconomic status of the community, peer effects in the school and so forth which theory can help teachers to see. Because of the myriad interactions, doing educational theory in early childhood, teacher education seems very difficult (Nolan & Raban, 2015). However, using theory to develop teachers' inclusive practice in early childhood provides rich tools for understanding oneself against expectations or standards, personal and stakeholder values and an understanding of what professionalism of the early childhood teacher entails.

Makiguchi (1997) expressed that each individual child must be valued regardless of differences in their culture, gender, age or birth circumstances. The philosophy of Soka regards education as a humanistic tool for the lifelong pursuit of self-awareness, wisdom and development (Bethel, 1989). Thus, situating the quality of early childhood inclusive education in Soka theory, teachers can be positioned to support each child to bring forth his or her potential from deep within and the ability to empathize with other's feelings (Ikeda, 2010).

## IMPLICATIONS FOR INCLUSIVE EARLY CHILDHOOD EDUCATION

Soka education seeks to draw-out the unlimited potential of each teacher and child in the hope that they will ultimately contribute to society and ultimately make a positive contribution to world peace. From a Soka educational perspective, it is possible to see the goodness in others rather than focussing on their limitations. Soka education philosophy espouses that by focussing on the potential within others in addition to compassion, respect and tolerance, one can lead others to the construction of a harmonious and supportive society. Ikeda stated that 'a great human revolution in just a single individual will help achieve a change in the destiny of a nation, and further, can even enable a change in the destiny of all humankind' (Soka Gakkai International [SGI], 2014c, para. 1). Ikeda (2010) further explained the possibility of inner transformation as a process of bringing forth our full human potential which can lead to individual empowerment and constructive action. Ultimately, the goal of Soka education is to develop teachers towards creating a peaceful, happy and sustainable world through education.

This belief in individuals must be connected to how teacher training for inclusive practice can assist teachers to encourage children to value their own unlimited potential, as this can impact their self-esteem (individual feelings and attitudes toward oneself), self-efficacy (belief in one's capabilities), self-confidence (linked to initiative, self-motivation, resilience and empathy) and self-belief (Rhodes, 2012). Similarly, associating these perspectives with early year's education brings into focus how individual children can value themselves and how teachers should perceive the unlimited potential of each child. Rhodes argues that 'self-belief may be an important bridge between the potential to lead and subsequent high performance' (2012, pp. 439–440). The value of self-belief is an important part of a quality individual inner life, which is highlighted within the Soka education system, as this creates a sense of courage to overcome difficulties and challenges in life.

As we addressed at the beginning of this paper, although theoretical under-standing and the classroom practices of an educator may not always be aligned in the classroom, we believe that the discussion on the application of theory and classroom practices are inevitable and valuable in teacher training for inclusive education. From a Soka educational viewpoint, the belief in the Soka educational concept of unlimited potential is a major factor in classroom practice as teachers are the ones who ultimately decide the detailed direction of children's learning (Hong Kong Bureau of Education, 2013). Soka theoretical concept of unlimited potential for classroom practice can guide teachers to establish an inclusive environment, positive relationships and child-centred learning in a classroom setting.

## Inclusive Learning Environment

As we discussed earlier, when the attitudes of teachers are drawn from a Soka educational philosophy to embrace individual children with a perspective that each child has unlimited potential with different strengths or capabilities, this can potentially lead to establishing greater inclusive environments. The policy guide-lines in respect of inclusion provided by UNESCO (2009) state that successfully creating an inclusive environment is linked to teachers' attitudes and expectations (Chan, 2016). Teachers' respect for diversity and value for differences such as gender, cultural identities and language backgrounds can be informed by all the five lenses we have presented in this chapter. Respect for diversity leads to orchestrating an inclusive environment which respects as well as response to chil-dren's differences 'in ways that include them in, rather than exclude them from, what is ordinarily available in the daily life of the classroom' (Florian & Black-Hawkins, 2011, p. 814). We argue that when teacher learning incorporates codes of respect for the child and believe they all have unlimited potential and are unique, this may positively impact the teachers' perspectives in creating a more inclusive teaching practice. An inclusive environment is not simply for groups of children physically together in a classroom, but also includes the notion that each child has opportunities to embrace their own cultural values, contribute their thoughts and skills to promote equitable practices, which is thought to contribute to the enhancement of collaborative learning and development (Ikegami & Agbenyega, 2014; Klibthong, Fridani, Ikegami, & Agbenyega, 2014).

Monsen, Ewing, and Kwoka (2014, p. 113) illustrated that teachers can be trained to create classroom learning environments that enact 'satisfaction, cohesiveness and lowered levels of friction, competitiveness, and difficulty' through the ideas of greater self and happiness. This would subsequently lead to an inclusive environment where all children feel actively engaged, safe and welcome (Ikegami & Agbenyega, 2014). Training teachers for inclusive practice must focus on teacher's understanding of the learning environment that cele-brates differences as part of everyday life as well as striving to value and encourage a sense of diversity within each child (Agbenyega & Klibthong, 2020). Purdue, Gordon-Burns, Gunn, Madden, and Surtees (2009) emphasized that a perceived sense of respect for children is an essential element in creating an inclusive environment where children's potential is embraced and their voices are heard in the classroom setting, enabling them to contribute to a sense of belonging and well-being.

### Positive Relationships

From a Soka education philosophy perspective, it is important that teachers have adequate skills to support each child to develop and grow to achieve their unlimited potential and with a sense of happiness (Ikeda, 2010). Makiguchi (2006), cited in Ikegami and Grieshaber (2017), argued that people are shaped by interactions with other people, and there is no genuine education without earnest life-to-life interactions and inspirations. Inspirations refer to each person having a positive influence and tapping into one's other lives. These interactions and inspirations simulate supportive and positive relationships.

It is argued that supportive and positive teacher-child relationships can reduce the risk of a child failing at school and are correlated with successful education (Hamre & Pianta, 2001). Similarly, positive relationships can contribute to children's cognitive and social-emotional outcomes (Klibthong et al., 2014; Spilt, Koomen, & Mantizcopoulos, 2010). Studies highlight that the interrelated teacher-child relationship encourages a child to actively participate and make active decisions which are also an important element of quality early childhood education (Theobald, Danby, & Ailwood, 2011). Rey, Smith, Yoon, Somers, and Barnett (2007) predicted that positive reinforcement for young children would lead to greater interest and involvement in learning as well as resulting in better behaviour. Importantly, children would value themselves and create changes within themselves, so a powerful transformation takes place (Suleiman-Gonzalez, 2004). Therefore, this is essential for teachers to value each child's unlimited potential and to appreciate a child's perspectives and ultimately to cultivate supportive and respectful relationships.

### Child-Centred Learning

As discussed, ascribing to the notion that every child has unlimited potential, has implications for child-centred inclusive practices. Child-centred learning refers to children having some level of control of their own learning (Hong Kong Bureau of Education, 2013). This may involve negotiated agreements in respect of the children's roles, rights and responsibilities relating to their learning (Arthur, Beecher, Death, Dockett, & Farmer, 2014). When teachers respect and appreciate that each child has unlimited potential, they embrace that individuals learn differently and create space to genuinely listen to children's voices. Child-centred learning often occurs when children have opportunities to voice their thoughts during a learning process and contribute their views to their learning (Humphreys, 2012). Effective learning recognizes that children are able to generate knowledge with others, instead of simply focussing on independent knowledge acquisition (Watkins, Carnell, & Lodge, 2007). Humphreys (2012, p. 437) identifies child-centred learning in the classroom as the essence of promoting effective learning which may create a participative-style of teaching that involves 'collaborative learning and student decision making'.

Indeed, there has been an increase in research into how children's views and voices contribute to meaning-making with adults (Humphreys, 2012; Watkins et al., 2007). The level of child-centred learning found within early childhood education settings varies across a wide range of classroom approaches. For example, teachers who believe that children have unlimited potential allow them to select activity and materials, make choices of activities in which to participate, have input into learning modes and influence curriculum planning. The common thread found in these different expressions focuses on allowing children to make decisions and to provide opportunities for them to provide input and have their voices recognized and learning aligned with their interests.

As media technology is now widely used throughout contemporary society—children often have opportunities to access information that was once the exclusive domain of adults (Kincheloe, 2004). Taking into consideration the notion of unlimited potential, teachers can rethink and reshape their roles to address changes in society (Kincheloe, 2004). This means they can participate in, support children's learning and engage in critical thinking instead of dominating children. Makiguchi (2006) emphasized that teachers must be aware that education should be embedded in humanity to enhance the happiness and value of others in society. Soka educational philosophy engages education on the primacy of the child and does not simply fulfil the needs of authority, commerce, teachers or parental expectations and demands. Therefore, teachers who engage in child-centred learning are not simply providing top-down directives to children, without any questions or reflections. Teachers can be viewed as researchers and knowledge generators who work with children (Kincheloe, 2008). This is in contrast to the traditional role of teachers who often use a transmission approach to teaching children.

## CONCLUSION

This chapter addresses Nichiren Buddhist philosophy as applied to Soka education and the potential implications for teacher education for inclusion and practices in early childhood settings. Nichiren Buddhist philosophies and Soka theoretical perspectives can be made visible in practice through a theory-driven program planning; theory-driven pedagogy; theory-driven assessment; and theory-driven reflections on teaching and children's learning. Ultimately, the concepts of happiness, greater self, human revolution and unlimited potential have benefits for establishing inclusive environments, increased positive relationships and encouraging child-centred learning. Nichiren Buddhist philosophy and Soka education approaches provide alternative theoretical perspectives that facilitate positive changes leading to teachers becoming open to alternative interpretations, new meanings and new configurations in classroom practices

(Dahlberg et al., 2013). Theory can help teachers transform children's learning beyond the prescribed curriculum, procedures, teacher's qualifications and educational policy directives, enabling all children to become ethical global citizens.

# REFERENCES

Agbenyega, J. S., & Klibthong, S. (2020). Exploring Thai early childhood teachers' experiences of inclusive teaching practices: A qualitative study. *Australian Education Researcher*. doi:10.1007/s13384-020-00380-1.

Arthur, L., Beecher, B., Death, E., Dockett, S., & Farmer, S. (2014). *Programming and planning in early childhood settings* (6th ed.). South Melbourne, VIC: Cengage Learning Australia.

Bethel, D. (1989). Introduction. In D. Bethel (Ed.), *Education for creative living: Ideas and proposals of Tsunesaburo Makiguchi* (pp. 3–14). Ames, IA: Iowa State University Press.

de Boer, A., Pijl, S. J., & Minnaert, A. (2011). Regular primary schoolteachers' attitudes towards inclusive education: A review of the literature. *International Journal of Inclusive Education, 15*, 331–353.

Boyd, W., & Cutcher, L. (2015). Learning from early childhood philosophy, theory and pedagogy: Inspiring effective art education. *Australasian Journal of Early Childhood, 40*(1), 91–98.

Carrington, S., MacArthur, J., Kearney, A., Kimber, M., Mercer, L., Morton, M., & Rutherford, G. (2012). Towards an inclusive education for all. In S. Carrington & J. MacArthur (Eds.), *Teaching in inclusive school communities* (pp. 3–38). Milton, QLD: John Wiley & Sons Australia Ltd.

Chan, W. L. (2016). The discrepancy between teachers' beliefs and practices: A study of kindergarten teachers in Hong Kong. *Teacher Development, 20*(93), 417–433.

Dadvand, B. (2015). Teaching for democracy: Towards an ecological understanding of preservice teachers' beliefs. *Australian Journal of Teacher Education, 40*(2), 77–93.

Dahlberg, G., Moss, P., & Pence, A. (2013). *Beyond quality in early childhood education and care: Languages of evaluation* (3rd ed.). London: Taylor & Francis Ltd.

Desimone, L. M., & Garet, M. S. (2015). Best practices in teachers' professional development in the United States. *Psychology, Society, & Education, 7*, 252–263.

Florian, L., & Black-Hawkins, K. (2011). Exploring inclusive pedagogy. *British Educational Research Journal, 37*(5), 813–828.

Garrison, J., Hickman, L., & Ikeda, D. (2014). *Living as learning*. Cambridge, MA: Dialogue Path Press.

Goulah, J., & Ito, T. (2012). Daisaku Ikeda's curriculum of soka education: Creating value through dialogue, global citizenship, and "Human Education" in the mentor-disciple relationship. *Curriculum Inquiry, 42*(1), 56–79.

Hamre, B. K., & Pianta, R. C. (2001). Early teacher-child relationships and the trajectory of children's school outcomes through eighth grade. *Child Development, 72*(2), 625–638.

Hong Kong Education Bureau. (2013). Quality review reports: Hong Kong Soka Kindergarten. Retrieved from http:www.edb.gov.hk/attachment/tc/edu-sustem/preprimary-kindergarten/quality-assurance-framework/qr/qr-report/HKSoka.pdf

Humphreys, C. K. (2012). Developing student character: Community college professors who share power. *Community College Journal of Research and Practice, 36*(6), 436–477.

Ikeda, D. (1987). *Buddhism and daily life* (Vol. 1). Singapore: Nichiren Shoshu Buddhist Association.

Ikeda, D. (2010). *Soka education: For the happiness of the individual*. Santa Monica, CA: Middleway Press.

Ikegami, K., & Agbenyega, J. S. (2014). Exploring educator's perspectives: How does learning through happiness promote quality early childhood education?. *Australian Journal of Early Childhood Education. 39*(3), 46–55.

Ikegami, K., & Grieshaber, S. (2017). Re-conceptualising quality early childhood education: What does Soka education have to offer?. In M. Li, J. Fox, & S. Grieshaber (Eds.), *Contemporary issues and challenges in early childhood education in the Asia-pacific region.* Dordrecht: Springer.

Kincheloe, J. L. (2004). The new childhood and critical thinking. In J. Kincheloe & D. Weil (Eds.), *Critical thinking and learning: An encyclopedia for parents and teachers* (pp. 101–104). London: Greenwood Press.

Kincheloe, J. L. (2008). *Knowledge and critical pedagogy: An introduction.* London: Springer.

Klibthong, S., Fridani, L., Ikegami, K., & Agbenyega, J. S. (2014). The relationship between quality early childhood programs and transition services in inclusive education of young children. *Asian Journal of Inclusive Education, 2*(1), 35–55.

Makiguchi, T. (1989). Reflections on purpose in education (A. Birnbaum Trans.). In D. Bethel (Ed.), *Education for creative living: Ideas and proposals of Tsunesaburo Makiguch.* Ames, IA: Iowa State University Press.

Makiguchi, T. (1997). *Soka Kyoikugaku Taikei: The system of value-creating pedagogy. Makiguchi Tsunesaburo zenshu* (2nd ed.). Tokyo: Daisan Bunmerisha.

Makiguchi, T. (2004). *Soka education system* (K. H. Kiu Trans.) (Vol 1). Taipei City: Cheng Yin Culture.

Makiguchi, T. (2006). *Soka education system* (K. H. Kiu Trans.) (Vol. 2). Taipei City: Cheng Yin Culture.

Mergler, A., Carrington, S., Kimber, M., & Bland, D. (2016). Inclusive values: Exploring the perspectives of pre-service teachers. *Australian Journal of Teacher Education, 41*(4), 19–38.

Monsen, J., Ewing, D. L., & Kwoka, M. (2014). Teachers' attitudes towards inclusion, perceived adequacy of support and classroom learning environment. *Learning Environments Research, 17*(1), 113–126.

Nolan, A., & Raban, B. (2015). *Theories into practice: Understanding and rethinking our work with young children.* Blairgowrie, VIC: Teaching Solutions.

Purdue, K., Gordon-Burns, D., Gunn, A., Madden, B., & Surtees, N. (2009). Supporting inclusion in early childhood settings: Some possibilities and problems for teacher education. *International Journal of Inclusive Education, 13*(8), 805–815.

Rey, R. B., Smith, A. L., Yoon, J., Somers, C., & Barnett, D. (2007). Relationships between teachers and Urban African American children: The tole of informant. *School Psychology International, 28*(3), 346–364.

Rhodes, C. (2012). Should leadership talent management in school also include the management of self-belief?. *School Leadership & Management, 32*(5), 439–451.

Rock, D. (2009). *Your Brain at Work: Strategies for overcoming distraction, regaining focus, and working smarter all day long.* New York, NY: Harper Business.

Soka Gakkai. (1999). *The writings of Nichiren Daishonin.* Tokyo: Soka Gakkai.

Soka Gakkai. (2002). *The Soka Gakkai dictionary of Buddhism.* Tokyo: Soka Gakkai.

Soka Gakkai International [SGI]. (2013a). Tsunesaburo Makiguchi: First president of Soka Gakkai. Retrieved from http://www.sgi.org/about-us/history-of-sgi/tsunesaburo-makiguchi-first-president-of-the-soka-gakkai.html

Soka Gakkai International [SGI]. (2013b). Josei Toda: Second president of Soka Gakkai. Retrieved from http://www.sgi.org/about-us/history-of-sgi/josei-toda-second-president-of-the-soka-gakkai.html

Soka Gakkai International [SGI]. (2013c). Who is a Buddha?. Retrieved from http://www.sgi.org/about-us/buddhism-in-daily-life/who-is-a-buddha.html

Soka Gakkai International [SGI]. (2014a). *The Lotus Sutra.* Retrieved from http://www.sgi.org/buddhism/buddhist-cpncepts/the-lotus-sutra.html

Soka Gakkai International [SGI]. (2014b). *Human revolution.* Retrieved from http://www.sgi.org/about-us/buddhism-in-daily-life/human-revolution.html

Soka Gakkai International [SGI]. (2014c). *A great human revolution.* Retrieved from http://www.sgi.org/about-us/president-ikedas-writings/human-revolution.html

Soka Gakkai International [SGI]. (2015). Changing poison into medicine. Retrieved from http://www.sgi.org/about-us/buddhism-in-daily-life/changing-posion-into-medicine.html

Soka Gakkai International [SGI]. (2017a). The oneness of mentor and disciple. Retrieved from http://www.sgi.org/about-us/buddhism-in-daily-life/the-oneness-of-mentor-and-disciple.html

Soka Gakkai International [SGI]. (2017b). The greater self. Retrieved from http://www.sgi.org/about-us/buddhism-in-daily-life/the-greater-self.html

Soka Gakkai International [SGI]. (2017c). Creating value. Retrieved from http://www.sgi.org/about-us/buddhism-in-daily-life/creating-value.html

Soka Gakuen Educational Foundation. (2009). *Soka Gakuen: A system for cultivating human values.* Tokyo: Author.

Soriano, V., & Hughes, G. (2018). *Promoting common values and inclusive education: Reflections and messages.* European Agency for Special Needs and Inclusive Education. Retrieved from www.european-agency.org

Spilt, J. L., Koomen, H. M. Y., & Mantzicopoulos, P. Y. (2010). Young children's perceptions of teacher-child relationships: An evaluation of two instruments and the role of child gender in kindergarten. *Journal of Applied Developmental Psychology, 31*(6), 428–438.

Suleiman-Gonzalez, L. P. (2004). Youth development: Critical perspectives. In J. Kincheloe & D. Weil (Eds.), *Critical thinking and learning: An encyclopedia for parents and teachers.* London: Greenwood Press.

Tarabini, A., Jacovkis, J., & Montes, A. (2018). Factors in educational exclusion: Including the voice of the youth. *Journal of Youth Studies, 21*(6), 836–851.

Theobald, M., Danby, S., & Ailwood, J. (2011). Child participation in the early years: Challenges for education. *Australasian Journal of Early Childhood, 36*(3), 19–26.

UNESCO. (2009). *Policy guidelines on inclusion in education.* Paris: Author. Retrieved from http://unesdoc.unesco.org/images/0017/0001778/177849e.pdf. Accessed on May 3, 2017.

Watkins, C., Carnell, E., & Lodge, C. (2007). *Effective learning in classrooms.* London: Paul Chapman Publishing.

Young, P., & Tyre, C. (1995). *Gifted or able? Realizing children's potential.* Buckingham: Open University Press.

# TEACHER TRAINING FOR INCLUSIVE EDUCATION IN GERMANY: STATUS QUO AND CURRICULAR IMPLEMENTATION

Saskia Liebner and Claudia Schmaltz

## ABSTRACT

*The transformation of the German education system because of the ratification of the UN Convention on the Rights of Persons with Disabilities (United Nations, 2006) has also reached the domain of teacher training. Professional competences and their development are brought into focus (e. g., Trautmann, 2017). Since 2013, all prospective teachers in Germany have to be qualified in the field of heterogeneity, inclusion and diagnostics, mainly in the educational science part of the teacher training programmes (KMK, 2013a, 2013b, 2013c, 2013d, 2013e, 2015). However, there is a great heterogeneity regarding the content and structures of this teacher training for inclusion in Germany. Despite the formal anchoring of inclusion and heterogeneity in teacher training in Germany, an overview of the current status of the curricular implementation of inclusion-oriented teacher training is missing. The aim of this study is to fill this gap and, to do so, investigates in a first step the educational science parts of the curricula. Therefore, the study and examination regulations of all general education teacher training programmes (primary, secondary I and II) at German universities were analyzed by means of qualitative content analysis. The results show differences in the extent of the curricula regarding heterogeneity and inclusion between the states and universities on the one hand and the various study programmes on the other hand.*

Resourcing Inclusive Education
International Perspectives on Inclusive Education, Volume 15, 133–145
Copyright © 2021 by Emerald Publishing Limited.
ISSN: 1479-3636/doi:10.1108/S1479-363620210000015011

**Keywords**: Inclusion; heterogeneity; teacher training; Germany; professional development; qualitative content analysis

## TEACHER TRAINING FOR INCLUSIVE EDUCATION

At least since the ratification of the UN Convention on the Rights of Persons with Disabilities (United Nations, 2006), inclusive education is the subject of pedagogical, political and public discourse. This applies equally to Germany and internationally. For Germany, this has also resulted in a restructuring of the school system, for example, by anchoring inclusive education in the school laws of the 16 regional states. Thus, a long-term process was started with the requirement to align all current and future decisions and actions with the goal of inclusive education (Döbert & Weishaupt, 2013, p. 7; EADSNE, 2011, p. 77). The expected and necessary reforms have, with some delay, also reached teacher training at the universities. Currently, questions of curricular integration of inclusive education in teacher training as well as the competence development of pre- and in-service teachers regarding inclusion are discussed (EADSNE, 2010, 2012; Pabst, 2015; Trautmann, 2017).

The European Agency on Special Needs Development (EADSNE, 2012) has developed a profile of competences that are essential for inclusive education 'as a guide for the design and implementation of initial teacher education programmes for all teachers' (EADSNE, 2012, p. 20). It describes the central contents and values of inclusion-oriented teacher training but not how these should be imparted. The four core values are (1) valuing learner diversity, (2) supporting all learners, (3) working with others and (4) continuing professional development.

Regarding the structures and organizational forms of inclusion-oriented teacher education, Pugach und Blanton (2009) distinguish three models: discrete, integrated and merged. Whereas in discrete models, basically unchanged courses are supplemented by one or more courses on inclusion, in integrated models a systematic interweaving of general pedagogic and inclusive education content takes place both in the curriculum and at the level of individual courses. Merged models are based on the conception of new courses of study with a common curriculum for all teachers and thus on the replacement of the binary distinction between regular and special needs teachers. This system is based on the one previously presented by Stayton und McCollun (2002) who distinguished between the 'Infusion model', the 'Collaborative Training model' and the 'Unification model'. The EADSNE (2010, p. 21) describes these models as follows:

> In the Infusion model, students take 1 or 2 courses that cover inclusive education. In the Collaborative Training model, many more courses deal with teaching inclusive classes, and mainstream teaching students and special education students do all or part of their practical experiences together. In the Unification model, all students study the same curriculum that trains them for teaching mainstream education with a focus on pupils with special needs.

To identify differences between different teacher training programmes and a deeper understanding of the three described models, Pugach and Blanton (2009) cite the five criteria (1) curricular coherence, (2) faculty collaboration, (3) depth of knowledge, (4) performance/portfolio assessments and (5) PK-12 partnerships. Using these five criteria for research on teacher training for inclusion may help to establish a common language and structure for initiating a cohesive research.

## TEACHER TRAINING IN GERMANY

Regarding teacher training in Germany, it must first be noted that, due to the cultural sovereignty of the federal states, there are in some cases large differences between them. In their expertize on the regulations of the federal states for teacher training, Walm and Wittek (2014) conclude that this is implemented differently everywhere. Significant differences regarding the desired degree and the duration and content of study programme can be noticed. Most of the federal states have organized teacher training in consecutive bachelor's and master's programmes, while in some cases the state examination is still or again the pursued degree. Besides subject-specific pedagogy and discipline studies, the syllabus includes between 10 and 33% educational sciences and between 5 and 12% school internships (Walm & Wittek, 2014, p. 51). Overall teacher training programmes at universities have undergone and will continue to undergo reforms, without, so far, fundamentally restructuring and redesigning itself.

Although education in Germany falls under the sovereignty of the federal states, the KMK (Standing Conference of the Ministers of Education and Cultural Affairs of the Länder in the Federal Republic of Germany) formulates transnational regulations and recommendations for teacher training in Germany. These are of particular interest considering the outlined differences between the federal states and might be used as a base for the discussion of teacher training for inclusion in Germany. Following the ratification of the UN-CRPD in 2008 (BGBl. II 2008, 1419), these recommendations and standards were revised and further developed in the following years with regard to the requirements of heterogeneity and inclusion.

In a first step, the framework agreements for all teaching profession types were supplemented by a basic formulation for dealing with heterogeneity, inclusion and support diagnostics, which are thus highlighted as being particularly significant (KMK, 2013a, 2013b, 2013c, 2013d, 2013e). These framework agreements ensure that teacher training in the federal states takes the objectives of the relevant school types into account and leads to professional and pedagogical competence. Therefore, they are of particular importance for the recognition of qualifications and the mobility of teachers between the federal states (Pabst, 2015). In addition, the standards for teacher training in educational sciences were revised in 2014 and describe the professional competencies that a teacher should have to cope with the professional tasks in the field of inclusive education. Diversity and heterogeneity as conditions of school and teaching is thus declared one central part of the educational science curricula in all teacher training programmes in Germany (KMK, 2014). Finally, the joint recommendation of the KMK and the HRK (German Conference of Presidents and Rectors of Universities and Other Higher Education Institutions) on teacher training for a school of diversity from 2015 can be considered. This recommendation addresses especially universities, ministries and authorities and is intended to provide guidance for teacher education. Taking the models for teacher training for inclusion according to Pugach und Blanton (2009) as a starting point, discrete or integrated models are addressed as possible forms of implementation, whereby it is recommended to supplement discrete by integrated concepts and to implement an inclusive general conception (KMK & HRK, 2015).

In the overall view of the resolutions and recommendations of the KMK and HRK, inclusive education is thus described as the responsibility of all teachers, regardless of the school type. It also becomes apparent that inclusive education does not only refer to pupils with disabilities, which is in line with the understanding of United Nations Educational Scientific and Cultural Organization (UNESCO, 2003). Rather, as formulated by Kiuppis und Hausstätter (2014) under the slogan 'Inclusive education for all, and especially for some', diversity is addressed in a comprehensive sense, whereby various learning and achievement prerequisites and educational biographies, in terms of heterogeneity, are taken into account. This leads in particular to the conclusion that teacher training for inclusion must not only include special education.

## RESEARCH ISSUE

As shown above, since 2013 all prospective teachers have to be qualified in the field of heterogeneity, inclusion and diagnostics, mainly in the educational science part of the teacher training programmes (KMK, 2013a, 2013b, 2013c, 2013d, 2013e, 2015). Regarding the content and structures of this teacher training for inclusion in Germany, there is great heterogeneity (Lindmeier, 2015; Radhoff & Ruberg, 2017; Walm & Wittek, 2014). A systematization of the national state of research on teacher education in Germany has shown that the topics of inclusion, integration and special needs education have not been of central importance and have therefore hardly been considered (Hillenbrand, Melzer, & Hagen, 2013; Laubner & Lindmeier, 2017). This is barely surprising, as the papers included were published between 2002 and 2012, but the resolutions and recommendations of the KMK and HRK have not been revised until 2013. The implementation was therefore only possible hereafter. Since no specific curriculum results from the presented specifications and recommendations, this had to be developed subsequently by the individual universities. In 2015, it was recorded for all federal states how inclusion-oriented teacher training is currently implemented and what plans are currently in preparation (Monitor Lehrerbildung, 2015).

Despite the described formal anchoring of inclusion and heterogeneity in teacher training in Germany, an up-to-date overview of the current curricular implementation of inclusion-oriented teacher training is still missing. Until today, since only concepts of individual universities are described comprehensively (e. g. University of Dortmund: Hußmann & Welzel, 2018; University of Bielefeld: Lütje-Klose, Miller, & Ziegler, 2014), it remains unclear how the universities have designed their curricula. There are numerous empirical studies on various aspects of teacher training for inclusion e.g. on pre-service teachers' attitudes (Sharma, Moore, & Sonawane, 2009), their career choice motives (Kiel, Weiß, & Braune, 2012) or the impact of university courses on their competence development (Opalinski & Scharenberg, 2018). However, these are difficult to interpret due to the lack of an overview of the formal anchoring and curricular design of teacher training for inclusion in Germany (Laubner & Lindmeier, 2017, p. 191). This study seeks to obtain data, which will help to address this research gap. In this paper, attention is first directed to the implementation of the nationwide structural specifications in the teacher training programmes of the universities in the 16 federal states.

## METHODS

In a first step, all general teacher training programmes at German universities as well as their study and examination regulations and/or module catalogues were researched. The documents included were in force at the time of the research (summer semester 2019). Regarding the complexity of teacher training programmes, which usually comprise two or more subjects, and the resolutions and recommendations of the KMK, the focus was placed on the educational sciences, which are part of all teacher training programmes in Germany. Overall, we found 230 documents (sampling units) from 74 universities, which were analyzed in a second step by means of qualitative content analysis (Kuckartz, 2016) using MAXQDA 18 (VERBI Software, 2018). For this purpose, coding was carried out regarding the four aspects (1) study programme, (2) desired degree, (3) heterogeneity as part of the curriculum and (4) inclusion as a part of the curriculum, using deductive and inductive categorization. The respective study programme was inductively coded. Because of the cultural sovereignty of the Länder, 16 differently structured school systems with corresponding school types can be distinguished for the analyses. For the coding of the school-type specific study programme, we followed the International Standard Classification of Education (ISCED) (UNESCO, 2011). We identified study programmes for teaching at (1) primary level (ISCED 1), (2) secondary level I (not grammar school) (ISCED 2), (3) secondary level I and II (ISCED 2 and 3), (4) secondary level I and II (grammar school, ISCED 2 and 3) and (5) primary and secondary level I (not grammar school, ISCED 1 and 2). The desired degree was also coded inductively and led to three categories: bachelor, master and state examination. Deductive coding was used for inclusion and heterogeneity as parts of the curriculum, using the following coding rules: Only compulsory modules or courses were included. Furthermore, inclusion or heterogeneity had to be mentioned in the module or course title. In case of double naming, it was coded as inclusion. This resulted in 10 categories of 1 ECTS credit up to 10 or more ECTS credits for each of these two subject areas. 'The European Credit Transfer and Accumulation System (ECTS) is a tool of the European Higher Education Area (EHEA) for making studies and courses more transparent and thus helping to enhance the quality of higher education' (European Union, 2015, p. 6). One credit refers to 25–30 hours of students' work.

## RESULTS

As the results differ between heterogeneity and inclusion as subject areas they are presented separately, starting with heterogeneity (see Table 1). In 31 of the 230 documents, 35 modules or courses with the word part heteroge* in the title were identified. The spectrum ranges from 1 to 10 or more ECTS credits.

Looking at the different study programmes, in the sense of different school types, clear differences become apparent. While there are no (Prim + Sec I not grammar) or only 2 (Sec I not grammar) or 3 (Sec I + II grammar) corresponding

*Table 1.* Results for Heterogeneity.

| Category | N | % | Prim | Prim + Sec I (not Grammar) | Sec I (not Grammar) | Sec I + II | Sec I + II (Grammar) | General |
|---|---|---|---|---|---|---|---|---|
| Analyzed documents | 230 | 100 | 60 | 6 | 44 | 63 | 50 | 7 |
| Documents without codings | 199 | 86.5 | - | - | - | - | - | - |
| Documents with codings | 31 | 13.5 | - | - | - | - | - | - |
| 1 ECTS | 2 | 0.9 | 1 | | | | | 1 |
| 2 ECTS | 5 | 2.2 | 2 | | | 2 | | 1 |
| 3 ECTS | 4 | 1.7 | 2 | | | 2 | | |
| 4 ECTS | 3 | 1.3 | 1 | | | 2 | | |
| 5 ECTS | 6 | 2.6 | 2 | | 1 | 1 | 2 | |
| 6 ECTS | 3 | 1.3 | 2 | | | 1 | | |
| 7 ECTS | 0 | 0 | | | | | | |
| 8 ECTS | 1 | 0.4 | | | | 1 | | |
| 9 ECTS | 7 | 3.0 | 3 | | 1 | 2 | 1 | |
| 10+ ECTS | 4 | 1.7 | 1 | | | 3 | | |

***Table 2.*** Results for Inclusion.

| Category | N | % | Prim | Prim + Sec I (not Grammar) | Sec I (not Grammar) | Sec I + II | Sec I + II (Grammar) | General |
|---|---|---|---|---|---|---|---|---|
| Analyzed documents | 230 | 100 | 60 | 6 | 44 | 63 | 50 | 7 |
| Documents without codings | 155 | 67.4 | - | - | - | - | - | - |
| Documents with codings | 75 | 32.6 | - | - | - | - | - | - |
| 1 ECTS | 10 | 4.3 | 2 | | | 8 | | |
| 2 ECTS | 12 | 5.2 | 2 | | 2 | 6 | 1 | 1 |
| 3 ECTS | 9 | 3.9 | 4 | | 2 | 1 | 2 | |
| 4 ECTS | 4 | 1.7 | 2 | | | 1 | 1 | |
| 5 ECTS | 15 | 6.5 | 4 | 1 | 4 | 2 | 4 | |
| 6 ECTS | 19 | 8.3 | 5 | 1 | 4 | 5 | 4 | |
| 7 ECTS | 2 | 0.9 | 1 | | | | 1 | |
| 8 ECTS | 5 | 2.2 | 2 | | 1 | 2 | | |
| 9 ECTS | 6 | 2.6 | 2 | | 2 | | 2 | |
| 10+ ECTS | 3 | 1.3 | 1 | | | 1 | 1 | |

courses/modules for those study programmes, these are more common for the study programmes at primary level and Sec I + II and range from 1 to 10 or more ECTS credits.

Considering the results for inclusion (see Table 2), 75 of the 230 documents were coded with modules or courses covering 1 to 10 or more ECTS credits with the word part inclusi* in their title.

Once again, clear differences between different study programmes become apparent. There are only few codings for the combined study programmes regarding teacher training for primary and non-grammar secondary I level as well as general teacher training programmes but several codings for the other four types of study programmes.

A detailed examination of the 16 German states (see Table 3) shows remarkable differences, even when considering the different number of documents involved. Overall, we have no codings in Hesse and Saarland, neither for heterogeneity nor for inclusion, and 52 codings for North Rhine-Westphalia.

A closer look reveals further that there is one coding each for Hamburg, Saxony and Saxony-Anhalt, two codings each for Bavaria and Thuringia and three codings each for Brandenburg, Berlin, Bremen, Mecklenburg Western Pomerania and Lower Saxony. The other German states (Baden-Wuerttemberg, North Rhine-Westphalia, Rhineland Palatinate and Saxony-Anhalt) have four or more codings with the maximum of 52 codings for North Rhine-Westphalia.

*Table 3.* Results for Heterogeneity (H) and Inclusion (I) for the 16 German States.

| Category | BB | | BW | | BY | | BE | | HB | | HH | | HE | | MV | | NI | | NW | | RP | | SL | | SN | | ST | | SH | | TH | |
|---|---|---|---|---|---|---|---|---|---|---|---|---|---|---|---|---|---|---|---|---|---|---|---|---|---|---|---|---|---|---|---|---|
| Analyzed documents | 5 | | 41 | | 36 | | 10 | | 5 | | 2 | | 11 | | 5 | | 19 | | 67 | | 6 | | 1 | | 7 | | 6 | | 6 | | 5 | |
| | H | I | H | I | H | I | H | I | H | I | H | I | H | I | H | I | H | I | H | I | H | I | H | I | H | I | H | I | H | I | H | I |
| 1 ECTS | | | | | | | | | | | 1 | | | | | | | | 1 | 16 | | | | | | | | | | | | |
| 2 ECTS | | | 1 | | 1 | | 1 | 3 | | | | | | | | | 3 | | 3 | 6 | | | | | | | | | 1 | 1 | | |
| 3 ECTS | | | 4 | | | | | 1 | | | | | | | 4 | | 2 | 2 | 2 | 2 | 2 | 2 | | | | | | | | | | |
| 4 ECTS | | | 1 | | | | 1 | | | 1 | | | | | | | 2 | 1 | 2 | 1 | 1 | | | | | | | | | | | |
| 5 ECTS | 3 | | 4 | | | | | 2 | 2 | | | | | | | | 3 | | 2 | | | | | | 2 | | 5 | | 2 | 1 | | 1 |
| 6 ECTS | 1 | | 8 | | | | | | | | | | | | 6 | | 1 | 1 | 1 | 6 | | | | | | | | | | | | 1 |
| 7 ECTS | | | 1 | | | | | | | | | | | | | | | | 1 | | | | | | | | | | | | | |
| 8 ECTS | | | 2 | | | | | | | | | | | | | | | | 3 | | | | | | | | | | | | | |
| 9 ECTS | 2 | | 2 | 1 | | | | | 3 | | | | | | 1 | | 2 | 1 | 4 | 1 | 1 | | | | | | | | | | | |
| 10+ ECTS | 1 | | | | | | | | | | | | | | | | | | 1 | | | | | | | | | | | | 1 | |

*Note:* Number of codings for each of the German States for heterogeneity (H) in the left column and inclusion (I) in the right column. BB = Brandenburg; BW = Baden-Württemberg; BY = Bavaria; BE = Berlin; HB = Bremen; HH = Hamburg; HE = Hesse; MV = Mecklenburg Western Pomerania; NI = Lower Saxony; NW = Northrhine-Westphalia; RP = Rhineland Palatinate; SL = Saarland; SN = Saxony; ST = Saxony-Anhalt; SH = Schleswig-Holstein; TH = Thuringia.

# DISCUSSION

While Hillenbrand, Melzer, and Hagen concluded in 2013 (p. 36) that inclusion was hardly an issue in teacher training in Germany, a more differentiated picture can currently be drawn, revealing considerable differences between the federal states. It can be summarized that pre-service teachers in Hesse and Saarland seem not engaged to deal with the topics of heterogeneity and inclusion within the curricula of compulsory educational science modules/courses. Pre-service teachers in Bavaria, Hamburg, Lower Saxony, Saxony and Thuringia appear to be partly confronted with the two topics. Finally, for the federal states of Brandenburg, Baden-Wuerttemberg, Bremen, Mecklenburg Western Pomerania, North Rhine-Westphalia, Rhineland Palatinate and Schleswig-Holstein, it can be assumed that all prospective teachers deal with both topics within the framework of the compulsory education studies, in some cases to the extent of 10 or more ECTS credits. The results of this first analysis do not yet provide a conclusion regarding the models of Pugach and Blanton. Following the KMK (2013a, 2013b, 2013c, 2013d, 2013e) all prospective teachers in Germany have to be qualified in the field of heterogeneity, inclusion and diagnostics, mainly in the educational science part of the teacher training programmes. In light of the results of our study, the practical implementation of this requirement must be critically reviewed, at least in some of the 16 federal states.

Beyond that, the lack or low level of embedding the topics heterogeneity and inclusion in the curricula of compulsory educational science in some federal states must be problematized to the extent that the school experience of prospective teachers in Germany has to date essentially been acquired in a segregated, non-inclusive school system (Laubner & Lindmeier, 2017, p. 170). In the 2017/2018 school year, the inclusion rate in the national average was 41.7%, with a range of 29.6% in Hesse and 84.7% in Bremen (own calculations based on KMK statistics; KMK, 2019a, 2019b). This becomes even more serious when one considers that school inclusion has only been implemented to a limited extent in grammar schools, where most students acquire a higher education entrance qualification.

# LIMITATIONS AND OUTLOOK

When considering the findings, it must be noted that they result from the first analysis step, which is more oriented towards the surface structures. For this reason, it should not be summarized that in some federal states prospective teachers are not at all trained on questions of how to deal with heterogeneity and inclusion. Rather, it can only be stated that this does not appear to take place in the compulsory part of the education science curriculum. Based on this, it can be assumed that inclusive education content is anchored in the study and examination regulations of the subject-specific pedagogy and discipline studies.

Taking this into account, the next steps of the analysis will first consider other relevant keywords, such as diversity, and include the elective curricula of educational science studies. In addition, country-specific regulations for the teacher training regarding inclusion are also considered. In the further analyses, the specifications of the teacher training programmes at selected universities in each of the 16 federal states of Germany are then analyzed more in detail with regard to the implementation of inclusive education in the curricula. This will definitely include the curricula of the subject-specific pedagogy and discipline studies. The implementation of inclusive education in schools must not only be addressed in terms of educational science but also in terms of subject specifics. As suggested by Pugach und Blanton (2009) curricular coherence, depth of knowledge (in terms of learning and competence objectives) as well as described performance assessments will be used as analysis criteria.

Notwithstanding the limitations described above, these results provide an up-to-date overview of the curricular implementation of inclusion-oriented teacher training in Germany, which can be used as a base for further research and for the interpretation of findings, e.g., on the competence development of prospective teachers.

# REFERENCES

Döbert, H., & Weishaupt, H. (2013). Einleitung [Introduction]. In H. Döbert, & H. Weishaupt (Eds.), *Inklusive Bildung professionell gestalten. Situationsanalyse und Handlungsempfehlungen* (pp. 7–10). Münster: Waxmann.

European Agency for Development in Special Needs Education (EADSNE). (2010). Teacher education for inclusion – international literature review. Retrieved from https://www.european-agency.org/sites/default/files/TE4I-Literature-Review.pdf. Accessed on July 8, 2019.

European Agency for Development in Special Needs Education (EADSNE). (2011). Teacher education for inclusion across europe – challenges and opportunities. Retrieved from https://www.european-agency.org/sites/default/files/te4i-challenges-and-opportunities_TE4I-Synthesis-Report-EN.pdf. Accessed on November 8, 2018.

European Agency for Development in Special Needs Education (EADSNE). (2012). Teacher education for inclusion. Profile of inclusive teachers. Retrieved from https://www.european-agency.org/sites/default/files/Profile-of-Inclusive-Teachers.pdf. Accessed on July 8, 2019.

European Union. (2015). ECTS users' guide. Retrieved from https://ec.europa.eu/education/ects/users-guide/docs/ects-users-guide_en.pdf. Accessed on May 3, 2020.

Gesetz zu dem Übereinkommen der Vereinten Nationen vom. (2006, Dezember, 13). über die Rechte von Menschen mit Behinderungen sowie zu dem Fakultativprotokoll vom 13. Dezember 2006 zum Übereinkommen der Vereinten Nationen über die Rechte von Menschen mit Behinderungen. (21.12.2008) (BGBl. II 2008, 1419) [Law on the United Nations Convention on the Rights of Persons with Disabilities of 13 December 2006 and the Optional Protocol of 13 December 2006 to the United Nations Convention on the Rights of Persons with Disabilities. (21.12.2008) (Federal Law Gazette II 2008, 1419)].

Hillenbrand, C., Melzer, C., & Hagen, T. (2013). Bildung schulischer Fachkräfte für inklusive Bildungssysteme [Education of school professionals for inclusive education systems]. In H. Döbert, & H. Weishaupt (Eds.), *Inklusive Bildung professionell gestalten. Situationsanalyse und Handlungsempfehlungen* (pp. 33–68). Münster: Waxmann.

Hußmann, S. & Welzel, B. (Hrsg.). (2018). *DoProfiL – Das Dortmunder Profil für inklusionsorientierte Lehrerinnen- und Lehrerbildung [DoProfiL - the Dortmund profile for inclusion-oriented teacher training.]* Münster: Waxmann.

Kiel, E., Weiß, S., & Braune, A. (2012). Sonderpädagogische Professionalität und Inklusion: Welchen Beitrag leistet das Studium der Sonderpädagogik? [Special education professionalism and inclusion: What contribution is made by studying special education?] In U. Heimlich, & J. Kahlert (Eds.), *Inklusion in Schule und Unterricht. Wege zur Bildung für alle* (pp. 191–199). Stuttgar: Kohlhammer.

Kiuppis, F., & Hausstätter, R. S. (2014). Inclusive education for all, and especially for some? On different interpretations of who and what the "salamanca process" concerns. In F. Kiuppis, & R. S. Hausstätter (Eds.), *Inclusive education twenty years after salamanca* (pp. 1–5). New York, NY: Peter Lang Publishing.

Kuckartz, U. (2016). *Qualitative inhaltsanalyse. Methoden, Praxis, Computerunterstützung [Qualitative content analysis. Methods, practice, computer support]* (3. Ed.). Weinheim: Beltz Juventa.

Laubner, M., & Lindmeier, C. (2017). Forschung zur inklusionsorientierten Lehrerinnen- und Lehrerbildung in Deutschland. Eine Übersicht über die neueren empirischen Studien zur ersten, universitären Phase [Research on inclusion-oriented teacher education in Germany. An overview of recent empirical studies on the first, university phase]. In C. Lindmeier, & H. Weiß (Eds.), *Pädagogische Professionalität im Spannungsfeld von sonderpädagogischer Förderung und inklusiver Bildung. 1. Beiheft Sonderpädagogische Förderung heute* (pp. 154–201). Weinheim: Beltz.

Lindmeier, C. (2015). Herausforderungen einer inklusionsorientierten Erneuerung der deutschen Lehrer*innenbildung [Challenges of an inclusion-oriented reform of German teacher education]. In H. Redlich, L. Schäfer, G. Wachtel, K. Zehbe, & V. Moser (Eds.), *Veränderung und Beständigkeit in Zeiten der Inklusion. Perspektiven Sonderpädagogischer Professionalisierung* (pp. 112–132). Bad Heilbrunn: Verlag Julius Klinkhardt.

Lütje-Klose, B., Miller, S., & Ziegler, H. (2014). Professionalisierung für die inklusive Schule als Herausforderung für die LehrerInnenbildung [Professionalism for inclusvie schooling as a challenge for university education of teachers]. *Soziale Passagen, 6*(1), 69–84.

Monitor Lehrerbildung. (2015). Inklusionsorientierte Lehrerbildung – vom Schlagwort zur Realität?! Eine Sonderpublikation aus dem Projekt "Monitor Lehrerbildung" [Inclusion-oriented teacher training – from catchword to reality?! A special publication from the project "Monitor Lehrerbildung"]. Retrieved from https://www.monitor-lehrerbildung.de/web/.content/Downloads/Monitor_Lehrerbildung_Inklusion_04_2015.pdf. Accessed on November 17, 2018.

Opalinski, S., & Scharenberg, K. (2018). Veränderung inklusionsbezogener Überzeugungen bei Studierenden durch diversitätssensible Lehrveranstaltungen [Development of student teachers' beliefs towards inclusion by means of diversity-sensitive teaching]. *Bildung und Erziehung, 71*(4), 449–464.

Pabst, A. (2015). Inklusive Lehrerinnen- und Lehrerbildung – Positionen und Aktivitäten der Kultusministerkonferenz [Inclusive teacher education – positions and activities of the Conference of Ministers of Education and Cultural Affairs]. In T. Häcker, & M. Walm (Eds.), *Inklusion als Entwicklung. Konsequenzen für Schule und Lehrerbildung* (pp. 135–148). Bad Heilbrunn: Verlag Julius Klinkhardt.

Pugach, M., & Blanton, L. (2009). A framework for conducting research on collaborative teacher education. *Teaching and Teacher Education, 25*(4), 575–582.

Radhoff, M., & Ruberg, C. (2017). Inklusion in der Lehrerausbildung. Aktuelle Strukturen und die Rolle der Universität [Inclusion in teacher training. Current structures and the role of the university]. In S. Greiten, G. Geber, A. Gruhn, & M. Köninger (Eds.), *Lehrerausbildung für Inklusion. Fragen und Konzepte zur Hochschulentwicklung* (pp. 64–76). Münster: Waxmann.

Sekretariat der Ständigen Konferenz der Kultusminister der Länder in der Bundesrepublik Deutschland (KMK). (2013a). Rahmenvereinbarung über die Ausbildung und Prüfung für ein Lehramt der Grundschule bzw. Primarstufe (Lehramtstyp 1). Beschluss der Kultusministerkonferenz vom 28.02.1997 i. d. F. vom 07.03.2013. [Framework agreement on the training and examination for a primary school or primary level teacher (type 1). Resolution of the Conference of Ministers of Education and Cultural Affairs of 28.02.1997 as amended on 07.03.2013]. Berlin.

Sekretariat der Ständigen Konferenz der Kultusminister der Länder in der Bundesrepublik Deutschland (KMK). (2013b). Rahmenvereinbarung über die Ausbildung und Prüfung für ein Lehramt der Sekundarstufe I (Lehramtstyp 3). Beschluss der Kultusministerkonferenz vom 28.02.1997 i. d. F. vom 07.03.2013. [Framework agreement on the training and examination for a secondary level I teacher (type 3). Resolution of the Conference of Ministers of Education and Cultural Affairs of 28.02.1997 as amended on 07.03.2013]. Berlin.

Sekretariat der Ständigen Konferenz der Kultusminister der Länder in der Bundesrepublik Deutschland (KMK). (2013c). Rahmenvereinbarung über die Ausbildung und Prüfung für ein Lehramt der Sekundarstufe II (allgemein bildende Fächer) oder für das Gymnasium (Lehramtstyp 4). Beschluss der Kultusministerkonferenz vom 28.02.1997 i. d. F. vom 07.03.2013. [Framework agreement on the training and examination for a teaching profession at upper secondary level (general subjects) or for grammar school (type 4). Resolution of the Conference of Ministers of Education and Cultural Affairs of 28.02.1997 as amended on 07.03.2013]. Berlin.

Sekretariat der Ständigen Konferenz der Kultusminister der Länder in der Bundesrepublik Deutschland (KMK). (2013d). Rahmenvereinbarung über die Ausbildung und Prüfung für ein Lehramt der Sekundarstufe II (berufliche Fächer) oder für die beruflichen Schulen (Lehramtstyp 5). Beschluss der Kultusministerkonferenz vom 13.05.1995 i. d. F. vom 07.03.2013. [Framework agreement on the training and examination for a teaching profession at upper secondary level (vocational subjects) or for vocational schools (teaching profession type 5). Resolution of the Conference of Ministers of Education and Cultural Affairs of 13.05.1995 as amended on 07.03.2013]. Berlin.

Sekretariat der Ständigen Konferenz der Kultusminister der Länder in der Bundesrepublik Deutschland (KMK). (2013e). Rahmenvereinbarung über die Ausbildung und Prüfung für übergreifende Lehrämter der Primarstufe und aller oder einzelner Schularten der Sekundarstufe I (Lehramtstyp 2). Beschluss der Kultusministerkonferenz vom 28.02.1997 i. d. F. vom 07.03.2013. [Framework agreement on training and examinations for cross-curricular teaching posts at primary level and all or individual types of secondary level I schools (type 2). Resolution of the Conference of Ministers of Education and Cultural Affairs of 28.02.1997 as amended on 07.03.2013]. Berlin.

Sekretariat der Ständigen Konferenz der Kultusminister der Länder in der Bundesrepublik Deutschland (KMK). (2014). Standards für die Lehrerbildung: Bildungswissenschaften (Beschluss der Kultusministerkonferenz vom 16.12.2004 i. d. F. vom 12.06.2014). [Standards for teacher training: Educational Sciences (Resolution of the Conference of Ministers of Education and Cultural Affairs of 16.12.2004 as amended on 12.06.2014)]. Retrieved from http://www.kmk.org/fileadmin/veroeffentlichungen_beschluesse/2004/2004_12_16-Standards-Lehrerbildung.pdf. Accessed on May 13, 2014.

Sekretariat der Ständigen Konferenz der Kultusminister der Länder in der Bundesrepublik Deutschland (KMK). (2015). Lehrerbildung für eine Schule der Vielfalt. Gemeinsame Empfehlung von Hochschulrektorenkonferenz und Kultusministerkonferenz. (Beschluss der Kultusministerkonferenz vom 12.03.2015/Beschluss der Hochschulrektorenkonferenz vom 18.03.2015). [Teacher training for a school of diversity. Joint recommendation of the German Rectors' Conference and the Conference of Ministers of Education and Cultural Affairs. (Resolution of the Standing Conference of Ministers of Education and Cultural Affairs of 12.03.2015/ Resolution of the German Rectors' Conference of 18.03.2015)]. Retrieved from https://www.kmk.org/fileadmin/Dateien/veroeffentlichungen_beschluesse/2015/2015_03_12-Schule-der-Vielfalt.pdf. Accessed on October 18, 2016.

Sekretariat der Ständigen Konferenz der Kultusminister der Länder in der Bundesrepublik Deutschland (KMK). (2019a). Sonderpädagogische Förderung in allgemeinen Schulen (ohne Förderschulen) 2017/2018 [Special educational support in general schools (excluding special schools) 2017/2018]. Retrieved from https://www.kmk.org/fileadmin/Dateien/pdf/Statistik/Dokumentationen/Aus_SoPae_Int_2017.pdf. Accessed on December 19, 2019.

Sekretariat der Ständigen Konferenz der Kultusminister der Länder in der Bundesrepublik Deutschland (KMK). (2019b). Sonderpädagogische Förderung in Förderschulen (Sonderschulen) 2017/2018 [Special educational support in special schools (special schools) 2017/2018]. Retrieved from https://www.kmk.org/fileadmin/Dateien/pdf/Statistik/Dokumentationen/Aus_Sopae_2017.pdf. Accessed on December 19, 2019.

Sharma, U., Moore, D., & Sonawane, S. (2009). Attitudes and concerns of pre-service teachers regarding inclusion of students with disabilities into regular schools in Pune, India. *Asia-Pacific Journal of Teacher Education*, 37(3), 319–331.

Stayton, V. D., & McCollun, J. (2002). Unifying general and special education: What does the research tell us? *Teacher Education and Special Education*, 25(3), 211–218.

Trautmann, M. (2017). Lehrerausbildung für die inklusive Schule. Eine Einschätzung zum Stand der Diskussion [Teacher training for the inclusive school. An evaluation of the state of the discussion]. In S. Greiten, G. Geber, A. Gruhn, & M. Köninger (Eds.), *Lehrerausbildung für Inklusion. Fragen und Konzepte zur Hochschulentwicklung* (pp. 37–47). Münster: Waxmann.

United Nations Educational Scientific and Cultural Organization (UNESCO). (2003). *Overcoming exclusion through inclusive approaches in education. A challenge & a vision.* Conceptual paper. Retrieved from http://unesdoc.unesco.org/images/0013/001347/134785e.pdf. Accessed on July 8, 2019.

United Nations Educational Scientific and Cultural Organization (UNESCO). (2011). International standard classification of education. ISCED 2011. Retrieved from http://uis.unesco.org/sites/default/files/documents/international-standard-classification-of-education-isced-2011-en.pdf. Accessed on May 3, 2020.

United Nations. (2006). Convention on the rights of persons with disabilities. Retrieved from http://www.un.org/disabilities/documents/convention/convention_accessible_pdf.pdf. Accessed on February 22, 2018.

VERBI Software. (2018). MAXQDA 2018. Retrieved from maxqda.com

Walm, M., & Wittek, D. (2014). *Lehrer_innenbildung in Deutschland im Jahr 2014. Eine phasenübergreifende Dokumentation der Regelungen in den Bundesländern. Eine Expertise im Auftrag der Max-Traeger-Stiftung (2. Aufl.)* [Teacher training in Germany in 2014, a cross-phase documentation of the regulations in the federal states. An expertise commissioned by the Max Traeger Foundation] (2nd ed.). Retrieved from https://www.gew.de/fileadmin/media/publikationen/hv/Hochschule_und_Forschung/Ausbildung_von_Lehrerinnen_und_Paedagogen/Zukunftsforum_Lehrer_innenbildung/Lehrer-Innenbildung_2014_A4_web.pdf. Accessed on April 12, 2019.

# ENHANCING TEACHER EDUCATION BY UTILIZING A REVISED PGDE CURRICULUM AS A FUNDAMENTAL RESOURCE FOR INCLUSIVE PRACTICES IN MACAO

Elisa Monteiro and Chris Forlin

## ABSTRACT

*A critical resource for inclusive education is ensuring that an effective curriculum is in place for preparing teachers. Reviewing an existing curriculum and revising it to meet this need is an important aspect of every teacher training institution. The purpose of this chapter is to investigate the effect of a revised Post-Graduate Diploma in Education programme on teachers' pedagogical practice and knowledge transfer for inclusive education. Following completion of the programme, this was investigated from the perspective of teachers' implementation of knowledge transfer to their teaching through various pedagogical strategies, classroom management and perceived personal awareness of student needs. In addition, teachers responded regarding the programme design. While strong support was found for the programme, significant differences were found, however, between teachers working in Chinese and English medium of instruction schools, age and teaching experience following participation in the programme. Implications are discussed within the context of responding to the new curriculum framework for formal education in Macao Special Administration Region, which promotes more inclusive schools.*

**Keywords**: Inclusive education; knowledge transfer; pedagogical practice; post-graduate diploma in education; programme design; teachers

Resourcing Inclusive Education
International Perspectives on Inclusive Education, Volume 15, 147–164
Copyright © 2021 by Emerald Publishing Limited.
All rights of reproduction in any form reserved
ISSN: 1479-3636/doi:10.1108/S1479-363620210000015012

# INTRODUCTION

Since 1999, Macao has been a Special Administration Region (SAR) of China. Macao covers a very small area of 30 square km, yet it is perceived to be the most densely populated region in the world (DSEC, 2017). The majority of the population are Chinese (95%), with the remainder being of various ethnic groups including immigrants from Portugal, Indonesia, Philippines and Myanmar, among others. The education system in Macao has a long history without a unified educational system. In the 2016/17 academic year, of the 74 regular schools, all but 10 were private schools. The majority of teachers are, thus, employed in private schools. This predominance of private schools impacts on expectations for implementing new initiatives promoted by the Government.

One such new initiative implemented in 2011 is a new curriculum framework outlining the learning standards and key learning areas for school students (DSEJ, 2014). This has far reaching implications as it is now expected that all government and private schools under the free education school system (providing free education), who originally had their own curriculum, should now adopt the new curriculum framework for formal education (DSEJ, 2014). Initially, the framework commenced with Kindergarten with it being extended to Primary Years 1 – 3 in 2016 and to Primary 4 - 6 and the first two years of Junior and Senior Secondary in 2018. Full implementation is due for the 2019/2020 academic year. Preparing and educating teachers, both prospective and practicing has, therefore, become a key focus of the Government in relation to ensuring they have the capacity to implement the new curriculum framework. The Macao Department of Education reform now focuses more prominently on promoting holistic development of students, establishing benchmarks for inclusive education, enhancing the effectiveness and quality of education and optimizing the new curriculum structure through a student-centred approach (DSEJ, 2014). There is little doubt that teachers are the best resource for enabling effective inclusive education. Providing them with an appropriate curriculum is essential if they are to be able to act as an effective resource for supporting all learners in Macao (Forlin & Sin, 2019). This research therefore investigated teachers' pedagogical practice (TPP) and knowledge transfer in response to undertaking a revised Post-Graduate Diploma in Education (PGDE) at one higher education institute designed to address the new curriculum framework for formal education in Macao SAR. A revised PGDE curriculum was deemed to be critical if this was to act as a catalyst for improving quality of teachers to become an effective resource to implement inclusive education.

# TEACHER PREPARATION AS A RESOURCE FOR INCLUSIVE EDUCATION

Preparing teachers for today's classrooms, schools and the modern economy demand different approaches. Teacher education must equip teachers to meet these demands effectively and to be able to cope with changes instigated by local governments. There is substantial literature (e.g., Clarke & Hollingsworth, 2002; Evans, 2014; Opfer & Pedder, 2011) on the process of teachers' professional development and learning and a number of models have been proposed and analyzed (Boylan, Coldwell, Maxwell, & Jordan, 2018). Zeichner (2010) suggests that traditionally, academic knowledge is viewed as the primary source of knowledge for preparing teachers. He argues, however, that expanded learning opportunities for prospective teachers are essential to enable improved complex teaching practices in the current educational climate.

To become an effectual resource for inclusive education, teachers must be provided with a curriculum that includes appropriate opportunities to practice what they have learned during their preparation in schools, while receiving constructive feedback. Many reforms of teacher education include enhanced field experiences, which are now a significant part of teacher preparation. Field experiences are considered key mechanisms in preparing prospective teachers to bridge theory and practice and develop pedagogical and curricular strategies (Hollins & Guzman, 2005). In many parts of the world, service-learning in primary and secondary schools has become popular with advancing teacher preparation. Indeed, Darling-Hammond (2010) suggests extensive fieldwork, intensive supervision, expert modeling of practice and using pedagogies linking theory and practice are critical in preparing pro-spective teachers to learn and organize their experiences so that they can integrate and use their knowledge to adapt their practice in a well-grounded and innovating way to meet the specific classroom contexts they later encounter in real school settings.

In England, for example, coaching and mentoring to develop classroom practice has become a provision of professional development and teacher edu-cation (Lofthouse, 2018). These provisions include improvements in the quality of teaching, professional learning and the facilitation of professional working relationships between teachers and the wider school community. Coaching has increasingly been recognized as an effective way to enhance teachers' self-efficacy (e.g., Shidler, 2008; Trautwein & Ammerman, 2010) and their capacity to improve teaching practice and skills and student outcomes. This approach has arisen to inspire motivation, reflective practice and mastery of teaching. Tschannen-Moran and Tschannen-Moran (2010) suggest a coaching model which they term 'evocative coaching'; a model that encompasses concern for consciousness (increased self-awareness, self-knowledge and self-monitoring), concern for connection (connection with teachers and the school environment), concern for competence (master the art and science of teaching and expert knowledge), concern for contribution (make contribution to the learning and well-being of students) and concern for creativity (unleash creativity). Coaching has thus become an integral part of teacher preparation in many parts of the world and can provide the necessary support required to improve the quality of teachers as inclusive practitioners. In Macao, curriculum reform must ensure that teachers have the initiative as well as the ability to use their talents to implement the proposed move to a more inclusive paradigm, as outlined in the new framework for education.

While most regions are engaged in regular curriculum reform, the lack of supports for teachers to adjust to new practices is frequently insufficient (Camburn & Han, 2015). Invariably, the initial introduction of new ideas is presented to teachers utilizing traditional approaches (Desimone, 2011). While many factors influence student academic achievements and outcomes in schools that serve diverse student populations, one of the major factors is teacher quality (Hollins & Guzman, 2005). As promoted in the *Education For All Global Monitoring Report 2013/1* (UNESCO, 2013/2014, 11th EFA Report, p. 30) 'All children must have teachers who are trained, motivated and enjoy teaching, who can identify and support weak learners, and who are backed by well-managed education systems'.

More innovative teacher preparation, therefore, is needed if newly graduated teachers are to be able to implement effective practices that accommodate the changing needs of diverse student populations. This is especially relevant in the Asia-Pacific region where there is an enormous variation in cultural diversity (Forlin, 2018). Effective teacher preparation across this region requires much greater consideration of cultural differences and how educational reforms can be implemented within a range of potential constraints such as large class sizes, limited access to ongoing professional learning and often limited or no links between universities and schools. A further constraint is consistently the lack of good practice schools for pre-service teachers to observe best practice teaching.

It has increasingly become accepted that knowledge production has moved out of universities to a greater emphasis on learning within the work environment. There is an increased expectation for teacher education to occur within a situated pedagogy, where teachers can develop an understanding of real classroom practices and application (Bloomfield, Taylor, & Maxwell, 2004). The importance of teaching practice in schools with strong links between university theory and school pedagogy has been well-documented (Cochran-Smith & Lytle, 2009; Darling-Hammond, 2010; Zeichner, 2010). There has, therefore, been an increase in university and school partnerships in recent years, acknowledging the value to be achieved through such collaborative links. Exemplary pre-service teacher programmes that have been found to produce well-prepared teachers include those that have robust university school relationships, with shared beliefs and common pedagogical knowledge (Darling-Hammond, 2010). Acting as a resource for inclusive education, curriculum that is provided for preparing teachers must be rigorous and quality assured to prepare the most efficacious teachers. To establish effective partnerships, high-quality learning support for students during teaching practice needs to be built upon shared understandings and expectations of both roles (Chambers & Armour, 2012).

Indeed, initial teacher education that includes professional experience that extends beyond university-based learning is widespread. In Australia, for example, the current review of initial teacher education is driven by the need to make teacher preparation programmes more practical to provide pre-service teachers with authentic opportunities to engage with professional learning communities (Morrison, 2016). This driver for change builds on critical understandings that cooperation between universities and schools are beneficial to prepare pre-service teachers for career entry rigorously. As Jackson and Burch

(2018) suggest, initial teacher education programmes in England could be more effective if they are collaborative, with the school and the university working together, rather than in parallel (p. 2). They also suggest creating a 'Third-Space' to enhance effective partnership between university and school-based teacher education.

## PEDAGOGICAL APPROACHES

A student-centred approach is now most favoured as a teaching pedagogy in many countries in Western cultures (e.g. Adkins, 2018; Lumpkin, Achen, & Dodd, 2015), and is increasingly being adopted in Asian regions. The movement has been from a teacher-centred emphasis where students were expected to be passive learners to a more constructivist approach involving students in their own learning. Student-centred learning methods have long been advocated as an effective and efficient form of teaching and learning (Adkins, 2018). The roots can be traced back to educational ideologies of student-centreness and discovery-based learning proposed by Dewey (Dewey, 1938). Teaching methods and curriculum design in Eastern Asian cultures are now being adopted although to a lesser extent than western counterparts.

The traditional Asian culture of learning has been underpinned by different philosophies about the nature of teaching (Hu, 2002). Teaching methods in many Asian cultures are largely teacher-centred (Watkins & Biggs, 1996). Cultural expectations consider that the teacher is there to 'tell' and to be the expert, while students are to listen and obey (Lee, 1996; Morrison, 2009). For example, in Taiwan, many schools adopt a more teacher-centred, information-based and test-driven instructional approach (Zhang, Peng, & Hung, 2009). In China and some other Asian cultures, Confucian principles still play an essential role in the educational system, whereby assumptions of teaching and learning are driven by hierarchical rules and transmission of knowledge (Brick, 1991; Jin & Cortazzi, 1995).

There still exists a dual Medium of Instruction (MOI) system of education in Macao, involving schools which teach in either Chinese or English, with a few adopting Portuguese as their instructional language. The majority of students, nevertheless, are educated in a Chinese schooling system, which generally promotes conformity to teachers' requirements to listen obediently and passively while the teacher teaches (Morrison, 2009). They are generally required to memorize and repeat information and to learn individually within a traditional didactic, transmission mode of teaching (Morrison & Tang, 2002). This approach epitomizes the familiar and contested concept of the 'Chinese learner' (Watkins & Biggs, 2001). The focus of teaching, therefore, in Chinese medium of instruction (CMI) schools in Macao is not on how students can construct and apply knowledge, but how knowledge is transmitted (Monteiro & Morrison, 2018). In English Medium of Instruction (EMI) schools in Macao, however, many of which are international schools, the pedagogical approach generally tends to follow much more closely to the Western student-centred model. Such polarization and generalized distinctions should be treated with caution. The concept of the Chinese learner has not only been contested but also it is not always prevalent and depends on the learner in context and learning *in situ*.

## REDESIGNING THE TEACHER
## PREPARATION PROGRAMME

The initial preparation of pre-service and in-service teachers is offered at four higher education institutions in Macao, and programmes vary from institution to institution. This preparation takes the form of a one-year part-time PGDE or a four-year full-time bachelor's degree in education. Teacher preparation in Macao is offered in either Chinese or English to accommodate the needs of participants who will be aiming to teach in either a CMI or an EMI school.

The PGDE programme at one of the universities in Macao has revised its curriculum to reflect and to contribute to evolving knowledge grounded upon evidence-based teaching practices and principles within a student-centred approach and alternative forms of student assessment. This is pertinent, as the Macao Government's new educational reform requires all teachers to have a teaching degree that provides for improved teaching to align with the new reform and curriculum framework (DSEJ, 2014). Effective teachers prepared for this new government curriculum must be resourceful if they are to the meet the new student-centred framework that supports a more inclusive approach to education.

The PGDE curriculum at this university has four primary goals for teacher development that served as guidelines when redesigning the programme in 2016. These goals oriented the programme towards a multidimensional image of teacher education and development. They were aimed at preparing teachers to achieve excellence in the classroom and helping them to become active agents of educational improvement. The first goal of the revised programme focused on developing teachers' pedagogical knowledge (i.e., curriculum development, instruction, classroom management, psychology of child development and responding to individual student needs). This was guided by a teacher-centred framework for classroom design and supported by faculty applying similar understandings of teaching and learning to their own roles as educators. The second goal was to prepare teachers to support equity and diversity in the classroom while providing differentiated learning. The philosophy of inclusive education is being increasingly adopted in Macao, necessitating a greater emphasis on this during teacher preparation. The programme adopts an infused approach to preparing teachers for inclusion. The third goal was learning how to create school cultures that are responsive to changing contexts and develop stronger links between schools, parents and communities. The fourth goal was to enable teachers to apply what they learned during their practicum to use this knowledge when teaching and commit to ongoing professional growth.

To ensure that all teachers completing the revised PDGE programme would be able to be active agents of change, the collaborative links between the university and teaching practice schools was considered an important element in the new structure. The practicum experiences, therefore, were organized in schools with direct links to participants' coursework. Supervising faculty of the university and a mentor teacher from the placement school managed student's professional experience within the schools. At the centre of the practicum framework was the teacher-as-learner, a professional striving to improve mastery of technical instructional practices and to enhance their capacity as reflective practitioners.

## THE RESEARCH

This study sought to obtain data from practicing teachers after completing the revised PGDE programme. The focus was on Goal 1 of pedagogical knowledge and Goal 4 of knowledge transfer between the university programme and school practice. The effect of the programme was investigated from the perspective of teachers' implementation of pedagogical strategies, classroom management and awareness of students' needs. Knowledge transfer issues examined application of the university-based programme to classroom practice related to the school culture and acceptance by staff and students of the new approaches. If curriculum change in teacher preparation is to be an effective resource for improving inclusive education, it is critical to investigate these knowledge transfer issues to ensure teachers are able to implement their new knowledge in classroom settings. Research questions were (1) what are teachers' perceptions regarding their implementation of student-centred pedagogical practices? and (2) what issues do teachers perceive influence their transfer of knowledge from the university-based programme to classroom practice?

## METHODOLOGY

The methodological approach adopted for this study was quantitative, employing a combination of items from two instruments, together with demographic data.

The first instrument *TPP* was developed before the commencement of the research with items based on the expected outcomes from the programme in pedagogical practice. These were related to teaching strategies, classroom management and personal awareness. An initial 30 items were piloted with a small number of PGDE graduates ($N = 19$). Two faculty experts also provided comments on the content validity of the items. Following feedback, minor changes were made to the wording to overcome potential ambiguities identified by the critics.

The second instrument was a modified version of the 50-item questionnaire developed and validated by Feixas et al. (2013). The original questionnaire CuestionarioSobreFactores de Transferencia de la Formación Docente (Questionnaire about transference factors of teacher's training) by the Equipo de Transferencia Formación Docente (UAB) (Team for the transference of teacher's training) was published in Spanish, thus for this research it was first translated into English and then into Chinese. A bilingual translator undertook the first iterations. For the second, it was back-translated from the Chinese into English by a second interpreter. Several experts reviewed the items and 10 were deleted as being considered not relevant to the context in Macao. The remaining 40 items were retained with minor changes to terminology. These included items related to three aspects of knowledge transfer, namely, support by the school culture, acceptance of new ideas by the students and the staff, and the Programme design and practicum supervisor support. Six items were written in the negative and were, therefore, recoded before analysis.

### Procedure

The final selected items from both instruments were combined into an online survey using Google Docs. A set of five demographic items were added related to the PGDE intake year (2013/14, 2014/15, 2015/6, 2016/17), gender, age (25 years or less, 26–35 years, 36–45 years, 66 years or above), programme MOI (English [(EMI] or Chinese [CMI]) and teaching level (kindergarten, primary, secondary). Following the completion of the programme, all teachers were emailed and invited to complete the online survey. In total, 233 teachers from the four cohorts were invited to participate, with the response rate calculated as 46%. Data were entered in Statistical Package for the Social Sciences (SPSS) for analysis.

## RESULTS

Of the 108 teachers who completed the questionnaires, the majority of 76% were females; nearly half were in the 26–35 age group, with 13% being older than 46 years and 14% less than 25 years. The remaining teachers were 36–45 years. Of the teachers, 70% undertook the Programme in English with the remainder taking the Chinese version. The numbers of questionnaires completed by teachers were from the 2013/14 cohort ($N = 9$), the 2014/15 cohorts ($N = 24$), the 2015/16 cohort ($N = 36$) and from the 2016/17 cohort ($N = 39$). Almost 64% were in their first five years of teaching with only 13% having more than 11 years of teaching experience. When asked what school level they were currently teaching, approximately 17% indicated kindergarten, 39% primary and 42% secondary.

### Teachers' Pedagogical Practice

The first section of the questionnaire asked teachers to respond to statements that related to their implementation of the pedagogical strategies they had been taught during the Programme. A generic question initially asked them how competent they considered themselves to be in using appropriate skills to teach kindergarten, primary or secondary classrooms after completing the PGDE. Responses ranged from 1 (not at all) to 5 (a very great deal). The mean response was 3.98 (SD = 0.68), indicating a reasonably positive response.

More detailed information was then sought regarding their perceptions of implementing teaching strategies, classroom management skills and perceived personal awareness. Of the 18 items related to the implementation of teaching strategies, an overall mean response of 3.73 (SD = 0.58) was recorded indicating quite strong agreement with the number of strategies they implemented during their teaching (Table 1).

***Table 1.*** Teachers' Pedagogical Practice for Implementing Teaching Strategies.

| | *M* | SD |
|---|---|---|
| Teaching Strategies (Alpha Cronbach = 0.906) | 3.73 | 0.58 |
| 12. I encourage student interaction. | 4.34 | 0.76 |
| 13. I use intrinsic motivation strategies (praise, social recognition, student autonomy, etc.). | 4.11 | 0.84 |
| 6. I give clear instructions and explanations of content or concepts. | 4.07 | 0.76 |
| 11. I provide opportunities for students to take responsibility for their own learning. | 4.03 | 0.73 |
| 5. I apply a range of teaching and learning methods. | 3.98 | 0.79 |
| 9. I encourage students to use a variety of problem-solving techniques. | 3.92 | 0.85 |
| 15. I prepare teaching strategies, teaching materials and assessment directly related to each ILO. | 3.81 | 0.85 |
| 7. I frequently use student-centred instruction. | 3.72 | 0.93 |
| 17. I use a variety of classroom assessment techniques-ongoing informal assessment strategies (e.g., minute paper, questioning, etc.) to measure student learning. | 3.60 | 0.99 |
| 14. I use extrinsic motivation strategies (e.g., rewards, bonus points, badges, tokens, stickers, etc.). | 3.57 | 1.13 |
| 4. I communicate a clear plan and ILOs at the start of every lesson. | 3.53 | 0.95 |
| 10. I am confident in designing differentiated learning tasks so that all students in the class are accommodated. | 3.52 | 0.99 |
| 16. I use a variety of assessment strategies (e.g., portfolio assessment, performance-based assessment, peer/self-evaluation, etc.) to measure student learning. | 3.50 | 1.09 |
| 1. I prepare a lesson plan for every lesson. | 3.50 | 1.00 |
| 2. I link lesson objectives to Macao's curriculum framework. | 3.50 | 1.04 |
| 3. I use Bloom's Taxonomy of Educational Objectives as a guide to develop intended learning outcomes (ILOs) for each lesson. | 3.39 | 1.03 |
| 8. I use Blooms' Taxonomy of Educational Objectives as a guide for questioning to probe students' knowledge and understanding. | 3.26 | 0.98 |
| 18. I keep a reflective teaching journal. | 2.76 | 1.22 |

*Note*: Range is 1= strongly disagree to 5 = strongly agree.

The teachers were most positive about their ability to encourage student interaction, use intrinsic motivation and to give clear instructions while providing opportunities for students to take responsibility for their own learning. The teachers were least positive about using Bloom's Taxonomy to support their pedagogical practices. Few teachers indicated that they kept a reflective teaching journal. When asked to respond to items about their classroom management skills, a similar overall response indicated quite strong agreement with all aspects (Table 2).

The final section of the Teachers Pedagogical Practice questionnaire included eight items related to teachers' perceived personal awareness of students and their ability to respond to the students' different developmental stages (Table 3). The teachers indicated a keen awareness of how their own behaviour affected students and their ability to treat each student as a unique individual. They, nevertheless, considered themselves less able to identify mental health problems in their students and to refer and to work collaboratively with other professionals.

Consideration was subsequently given to the impact of five independent variables on the three aspects of TPP. Independent-samples t tests were conducted on gender and programme MOI with equal variances not assumed. One-way between subjects Analysis of variance (ANOVA) was conducted on age, year of programme and teaching level.

Regarding the implementation of teaching strategies, significant differences were found between the teachers in the EMI schools and those in the CMI schools. Teachers in the EMI schools ($M = 3.89$, SD $= 0.53$) had significantly higher rates of strategy implementation than those in the CMI schools ($M = 3.55$, SD $= 0.58$), $t(95) = 2.96$, $p = <0.004$. No other significant differences were found for strategy implementation.

For the items pertaining to classroom management, four variables were found to be significant. Differences in gender were present between males ($M = 4.13$, SD $= 0.58$), who gave significantly higher ratings of classroom management skills than females ($M = 3.66$, SD $= 0.67$), $t(106) = 3.39$, $p = <0.001$, $d = 0.75$. School MOI was also found to be significant with those in the EMI schools ($M = 3.95$,

*Table 2.* Teachers' Classroom Management Skills.

|                                                                                      | $M$  | SD   |
|--------------------------------------------------------------------------------------|------|------|
| Classroom Management (Alpha Cronbach = 0.851)                                          | 3.78 | 0.68 |
| 21. I can manage disruptions in the classroom.                                        | 3.85 | 0.84 |
| 19. I can keep the students on task throughout a lesson.                              | 3.82 | 0.80 |
| 20. I am able to design an effective classroom management plan.                       | 3.81 | 0.81 |
| 22. I am able to correct inappropriate behaviour immediately, accurately and constructively. | 3.62 | 0.82 |

*Note*: Range is 1= strongly disagree to 5 = strongly agree.

***Table 3.*** Teachers' Perceived Personal Awareness of Their Students.

|  | M | SD |
|---|---|---|
| Perceived Personal Awareness (Alpha Cronbach = 0.851) | 3.94 | 0.58 |
| 25. I am aware of the way my own behaviour affects students. | 4.32 | 0.71 |
| 27. I can look to each student as a unique individual with specific physical, cognitive and psychosocial characteristics. | 4.22 | 0.77 |
| 26. I am aware of the way students' behaviours affect me. | 4.01 | 0.76 |
| 24. I take into account the ecological dimensions (i.e., family, peers, culture, relationship between family and school) of my students' environment when trying to understand their behaviour. | 3.94 | 0.85 |
| 23. I adjust my strategies and lesson content to the developmental stage of my students. | 3.89 | 0.82 |
| 28. I pay attention to my students' risk and resilient factors to better promote their learning and global development. | 3.85 | 0.88 |
| 30. I am able to identify developmental problems and to refer and to work collaboratively with other professionals. | 3.74 | 0.92 |
| 29. I am able to identify mental health problems and to refer and to work collaboratively with other professionals. | 3.58 | 0.94 |

*Note*: Range is 1 = strongly disagree to 5 = strongly agree.

SD = 0.72), indicating higher levels of classroom management skills than those from the CMI schools (M = 3.51, SD = 0.58), $t(95)$ = 3.15, $p$ = <0.002. In addition, classroom management skills also varied by age, $F(3, 102)$ = 9.90, $p<0.05$, $\eta^2$ = 0.23. Bonferroni's post hoc procedure indicated that the youngest group of teachers below 25 years of age (M = 3.50, SD = 0.73) were significantly less effective in classroom management than were those aged 36–45 years (M = 4.21, SD = 0.46). Similarly, those aged 26–35 years (M = 3.52, SD = 0.61) rated their classroom management skills significantly less than those aged 36–45 years or above 46 years. Year of programme further impacted on use of classroom management skills, $F(3, 104)$ = 4.37, $p<0.05$, $\eta^2$ = 0.11. Bonferroni's post hoc procedure identified that those who completed the Programme in 2013/14 (M = 4.23, SD = 0.86) were implementing significantly more classroom management skills than those who completed the programme most recently in 2016/17 (M = 3.52, SD = 0.65). No other significant differences were found for classroom management.

Personal awareness of students and teachers' perceived ability to respond to their students' different developmental stages were also impacted by the variables of school MOI and age. Teachers who were in the EMI schools (M = 3.63, SD = 0.49) had significantly greater awareness of the students than those in the CMI schools (M = 3.62, SD = 0.48), $t(95)$ = 5.29, $p$ = <0.000. Personal awareness also varied by age, $F$ (3, 102) = 4.50, $p<0.05$, $\eta^2$ = 0.12. While awareness increased linearly with age, Bonferroni's post hoc procedure indicated that the differences were significant between those in the age group of 26–35 ($M$ = 3.80, SD = 0.57) and those above 46 years ($M$ = 4.30, SD = 0.52). No other significant differences were found for personal awareness. The variable of teaching level found no significant differences for TPP regardless of whether they were teaching in a kindergarten, primary or secondary school.

## Knowledge Transfer

If the new teacher preparation curriculum is to be a useful resource, then knowledge gained by the teachers must be transferrable to practice. The second part of the questionnaire, therefore, sought information about the issues that teachers perceive to influence their transfer of knowledge from the university-based programme to classroom practice. There were five items related to knowledge transfer: support by the school culture, acceptance of new ideas by the students and the staff, and the programme design and supervisor support. Each of these were investigated to identify any significant differences according to the five independent variables of gender, age, programme MOI, year of completion and teaching level (Kindergarten, Primary, Secondary). Responses ranged from 1 = strongly disagree to 5 = strongly agree. No significant differences were found for gender or for those teaching in secondary schools. The programme MOI was found to be significant across most aspects of knowledge transfer with other variables impacted in some areas.

The overall mean response for the 10 items about support from the school culture was 3.70 (SD = 0.44) indicating that the teachers held a fairly strong agreement with the support provided by the school in enabling them to transfer the knowledge they had learned during the PGDE into their school practice. The only item that teachers indicated a concern with was about their teaching workload, which they implied impacted to some degree on their ability to implement what they had learned ($M$ = 2.76, SD = 1.11). When considering any differences in responses for the five independent variables, significant differences were found for school support by school MOI. Teachers who were in an EMI school ($M$ = 3.44, SD = 0.54) indicated significantly greater support by their school in being able to implement the knowledge learned during their programme (e.g., human resources, facilities, department and technical support) than those in CMI schools ($M$ = 3.09, SD = 0.46), $t(94)$ = 3.35, $p$ = <0.001. Support by the school also varied for age with older teachers reporting more support than the younger teachers, $F$ (3, 102) = 2.78, $p<0.05$, $\eta^2$ = 0.075. Bonferroni's post hoc procedure indicated that the differences for age were significant between those in the age group of 26–35 ($M$ = 3.20, SD = 0.51) and those between 36–45 years ($M$ = 3.55, SD = 0.57). No other significant differences were found for school support.

The second set of five questions sought teachers' perceptions of how accepting they considered that their students were towards them implementing new strategies learned during the programme (e.g., cooperative/collaborative learning, inquiry-based learning, learning styles). The overall mean response was 3.63 (SD = 0.50), suggesting that they believed that students were accepting of the new ideas. Significant differences, nonetheless, were found according to age and for those working in kindergartens. Age differences showed greater support by students for the new strategies as teachers became older $F$ (3, 102) = 2.65, $p<0.05$, $\eta^2$ = 0.072. Bonferroni's post hoc procedure produced significant differences between teachers aged 26–35 years ($M$ = 3.51, SD = 0.47) and those aged 36–45 years ($M$ = 3.83, SD = 0.57). For this category of acceptance by students, there was also a significant difference with those teaching in kindergartens ($M$ = 3.86, SD = 0.49), perceiving greater acceptance by their students compared to the primary and secondary teachers ($M$ = 3.59, SD = 0.51), $t(104)$ = 2.05, $p$ = <0.05, $d$ = 0.54.

A further set of three questions asked for teachers' perceptions about acceptance by the staff of the new strategies they were implementing. The overall mean response was 3.49 (SD = 0.66) which, while still positive, was slightly lower than acceptance by the students. One significant difference was found for the cohort MOI with the EMI teachers ($M$ = 3.64, SD = 0.70), proposing greater acceptance by their staff than the Chinese teachers ($M$ = 3.32, SD = 0.55), $t(94)$ = 2.42, $p$ = <0.01. No other significant differences were found for staff acceptance.

The final two sets of questions sought information directly about the Programme design and the support teachers received from their supervisor during the practicum. Programme design had 14 items about the suitability of the content, the use of practical examples and strategies and the applicability of the programme design to preparing them for teaching. A positive mean response of 3.95 (SD = 0.53) indicated overall good satisfaction with the programme, although there were four areas of significant differences between groups. Teachers from the EMI schools ($M$ = 4.10, SD = 0.46) reported significantly stronger agreement with the effectiveness of the programme design than did those from the CMI schools ($M$ = 3.73, SD = 0.55), $t(94)$ = 3.61, $p$ = <0.000. Age also impacted significantly on perceptions of the effectiveness of the programme design with older teachers being more positive about the programme than the younger ones, $F$ (3, 102) = 7.38, $p<0.000$, $\eta^2$ = 0.178. No significant differences between the age groups were found by Bonferroni post hoc analysis. The ANOVA produced a significant result for the year of intake, $F$ (3, 103) = 2.68, $p<0.051$, $\eta^2$ = 0.072; although the $\eta^2$ was low, there was no distinguishable linear transition and Bonferroni post hoc did not reveal any significant differences between intake years. There was, however, a significant difference found between teaching levels $t(105)$ = 2.09, $p$ = <0.05, $d$ = 0.42, with those in primary school ($M$ = 3.82, SD = 0.54) indicating less satisfaction with the programme design for preparing them for teaching, compared to the other levels ($M$ = 4.04, SD = 0.51).

A further set of five items focussed on teachers' perceptions of the support provided by their practicum supervisors' during the programme. The mean response of 3.86 (SD = 0.70) was quite positive, although there was a significant difference for age $F$ (3, 102) = 3.30, $p<0.05$, $\eta^2$ = 0.088. Bonferroni post hoc did not reveal any significant differences between age groups, the $\eta^2$ was low, and there was no distinguishable linear transition.

# DISCUSSION

The new Government curriculum framework in Macao (DSEJ, 2014) is expected to be adopted by all schools under the free education school system. A key focus of this reform is promoting the holistic development of students through a student-centred approach. In addition to schools needing to restructure their curriculum, this also has implications for teacher preparation. This research was designed to investigate the impact of teachers' pedagogy and knowledge transfer after completing a revised PGDE programme that adopted a more student-centred approach to learning to align with the new Macao education framework. Attending to the PGDE curriculum and making changes to it is an important way of improving and enhancing its effectiveness as a resource for raising the capacity of teachers as inclusive practitioners. According to Darling-Hammond (2006), there are three critical components for effective teacher preparation programmes. These include:

> ... tight coherence and integration among programmes and between course work and clinical work in schools, extensive and intensely supervised clinical work integrated with course work using pedagogies that link theory and practice, and closer, proactive relationships with schools that serve diverse learners effectively and develop and model excellent teaching. (p. 300)

The revised programme had established a much stronger connection between the university and practicum schools and initiated more collaborative supervisor mentoring support. Revised content, greater use of practical examples and strategies and a new programme design were implemented to prepare teachers.

Results found that teachers' perceptions of their pedagogical practice to implement student-centred pedagogical practices were quite positive. They also proposed that they had sound classroom teaching management skills, although male teachers indicated significantly greater skills in this area. Their personal awareness of the needs of students was also quite good. No differences in pedagogical practice were found for teachers in kindergarten, primary or secondary schools.

Teachers' perceptions of their classroom management skills increased with age and teaching experience, as did their awareness of students' needs and the more positive support they were able to receive from their school when implementing the new strategies. Classroom management skills were also associated with the year of undertaking the programme. Teachers who graduated from the first cohort indicated that they were significantly more competent in classroom management skills than those from the later cohort. Clearly, practice is a critical element in improving classroom management. Revising the PGDE curriculum with a stronger focus on university school partnerships has improved its viability to act as a better resource for preparing teachers.

The significant differences in pedagogical practice were found between those teaching in CMI and EMI schools. In all instances, teachers working in the EMI schools expressed significantly higher application of teaching strategies such as student-centred instruction, encouraging student interaction and employing a range of approaches to involve students in higher order thinking. Teachers in

EMI schools were also more positive about implementing effective classroom management plans and engaging students in appropriate ways. Similarly, EMI teachers were significantly more aware of how their behaviour affected the students were able to respond to the students' developmental stages and to treat each student as a unique individual.

Significant differences were again found depending upon the MOI of the schools that the teachers were employed in. Compared to teachers working in CMI schools, those working in the EMI schools purported that they received greater support by the school in being able to introduce the new teaching methods learned during the programme. In the same way, they reported that they received stronger support by their colleagues for introducing changes and a greater willingness to exchange ideas.

There are many socio-cultural differences in the approaches teachers adopt and use to deliver and promote learning in their classrooms (Adkins, 2018). Given the significant differences found here between traditional Western approaches that have veered towards a more student-centred approach and the more teacher-centred perspective previously adopted by Asian cultures, the findings of differences between EMI and CMI teachers in their application of the new student-centred skills they had learned and the support they received to implement them, may be somewhat expected. A resourceful curriculum, therefore, needs to ensure that it addresses any potential cultural issues during the redevelopment stage. This must be treated with the same care and attention that is given to other resources if it is to be beneficial for preparing teachers to support the new inclusive paradigm being promoted for Macao.

The new PGDE programme was designed to be taught in either English or Chinese. Overall, all teachers were positive towards the programme design and the usefulness of the content in helping them to promote learning in the classroom. The teachers identified that the programme had deepened and updated their knowledge and was relevant and useful to their work. This finds resonance with Jackson and Burch's (2018) suggestions that teacher education should synthesize school and university expertise to adequately prepare pre-service teachers for everyday teaching. Teachers working in the EMI schools, nevertheless, still reported significantly higher agreeance with the effectiveness of the programme design. All teachers were, however, very positive about the support provided by their practicum supervisor during the programme. Supervisors were reported to be positive, encouraging and helpful in applying the new knowledge that teachers had learned. This perspective supports the view that coaching and mentoring in teacher education enhances learning, interprofessional learning, competencies and self-efficacy.

Two other significant differences were found in the data. The first was that kindergarten teachers found their students more accepting of their new practices. The second was that primary school teachers were less satisfied with the programme design compared to those in kindergarten and secondary schools. These differences will need to be addressed in the next programme review stage.

## LIMITATIONS OF THE STUDY

Regardless of follow-up efforts, the response rate was relatively low. Only half of the teachers invited to participate in the study responded to the online questionnaire. The findings may, therefore, not fully represent the effectiveness of the transfer of learning from the PGDE programme to classroom practice. In addition, the self-reporting measures employed in the questionnaire may be biased in favour of responses that are perceived as desirable to the teachers rather than objective evaluations of their own pedagogical practice. In spite of these limitations, the findings still provide several significant conclusions that are useful internationally when reviewing the effectiveness of teacher preparation programmes across different cultural climates.

## CONCLUSION

The results of this research highlighted the importance that the teachers placed on adopting active teaching methodologies learnt during their programme and the strong connection that was made with practice. Transference of knowledge was not an immediate consequence of the preparation, however, but seemed to be a process made of in vivo experience that gave teachers greater confidence in teaching. Implementation was also underpinned by a school's culture and the availability of support and encouragement to enable teachers to try their new skills.

Reviewing the implementation of the new programme structure in this university is an important next step. While the revised PGDE was designed to act as a resource to meet the aim of the newly released government curriculum framework, there are some mitigating circumstances that are currently impacting on this. Although schools are expected to adopt a more student-centred approach to the curriculum, teachers in the CMI schools found this more challenging to implement than those in the EMI schools. All teachers affirmed strong support for the PGDE programme design, the suitability of the content, the use of practical examples and strategies and the applicability of the programme to preparing them for teaching, regardless of whether they were undertaking the CMI or EMI programme. The impact of the new content and programme design was, nonetheless, deemed more beneficial by teachers working in EMI than in CMI schools. It would seem that the traditional didactic teacher-centred approach to pedagogy that has long been the philosophy for teaching in CMI schools in Macao is going to require considerable time and effort to reconfigure if students are to become actively engaged in their own learning through a more personalized constructivist curriculum.

When revising teacher preparation programmes, it is evident that much more significant consideration needs to be given to the reality and diversity of the schools in which the teachers will work. While preparing teachers by skilling them in the latest evidence-based pedagogical practices, unless schools are prepared and willing to support these changes, such preparation is going to be wanton. A revised PGDE curriculum should be seen as an important resource for supporting change in schools in Macao. Nevertheless, it is clear that a greater emphasis on working more intensely with schools during the practice sessions to support them in making whole school changes will be needed for these new practices to be implemented. This is not unique to Macao and the findings from this research have much to offer to other systems endeavouring to reform pedagogy and curriculum as a fundamental resource through updating their teacher preparation programmes.

## REFERENCES

Adkins, J. K. (2018). Active learning and formative assessment in a user-centered design course. *Information Systems Education Journal, 16*(4), 34–40.

Bloomfield, D., Taylor, N., & Maxwell, T.W. (2004). Enhancing the link between university and schools through action research on teaching practicum. *Journal of Vocational Education and Training, 56*(3), 355–372.

Boylan, M., Coldwell, M., Maxwell, B., & Jordan, J. (2018). Rethinking models of professional learning as tools: A conceptual analysis to inform research and practice. *Professional Development in Education, 44*(1), 120–139.

Brick, J. (1991). *China: A handbook in intercultural communication.* Sydney: Macquarie.

Camburn, E. M., & Han, S. W. (2015). Infrastructure for teacher reflection and instructional change: An exploratory study. *Journal of Educational Change, 16*(4), 511–533.

Chambers, F., & Armour, K. (2012). School–university partnerships and physical education teacher education student learning: A fruitful division of labour? *European Physical Education Review, 18*(2), 159–181.

Clarke, D., & Hollingsworth, H. (2002). Elaborating a model of teacher professional growth. *Teaching and Teacher Education, 18*(8), 947–967.

Cochran-Smith, M., & Lytle, S. (2009). *Inquiry as a stance: Practitioner research in the next generation.* New York, NY: Teachers College Press.

Darling-Hammond, L. (2006). *Powerful teacher education: Lessons from exemplary programmes.* San Francisco, CA: Jossey-Bass.

Darling-Hammond, L. (2010). Constructing 21st century teacher education. In V. Hill-Jackson & C. W. Lewis (Eds.), *Transforming teacher education: What went wrong with teacher training and how we can fix it* (pp. 223–247). Sterling, VA: Stylus Publishing, LLC.

Desimone, L. M. (2011). A primer on effective professional development. *Phi Delta Kappan, 92*(6), 68–71.

Dewey, J. (1938). *Experience and education.* New York, NY: Kappa Delta Pi.

Direcção dos Serviços de Educação e Juventude (DSEJ). (2014). Curriculum framework for formal education of local education system. Retrieved from https://portal.dsej.gov.mo/webdsejspace/internet/Inter_main_page.jsp?id=21248. Accessed on January 22, 2017.

Direcção de Serviços de Estatística e Censos (DSEC). (2017). Employment survey. Retrieved from https://www.dsec.gov.mo/zh-MO/Statistic?id=101. Accessed on January 22, 2017.

Evans, L. (2014). Leadership for professional development and learning: Enhancing our understanding of how teachers develop. *Cambridge Journal of Education, 44*(2), 179–198.

Feixas, M., Duran, M., Fernández, I., Fernández March, A., José Garcia San Pedro, M., Dolors Márquez, M., … Lagos, F. (2013). Cómo medir la transferencia de la formación en Educación Superior?: el Cuestionario de Factores de Transferencia. [*How to measure transfer of training in higher education: The questionnaire of transfer factors.*] October–December. *Revista ce Docencia Universitaria, 11*(3), 219–248. ISSN: 1887-4592.

Forlin, C. (2018). Teacher education and inclusion in the Asia Pacific region. In J. Lampert (Ed.), *Oxford research encyclopedia of global perspectives on teacher education.* Oxford: Oxford University Press.

Forlin, C., & Sin, K. S. (2019). In-service teacher training for inclusion: Best practice models for professional learning. In U. Sharma & S. Salend (Eds.), *The Oxford encyclopedia of inclusive and special education.* New York, NY: Oxford University Press.

Hollins, E., & Guzman, M. T. (2005). Research on preparing teachers for diverse populations. In M. Cochran-Smith & K.M. Zeichner (Eds.), *Studying teacher education: The report of the AERA panel on research and teacher education* (pp. 447–548). London: American Educational Research Association.

Hu, G. (2002). Potential cultural resistance to pedagogical imports: The case of communicative language teaching in China. *Language Culture and Curriculum, 15*, 93–105.

Jackson, A., & Burch, J. (2018). New directions for teacher education: Investigating school/university partnership in an increasingly school-based context. *Professional Development in Education, 45*(1), 138–150. doi:10.1080/19415257.2018.1449002

Jin, L.X., & Cortazzi, M. (1995). A cultural synergy model for academic language use. In P. Bruthiaux, T. Boswood, & B. Du-Babcock (Eds.), *Explorations in English for professional communication* (pp. 41–56). Hong Kong: City University of Hong Kong.

Lee, W. O. (1996). The cultural context for Chinese learners: Conceptions of learning in the confucian tradition. In D. A. Watkins & J. B. Biggs (Eds.), *The Chinese learner: Cultural, psychological and contextual factors* (pp. 25–41). Hong Kong: Comparative Education Research Centre and Melbourne: Australian Council for Educational Research Ltd.

Lofthouse, R. (2018). Coaching in education: A professional development process in formation. *Professional Development in Education, 45*(2), 1–13. doi:10.1080/19415257.2018.1529611

Lumpkin, A. L., Achen, R. M., & Dodd, R. K. (2015). Student perceptions of active learning. *College Student Journal, 49*(1), 121–133.

Monteiro, E., & Morrison, K. (2018). Challenges for collaborative blended learning in undergraduate students. In S. Martin & M. Notari (Eds.), *Technology-enhanced and collaborative learning* (pp. 49–76). Abingdon: Routledge.

Morrison, K. R. B. (2009). *Causation in educational research.* Abingdon: Routledge.

Morrison, C. M. (2016). Purpose, practice and theory: Teacher educators' beliefs about professional experience. *Australian Journal of Teacher Education, 41*(3), 105–125.

Morrison, K., & Tang, F. H. J. (2002). Testing to destruction: A problem in a small state. *Assessment in Education: Principles, Policy &Practice, 9*(2), 289–317.

Opfer, V. D., & Pedder, D. (2011). Conceptualizing teacher professional learning. *Review of Educational Research, 81*, 376–407.

Shidler, L. (2008). The impact of time spend coaching for teacher efficacy on student achievement. *Early Childhood Education Journal, 36*, 453–460.

Trautwein, B., & Ammerman, S. (2010). From pedagogy to practice: Mentoring and reciprocal peer coaching for preservice teachers. *Volta Review, 110*(2), 191–206.

Tschannen-Moran, B., & Tschannen-Moran, M. (2010). *Evocative coaching: Transforming schools one conversation at a time.* San Francisco, CA: Jossey-Bass.

UNESCO. (2013/2014). Education for all global monitoring Report 2013/1, 11th EFA Report. Retrieved from https://en.unesco.org/gem-report/report/2014/teaching-and-learning-achieving-quality-all

Watkins, D. A., & Biggs, J. B. (1996). Western misperceptions of the confucian heritage learning culture. In D. A. Watkins & J. B. Biggs (Eds.), *The Chinese learner: Cultural, psychological, and contextual influences* (pp. 45–67). Hong Kong; Melbourne: Comparative Education Research Centre; Australian Council for Educational Research.

Watkins, D. A., & Biggs, J. B. (2001). *Teaching the Chinese learner: Psychological and pedagogical perspectives.* Hong Kong: Hong Kong University Press.

Zeichner, Z. (2010). Rethinking the connections between campus courses and field experiences in college- and university-based teacher education. *Journal of teacher education, 61*(1–2), 89–99.

Zhang, K., Peng, S. W., & Hung, J. (2009). Online collaborative learning in a project-based learning environment in Taiwan: A case study on undergraduate students' perspectives. *Educational Media International, 46*(2), 123–135.

# INDEX